SO-EBA-141

Regulating Business:
The Search for an Optimum

REGULATING BUSINESS: THE SEARCH FOR AN OPTIMUM

Donald P. Jacobs, Editor

Chris Argyris
A. Lawrence Chickering
Penny Hollander Feldman
Richard H. Holton
Alfred E. Kahn
Paul W. MacAvoy
Almarin Phillips
V. Kerry Smith
Paul H. Weaver
Richard J. Zeckhauser

Institute for Contemporary Studies
San Francisco, California

353.0082
R344

Copyright© 1978 by the Institute for Contemporary Studies.
Second printing 1979.
Third printing 1979.

Printed in the United States of America. All rights reserved. No part of this book may be used or reproduced in any manner without written permission except in the case of brief quotations embodied in critical articles and reviews.

Copies of this book may be purchased from the Institute for $6.95. All inquiries, book orders, and catalog requests should be addressed to the Institute for Contemporary Studies, Dept. 424, 260 California Street, San Francisco, California 94111 — (415) 398-3010.

Library of Congress Catalog Number 78-50678

ISBN 0-917616-27-8

12/82

CONTENTS

I

Background

II

Area Studies

III

General Issues

IV

Postscript

CONTRIBUTORS

CHRIS ARGYRIS
James Bryant Conant Professor of Education and Organizational Behavior, Graduate Schools of Education and Business Administration, Harvard University

A. LAWRENCE CHICKERING
*Executive Director,
Institute for Contemporary Studies*

PENNY HOLLANDER FELDMAN
Director, Executive Program in Health Policy, Planning and Regulation, Harvard School of Public Health

RICHARD H. HOLTON
*Professor of Business Administration,
University of California, Berkeley*

DONALD P. JACOBS
*Dean, Graduate School of Management,
Northwestern University*

ALFRED E. KAHN
Chairman, Civil Aeronautics Board

PAUL W. MacAVOY
*Professor of Economics, Department of Economics
and School of Organization and Management, Yale University*

ALMARIN PHILLIPS
*Professor of Economics, Law and Public Policy,
University of Pennsylvania*

V. KERRY SMITH
*Fellow, Quality of the Environment Program,
Resources for the Future, Washington, D.C.*

PAUL H. WEAVER
Associate Editor, FORTUNE Magazine

RICHARD J. ZECKHAUSER
Professor of Political Economy,
Kennedy School of Government, Harvard University

PREFACE

Government regulation of business is a subject of heated controversy. Consumer groups, the academy, and recently even members of the government itself are taking aim at the older economic regulation of particular industries. Deregulation in such areas became a major interest toward the end of President Ford's administration and has continued under President Carter, the older regulations coming under fire primarily because of the harm they cause consumers and their tendency — according to many experts — to serve the interests of the regulated.

As the older regulations have fallen out of favor, a more recent form of "social regulation" has arisen. These newer regulations, promoted by consumer and environmental groups, are directed at problems of health and safety, and touch whole classes of business rather than individual industries. They are having, and promise to have, an enormous effect on the overall economy; but, because of their recent origin, academic evaluation of them is still relatively limited.

This volume, REGULATING BUSINESS: THE SEARCH FOR AN OPTIMUM, is directed primarily at economic regulation, with a succeeding volume—in development—to be devoted to social regulation. In approaching the problem, we deliberately avoided merely considering the merits of the issue in an ideal world. The inefficiencies in economic regulation have been studied at great length and depth, and our belief was and is that knowledge of *implementation*—of "how to get from here to there," as Alfred Kahn nicely puts it in his chapter title—lags far behind knowledge of the abstract ideal.

The policy question of regulatory reform includes both problems of politics and of substance related to the transition to increased competition. A major part of the policy problem involves the role of business itself. With few opportunities to participate constructively, industry representatives have often opposed deregulation and made its implementation all but impossible. To address this situation, we organized a program on regulation, in cooperation with the Graduate School of Management at Northwestern University, which attempted to involve business representatives in several ways. First, the program was arranged in the form of a lecture series, bringing together people from industry, government, the academy, and the media to encourage active participation by all groups. And second, we included special discussants drawn partly from industry; we have published excerpts of their remarks in the book, following the five "area study" chapters.

In putting together the study, we also noted that most studies on regulation have been done by economists, and that other disciplines concerned about public policy have not always been given equal time. With this in mind, we have included discussion on noneconomic aspects of regulation, which are important to an overall understanding of the subject.

The project, undertaken in collaboration with the Graduate School of Management at Northwestern, was designed to maximize its value for possible classroom use, including video presentations. Presented originally as a lecture series at Northwestern University during the fall of 1977, we were extremely pleased with that association.

The third printing of REGULATING BUSINESS comes at a time of continuing concern about the general problem of regulation and of intensifying interest in deregulation. Since the book was first released in early 1978, airline deregulation was completed under the firm guidance of CAB Chairman Alfred Kahn whose chapter in this volume concerns the problems of transition to self-control. The success of airline deregulation has now moved public and political attention to deal with trucking and other industries. Continued concern with regulation led to the institute's 1979 publication of BUREAUCRATS AND BRAINPOWER: GOVERNMENT REGULATION OF UNIVERSITIES, edited by UC-Berkeley political scientist Paul Seabury.

Many of the themes in these books remain at the top of the policy agenda. They are also likely to be hotly debated in the 1980 elections.

> H. Monroe Browne
> President
> Institute for Contemporary Studies

San Francisco, California
October 1979

INTRODUCTION

Anyone not familiar with the facts, but exposed to the rhetoric of politicans and regulatory officials, the media, or studies produced by some academics, might well conclude that the United States is moving toward a dramatic reduction of its massive regulatory apparatus.

The reality is quite different. While deregulation may be taking place on a modest scale in a few areas, new regulations and regulatory agencies are coming into being. Even in areas where the pressures for deregulation are greatest, new varieties of control are being enacted by Congress, and new regulations are being promulgated by agencies under previously enacted authority.

Clearly there is a gulf between the rhetoric of deregulatory expectation and the reality of regulatory growth. The disparities between appearance and reality were clear—and a matter of concern—to many faculty members conducting studies in a variety of fields in research centers connected with Northwestern University's Graduate School of Management. These scholars voiced their concern in seminars in which they discussed their findings, and it became evident to many of us at the school that the subject merited a broad and comprehensive effort toward clarification and wider understanding.

It was this recognition that brought the school and the Institute for Contemporary Studies together in a collaborative enterprise which culminated in this book. Herein are the lectures of a series cosponsored by the school and the Institute, held at Northwestern University's Graduate School of Management in the autumn of 1977, and dealing with regulatory issues on an industry-by-industry basis.

In developing the lecture program, the sponsors took cognizance of the fact that most efforts toward rationalizing the regulatory process dealt with the economic impacts of regulation or, occasionally, with its social effects. It is clear that the regulatory apparatus put into place in the United States in this century has had other pervasive effects, and has altered the nature and workings of business and government in many subtle and not easily discernible ways. For example, the consequences of modifications introduced by regulation in the organizational behavior of business and of government, and in the political process itself, remain largely unexplored.

Also, much of the information about regulation—the environment, the process, the effects—has been delivered in a form that cannot readily be digested by most audiences. Economists tend to communicate in a way that is most easily understood by other economists; lawyers and bureaucrats develop their own jargon.

Hence, the school and the Institute decided to seek expositions that would (1) explore the full dimensions of regulation, dealing not only with its economic and social effects, but also with its historical background, its impact upon the structure and behavior of business organizations and the bureaucracy, and upon the political process; (2) propose operational mechanisms for moving the deregulation process forward; and (3) be couched in language that would insure wide readership and comprehension.

Early in 1977 a committee was formed to advance these objectives. Kenneth M. Henderson, associate dean of the Graduate School of Management, chaired the committee, which included as members H. Monroe Browne, president, and A. Lawrence Chickering, executive director, of the Institute for Contemporary Studies; David P. Baron, professor of managerial economics and decision sciences; Douglas T. Hall, chairman, and Earl Dean Howard, professor of organization behavior; Morton I. Kamien, associate dean; Leon N. Moses, director of Northwestern University's Transportation Center; Kenneth R. Smith, professor of managerial economics and director of Hospital and Health Services Management; and Louis W. Stern, chairman, and A. Montgomery Ward, professor of marketing.

The committee sought to obtain, as lecturers in the series, people who had done original research in the areas to be explored, who could use reported research results to develop operational suggestions for altering the regulatory environment in a socially desirable manner, who would agree to prepare a paper on their subjects for publication, and who would appear at Northwestern and speak from their papers.

The lectures themselves, it was determined, would be delivered before an audience consisting of businessmen, government officials, and academics. Each paper would be discussed by an industry spokesman and a government spokesman, and there would be an opportunity for the audience to interact with the speaker and the discussants.

The lectures were delivered as planned, with audiences ranging in size from two hundred fifty to over four hundred persons. They were followed by spirited and stimulating discussions between the speakers and their discussants and, ultimately, members of the audience.

Discussions initiated at the lecture sessions were continued afterwards in small, select groups as the speakers and discussants joined industry and government leaders and academics at dinner.

We are pleased with the success of the lecture series, and optimistic about the probable impact of this volume. The series brought together some of the best minds that have grappled with the phenomenon of regulation, and it furnished them and their audiences with an opportunity for interaction.

Some of the excitement of the series cannot be communicated in this volume; the give-and-take of audience/speaker interaction is absent from these pages. But the core of thought that imbued each lecture with distinction and authority should be as evident on the printed page as it was on the speaker's platform. We hope that this work will furnish support to rational behavior in the direction of deregulation.

Donald P. Jacobs, Dean
Graduate School of Business,
Northwestern University

Evanston, Illinois
March 1978

I

Background

1

PAUL W. MacAVOY

The Existing Condition of Regulation and Regulatory Reform

The effect of regulation on corporate decisions. The costs of controls. The disruption of moving into an open market. Cross-subsidies. Safety, health, and environment. Industry reform proposals. Adverse effects of inflation. Working through and around regulations: natural gas controls.

The workability of various schemes in social governance cannot be determined without knowing where we are on the nature and extent of regulation, particularly by the federal agencies and boards and commissions. My views on the present condition may disagree with those of other analysts. If

so, then the need for additional work could not be more cogently stated.

The workings of regulation have left us with a good idea of
where we are, but not very much of a notion as to where we
are going. I will try to provide you with six typical professo-
rial aphorisms along that line. First, government regulation is
widely believed to be playing some role now in almost all
major corporate decisions in this economy—particularly, a
major role in hiring decisions, in the establishment of work
conditions, in prices, in quantities and qualities of goods and
services provided. Although some would not conclude that
this applies throughout the production sector of this economy,
there is agreement that controls have grown significantly in
the last decade, and that the newer controls are just as strong
as the direct price controls of the older independent commissions regulating transportation and communications. Direct
price controls apply to about 10 percent of the gross national
product, an increase of some 3 percent in the last five years.
The newer controls inherent in health and safety regulation,
that have many of the effects easily recognized in a public
utility industry, cover another 20 percent of industry so significantly that for all intents and purposes that sector is also
regulated. In other words, the control sector of the American
economy has probably grown from something like 7 percent
to close to 30 percent in the last decade. Elsewhere, the extent of controls is now not as great by any means, but it is
also not negligible. All of industry now undertakes pollution
and safety-related investments, checks price increases,
monitors output quality, with a federal agency in mind.

Second, this price control system did not have much effect
on performance in the 1960s, but since the early 1970s,
production of those regulated companies has probably been
reduced by the control system. The reductions have resulted
from cutbacks in investment and thereby in productivity
growth, which in turn has had some adverse impact on
growth of the economy as a whole. Indirect controls, the
health and safety, product quality, environmental controls,

have substantially increased prices in and of themselves. The higher prices have been accompanied by reduced production and increased investment—a contradiction except that the regulations mandate investments for health and safety reasons alone. But the reallocation of investment from productivity-increasing projects to regulation probably reduced overall GNP growth by one-quarter to one-half a percentage point per year alone. If you take this half percent a year of foregone productivity growth over a decade, you're going to find the economy essentially running 6 or 7 percent below its capacity potential because of these controls alone. Regulation thus has spread widely and effectively to encompass about a third of our output, and has thereby reduced our productivity growth significantly.

Third, there are apparently no commensurate benefits resulting from this activity. Until the advent of the sustained inflations of the 1970s, the general research literature indicated there were no direct benefits from public utility price regulation. Now the benefits are negative, because of the impact regulation is having on the growth of these industries. In the case of health, safety, and environmental controls, there are no findings of benefits whatsoever. Rivers are not cleaner, nor is the air of significantly greater quality. The general impression is that this regulatory activity now produces costs much greater than benefits, and that the costs are increasing rapidly in a way most adverse to the smaller organizations in the production sector of the economy.

Fourth, not surprisingly there has been widespread public antagonism to growing controls. In response, public interest institutions concerned with the regulatory phenomenon, and individuals as widely diverse in their views as Ralph Nader and Gerald Ford, have called for reduced regulation. These efforts to eliminate the excessive direct price controls where they clearly have had adverse effects have been unsuccessful. This applies to initiatives attempting to deregulate the Interstate Commerce Commission control of railroad and trucking rates, to efforts to change the Civil Aeronautics Board

procedures involving airline passenger fares, and to natural
gas field price controls. Controls in broadcasting, particularly
with respect to those that hamper the spread of cable television, have not been reduced in any way, although there were
widespread initiatives last year to do that. Even more omi-
nously, the newer energy control policies have taken these
activities in the opposite direction.

If deregulation initiatives have been put forward in railroads, trucking, airlines, gas, oil, and cable television, the
question is why we have not a single case of reduced controls. The fifth aphorism is that there are many good and
sufficient reasons for this state of affairs. Most of them have
to do with an inefficient or slow or procedurally constrained
Congress, but the reasons go deeper than procedural inefficiency. The congressional process for taking a case-by-case
approach to over-regulation is to take an initiative, either by
one of its members or by the president, calling for decontrol,
to a specialist subcommittee that has dealt for a number of
years with problems of the industry. In many cases, the
members of the subcommittee in the House or Senate wrote
the original bill which is being scolded and disparaged by the
proposals for decontrol. Their response is to go to those affected by regulation in the industry and ask them what would
happen if there were to be such decontrol as proposed. Industry reaction is that the proposals, whether by congressional or
White House staff members, are the worst rantings of
ideologues who have not worked in industry and have little
evidence or knowledge as to how the system really operates.
They stress that regulation is much more complex and, even
though there are indications of some ill effects, deregulation
would be worse.

These positions place the burden of proof on those proposing the initiative. That is, the burden ends up with those who
propose change, because members of Congress rely heavily
on industry expertise, and those in the industry affected by
the controls still say that they and the economy will be worse
off if we decontrol. Many individuals who make those state-

ments strongly believe in free enterprise principles. But they take the position that, even though an unregulated airline industry in the long run would be better for the economy and probably for the industry itself, the process of getting from here to there would be sufficiently disruptive as to destroy the industry. They argue that the technical dynamics of disequilibrium in moving from a fixed control system to an open market would be so perverse as to leave us much worse off.

There is also the "Grand Rapids argument"—namely, that Grand Rapids will be without food and clothing or whatever because there will be no trucking service or whatever as a result of decontrol. There'll be no rail service and no airline service for the same reason, so that you can't even leave as the food runs out. You have only to sit there and listen to network television—but that will go dark too, because there'll be no more local affiliated stations if cable television is allowed to wreak its havoc on the land. The argument is basically the notion that, in return for the control system, which involves certificates and licenses preventing competition, regulated companies have been operating widely and well to subsidize rural service, small town service, widow and orphan service, or whatever from the excess returns that are made as a result of the certificate on the large volume or bulk through-route service. Given the controls on entry into trucking and airlines, the providers of service deliver on schedule to Grand Rapids without remuneration because they make so much money on the Chicago-Los Angeles route.

This argument is logically correct, but it turns out to be factually of little importance. There is no such pattern of significant cross-subsidization. But that has to be indicated or proven in each case. The work required to bear that burden of proof is immense. In the case of the airlines, the president of Eastern Airlines, over Miami television, produced a list of those city pairs for which Eastern would terminate service if there were to be deregulation. John Snow, the Under Secretary of Transportation, reached out for the list, but only obtained half the page because Colonel Borman had such a strong grip. But on that half of the page there was listed the New York-Miami run, raising the question whether Colonel Borman was willing to argue that there is cross-subsidization from other services to the New York-Miami run, and if there were, why he doesn't sell that run to another airline because he's free to do that at this time. Such examples melt away as you go through them one by one—questions of equity and efficiency arise and quickly vanish because there is no long list of places that will lose service.

In the case of the airlines, Simat, Helliesen and Company, the consulting firm most often used by the airlines in Civil Aeronautics Board (CAB) proceedings, investigated over a hundred city pairs where there was potential loss of service and found, after detailed cost and revenue analysis, that less than a dozen were likely to sustain losses. As a result of this work, President Ford's airline regulatory reform bill proposed to subsidize those cities out of general revenues, because what was at issue in deregulation were billions of dollars of rate reductions in ransom for a few million dollars of cross-subsidies.

In cases of the proposed reform of regulation in the trucking industry, natural gas, crude oil, cable television, the maritime and the railroad industry, the burden of proof still lies on those making proposals for reform. This burden is not likely to be taken on successfully. As in Nelson's law, "The worse the results from present regulation, the less likely there will be reform"—because of the greater magnitude of the losses following reform for those now being advantaged by over-regulation. They will easily show losses which then would have to be discounted by the proponents as not disruptive of market operations, and such does not appear to be convincing.

The sixth aphorism is that efforts to improve safety, health, and environmental regulation have not been any more successful than elimination of excessive price and entry controls. Here, there is widespread initiative that is attempting to reform safety and health regulation primarily by changing the systems that are used to control behavior. The agencies have not worked well because the control systems now being used cannot, by their nature, be effective. It is not so much that the administrator at the Occupational Safety and Health Administration (OSHA) or the Environmental Protection Agency (EPA) is any worse a manager than a Yale University dean, but rather that even if he were twice as efficient he could not have a positive effect, because the systems that are built into the legislation, or that were established by rule-making in the early period of those organizations, cannot achieve that objective. The best example, of course, is OSHA. Here, the Senate required in 1971 legislation that there be rules and regulations curtailing unsafe conditions in the factories of this country within six months of passage of the bill, and it designated the source for those rules. The sources of existing rules were state occupational safety commissions and the voluntary industrial health associations in various industries in this country. Their "rules" were in good part, in fact, "guidelines" to be used along with occupational training programs to prevent accidents. The guidelines centered on physical work conditions such as the structure of the work floor and floor lighting which, combined with well-trained workers knowledgeable in safety hazards, could reduce accident rates. However, OSHA's rule-making made the guidelines the requirements themselves for specifications of work conditions, and this was done without reference to the training system of which they were part. That is how we got mandatory physical standards for conditions in the work place, including the description of ladder parts which fails to conjure up a ladder as a safe or unsafe tool. The procedure has been to designate the specific physical conditions of each piece of equipment in a factory, but this has only indirectly anything to do with accident rates. And OSHA, as a consequence, in its six years of operations, has had little effect on accident rates. This was not for lack of trying—special programs to enforce regulations in high accident-rate industries were undertaken; but where OSHA operations were, the accident rate increased slightly. The OSHA officers got in the way or, more likely, the quality of the data collected on the accidents improved. Either way, they had no effect of the type intended, because the process is directed toward objects rather than accident-creating behavior.

Research here and in environmental protection argues cogently that the proper direction of such legislation should be towards producing internal incentives for all parties to use whatever means to reduce accidents or environmental degradation. The incentives approach essentially uses taxes or fines or charges against the existence of whatever it is that you are trying to prevent. In the OSHA case, that would come essentially to a requirement that workers' compensation provide payments to injured workers through an insurance scheme based on higher premiums on those plants and those corporations where the accident rates are higher. We are many decades from such an improvement in workers' compensation, however, because the arguments have been denied by the safety professionals on grounds that it is still too early to tell, in the history of OSHA operations, whether there are significant malfunctions from the process. Those being regulated complain about the cost of meeting OSHA and EPA controls, but this does not exactly meet the issue of whether these procedures add more in cost than in social gains to the economy as a whole. In other words, all that we seem to be getting from industry is an estimate of costs, without meeting the question put by the professionals in this area as to whether benefits exceed costs.

Since the case-by-case approach to reform does not work, new approaches must be found. There are a number of attempts now occurring in Washington to do that. The most promising is to initiate comprehensive reform proposals along the lines of the Percy-Byrd-Ribicoff bill calling for specific schedules for comprehensive reduction and reorganization of all the regulations in each sector of the economy. This would require, for example, a White House staff report calling for reorganization and information of the transportation regulatory authorities within a specified period. Another paper would be due the next year calling for comprehensive reform of health, safety, and environmental regulatory authorities. There are a number of implications. One would be that each of the separate industry reform proposals would be enfolded into an across-the-board reform proposal for that sector of the economy. Congress would consider these as an integrated set of proposals, and if there were not a congressional decision according to the schedule, the reorganization and reform would go into effect on a due date. Thus the White House would initiate the program, and Congress would either accept or veto it across the board.

The procedure would likely not be that straightforward. The comprehensive reform proposals would still go through the same committees that, one by one, turn down specific reform proposals. That subcommittee of the Senate Commerce Committee that has dealt with the transportation regulation and has made it what it is in the last decade would have the opportunity to amend the proposal.

The most likely nonevent is that nothing will take place that could be called regulatory reform. In that case, what happens to the operations of the American economy? There would be reason to expect continuations of the loss of up to a half percentage point in GNP growth per year. That could be reduced, however, by the ingenuity within industry to find ways of working through regulation so as to greatly reduce its effect. We may be in a period now of maximum adverse regulatory effect because we are in a period of maximum inflation, and the lags of regulation behind an inflationary economy have adverse effects of the largest magnitude. We may also be in a period of maximum effect in health and safety regulations, because the agencies have only begun their activities and we have not learned to adapt to them.

The case of natural gas fuel price regulation is an example of how bad it can be, and yet how market enterprise learns to adapt and to work its way through. As bad as that looks to all of you, it looks very good to me. The Federal Power Commission (FPC) began wellhead natural gas price controls in 1954, when the Supreme Court stumbled on the totally unwarranted notion that gas production in the United States was characterized by natural monopoly of the public utility nature and therefore had to be regulated. The basis for that decision in the case literature and in the congressional reports on the natural gas act was very slim. The commission had to go into the business of regulating three to four thousand complicated field sales transactions involving hundreds of companies and joint ventures and companies that were producing gas and oil from the same well. Worse yet, this called for regulating essentially a resource which was being depleted, so that replacement costs exceeded historical costs on which prices are set. The ways of regulating, in fact, were amazingly inefficient, leading Dean Landes of the Harvard Law School to report to President Kennedy that the Federal Power Commission was administratively bankrupt.

This was not the end of the story. In the last ten years, great flexibility has been shown by company and commission in dealing with the worst of all controls. By rule-making, the FPC set aside the public utility price-setting approach, and designated specific price ceilings over regions in Texas, Oklahoma, or Louisiana. The first of these area rate-making approaches also took four years, a couple of hundred thousand pages of testimony, and came out with the decision that did very little more than freeze prices at that level that existed about the time the Supreme Court found the industry to be in need of regulation. This led into a ten-year long price freeze, during which the industry turned away from gas for interstate sales in order to develop oil abroad, or to develop natural gas within the states of Texas, Oklahoma, Louisiana, for use there by industry outside of price controls. There were no more new sales of newly discovered gas into regulated interstate markets of any great amount, so that gas delivered in the 1970s was from sales of old reserves contracted for before 1965. Thus, the industry did away with regulation by going out of business in the regulated sector.

This procedure has added to the rate of growth and the development of industry and employment in Texas to the detriment of Illinois. But essentially the American economy has worked its way out of regulation by doing all its business in the state of Texas. Proposals before Congress last year for emergency legislation to prevent Ohio and Illinois from running out during the great cold spell completed the fusion-like movement by declaring that Illinois and Ohio were part of Texas. They did so by allowing Illinois companies or Ohio companies to go to Texas to buy gas, and then to contract delivery by an interstate pipeline to the final point of use. That made Texas the location of purchase and sale, and limited regulation to the interstate transportation of the Ohio consumer's property.

Deregulating without telling can be carried out elsewhere, by using ingenuity to find a way out of other controls far less restrictive than field gas price controls. If this is effective, it would reduce regulation from reliance on Washington. But to be effective, there must be continued pressure from research results showing how bad present regulation is. And there must now be more of the comprehensive reform of the sort of the Percy-Byrd-Ribicoff bill, and not of the sort of the Carter reorganization of energy regulation which cancels much of the progress made in gas regulation.

II

Area Studies

2

DONALD P. JACOBS

Regulation of Deposit-Type Financial Institutions

Government regulation of financial institutions: interest rates, capital stability, insurance provisions. Functional partitioning. Pressure for deregulation and innovation. Computer technology and its influence on banking. Services offered by commercial and savings and loan institutions. The politics of deregulation. Fear of change. Nonfinancial businesses. Proposals for reform.

An enormous literature has developed on the regulation of deposit-type financial intermediaries, and academic writers generally agree that the proper direction of change is toward deregulation. Some easing has occurred in the last several years; but, given the formidable arguments favoring deregulation, progress has been disappointingly slow.

In this paper, I will briefly sketch the background of the existing regulatory framework, and then argue that changes in the economic milieu have weakened and/or altered the impact of major regulatory constraints. Consequently, regulation does not accomplish its original objectives, and in some instances its results are perverse. The implication is that deregulation would benefit both the public and the deposit intermediaries. In the concluding section, I will address the question of why efforts to deregulate have been stymied, and set forth some recommendations for renewing the momentum for deregulation. Although my proposals involve risks, barring a major crisis they involve smaller potential costs than those that may follow without reform.

THE EXISTING REGULATORY SYSTEM

The major features of the existing regulatory system were forged during the early 1930s and were clearly a response to prevailing aberrant conditions. Many commercial banks had failed because of the depressed economy. But bank failures were also common in the 1920s, when economic conditions were generally prosperous. Moreover, banks that continued to operate had large potential portfolio losses relative to available capital. In the banking acts of 1933 and 1935, Congress attempted to correct the perceived major problem of the industry—which was a socially pernicious and unacceptable failure rate.

Lowering Commercial Bank Risk-Taking and Increasing Capital

To reduce commercial bank risk-taking to socially acceptable levels, congressional legislation divorced commercial from investment banking, reduced real estate lending, and established many other restrictions on management prerogatives.

Increasing the capital position of the industry in the long run could only be accomplished by raising bank profitability. In the short run, some severely undercapitalized banks would be allowed to borrow from the Reconstruction Finance Corporation. Profitability would be increased by the prohibition of interest on demand deposits, regulation over the maximum rate which could be paid on time and savings deposits, and control over new entrants into the banking business. Because it was believed "excessive" competition for deposits raised costs and tempted bankers to reach for high-yielding, risky assets to return a profit, these regulations were also perceived as risk reducers.

Due to the precarious position of the industry, deposit insurance with a potential draw on the federal government was instituted. But Federal Deposit Insurance was not then accorded its present crucial position in defending the system. To round out the major elements of the regulatory framework of the banking system, it must be noted that the major structural determinant was accidently introduced by the McFadden Act in 1927. As an example of a regulatory quirk, this act was originally intended to force the comptroller to permit national banks to establish branches where state-chartered banks were given this power. At the present time, its major impact is to stop the comptroller from permitting national banks to set up branches in states that prohibit this practice.

Partly in response to the withdrawal of commercial banks from the real estate market, but also because of the depressed conditions and the social priority accorded to housing, the Federal Home Loan Bank Board was created, with a deposit insurance program to encourage the growth of deposit institutions that would specialize in financing residential real estate. This agency, modified by continuing changes in legislation, continues its original mandate: encouragement of the growth and viability of savings and loan associations (S&Ls).

Functional Partitioning of the Industry

In effect, the developing regulatory design called for a set of mission-oriented institutions, with each institution granted advantages in certain markets. Commercial banks would finance business and provide third-party transfers, and would rely mainly on transaction balances as their source of funds. And thrift institutions would specialize in financing residential real estate, and would tap the consumer savings markets for funds.

This functional partitioning worked tolerably well for more than two decades. Deposit intermediaries enjoyed the protection of the regulatory structure, and little criticism was heard. Economic conditions supported the thrift institutions, since the spread between short and long rates provided a comfortable margin of profitability. The thrift institutions were thus able to attract sufficient funds to finance the growing housing stock.

Growing Interest in Deregulation

This placid era ended for commercial banks around 1960. One hypothesis explaining the changed attitude of many bankers about this time is that many banks changed top management during the late 1950s, and replaced executives who had experienced the despair of the 1930s with others who knew only the prosperity of the late 1940s and 1950s. A second hypothesis is that by the late 1950s banks had dissipated the liquidity that had been accumulated, largely during World War II. Reduced liquidity meant that for the first time in two decades major banks became concerned about having lendable funds to meet the financing requirements of their traditional clientele. Depositors, especially businesses, had learned to economize on zero interest demand deposits, and commercial banks lost their share of the market among the deposit intermediaries. A third hypothesis suggests that the advent of a Comptroller of the Currency dedicated to deregulation—James Saxon—sparked latent but strong competitive inclinations in the industry. All three factors probably played a role.

Whatever the reason, the early 1960s witnessed increasing agitation within the industry for loosening of regulatory constraints. These efforts enjoyed some early success, but stern opposition arose to stymie deregulation. When deregulation faltered, the industry turned to innovation to serve their customers.

Innovation in the 1960s

The decade of the 1960s saw an extraordinary burst of innovative behavior by banks—first under the heading of liability management, and then through the holding company—which permitted functional, geographic, and financial diversification.

The thrift institutions—mutual savings banks and savings and loan associations—began to experience the more vigorous competition for savings during the 1960s. The growth rate in mutual savings banks and S&Ls slowed relative to commercial banks, but it was not until 1966, when interest rates rose rapidly, that the S&L industry became concerned with their regulatory environment.

The rise in interest rates demonstrated the inherent weakness of a business that borrows short and lends long. This weakness could prove fatal if depositors withdrew their funds when the institution failed to meet competitive offers, or if the cyclical timing of investments produced large losses.

Since 1966, the financial health of thrift institutions has been protected by allowing them a rate advantage over commercial banks through restriction of the maximum interest rates that deposit institutions could pay. Because of the continued specialization of S&Ls, the differential rate maxima have become crucial to their viability. In principle, the differential is an offset to the competitive advantage commercial banks enjoy through wider lending powers. When the rate maxima are below open market rates, the costs of deposits are reduced for all depository institutions, at least in theory.

Weakening of the Regulatory System

There is reason to believe that deposit rate regulation will not continue to protect the thrift institutions, given their present confined operating powers. Moreover, deposit rate regulation involves increasing social costs in terms of misallocation of resources and an increase in the fragility of capital markets. Most important, transactors have learned to adapt, reducing the power of rate regulation to defend the competitive position of the thrift institutions. Depositors invest their funds, circumventing financial intermediaries; and borrowers tailor securities to the taste of direct lenders. Through time, all the regulated deposit institutions are losing their share of the market.

In addition, technological change which increases the convenience of third-party payment services to households implies that the interest rate differential will have to be widened to continue the existing protection against commercial bank competition. The use of computer technology in funds-transfer, data storage, and analysis has already influenced the financial services delivered to households as well as the types of institutions delivering these services. And it is certain that the influence of this new technology will become increasingly pervasive. A dramatically different funds-transfer mechanism relying on electronic signals is replacing the paper-based system. This new payments system will broaden the geographic market that can be serviced by an office of a deposit intermediary. It will greatly increase the ability of institutions other than commercial banks to provide third-party payment services. It will facilitate transfers of interest-bearing assets—virtually identical to savings deposits—that are free of regulation on maximum interest payment. If the regulatory framework is not soon altered, these changes will certainly harm the competitive position of the regulated deposit inter-mediaries vis-à-vis the unregulated sector.

This discussion suggests a number of conclusions. The mission-oriented system of deposit intermediaries that evolved out of the 1930s worked tolerably well as long as the economy exhibited a high degree of economic stability and the banking industry had surplus lending capacity. With the economic instability since the mid-1960s, and with the newly developing funds-transfer technology, a number of problems have emerged. Savers have been inclined to forego the ser-vices of intermediaries because of artificially contained yields; financial institutions have overinvested in physical facilities to provide convenience because they cannot pay explicit interest; the possibility of financial crisis is increased because of the larger use of open-market rather than customer-relationship financing through intermediaries; new institutions are formed more often because the regulated firms cannot adapt to new market demands; and on and on.

For two entirely different reasons, one would expect that thoughtful commercial bankers and S&L managers should both favor substantial relaxation of regulatory constraints. Commercial banks now provide a wide range of services, but are prohibited from providing others which they could profit-ably produce. More important to them are the regulatory pro-hibitions which impinge on their ability to compete for de-posits. During the 1960s and early 1970s, the effects of these regulatory prohibitions have been forestalled by innovations in liability management and in the development of the bank holding company. But emerging electronic funds-transfer im-plies a major competitive setback if deposit payment regula-tions are not withdrawn or greatly altered. Thus, in the ab-sence of regulatory changes, commercial banks may face a greatly reduced growth rate.

The S&L industry is in a still more precarious position. The dramatic increase in interest rate instability implies a need to restructure balance sheets to achieve a more hedged maturity position. In addition, the advent of electronic funds-transfer means S&Ls must either offer funds-transfer services or enhance their income in order to offer a larger interest premium to their depositors.

Political Problems

Since all parties—commercial banks, S&Ls, mutual savings banks, and the public—could benefit from deregulation, it would seem that reform should be readily obtainable. Nevertheless, in recent years little has been accomplished from a number of major initiatives. The Hunt Commission blueprint, which intentionally balanced measured costs and benefits for the major deposit intermediaries, was given congressional review in the form of the Financial Institutions Act of 1973. This legislation got nowhere. During 1975, Senator McIntyre's Financial Institutions Subcommittee endorsed the Financial Institutions Act of 1975, which was subsequently passed by the Senate. But this legislation foundered in the House Banking Committee. The House Banking Committee's so-called FINE study led to the Financial Reform Act of 1976, which never got out of committee. None of these major reform packages came close to adoption. Before turning to my recommendation, it is important to explain why the existing system has been so slow to change.

POLITICAL PROBLEMS IN DEREGULATION

The problems encountered by regulatory reform efforts in the absence of a financial crisis are inherent in the present system. The mission-oriented structure, in which each type of institution is granted competitive advantages in the area of its mandated mission, establishes forces that undermine reform legislation; where legislation *has* been adopted, these forces reshape proposals to serve parochial ends. Some of the reasons for this negativism are widely understood, but I believe much ignorance exists about the strengths and weaknesses of the major participants in the legislative arena.

In understanding recent discussions of banking reform, the beginning of wisdom is recognition that there is no such thing as a commercial banking industry. Rather, commercial banking is a host of shifting alliances, depending on the proposals at hand. There are big banks and little banks, member banks and nonmember banks, domestic banks and international banks, money-market banks and regional banks, and on and on. Because of the enormous heterogeneity, it is virtually impossible to define an industry position for reform, but it is easy to find a subgroup eager to veto reform proposals.

The shifting alliances reflect the broad functional diversity among commercial banks. Individual banks specialize in some services and do not offer others; or some services are offered to a minor extent. Vital concerns to one type of bank may be of little concern to another. Also, because of differing strategies, locations, or market conditions, the interests of different banks result in differing trade-offs in legislative packages. Diversity within the banking industry is so great that, in the absence of outside forces, major industry disagreements about regulatory change would create basic realignments in industry organization. Although disagreements are aired in congressional and state legislative debates, their intensity is muted by the push for enlarged powers by the other deposit intermediaries. When such legislation comes up, the commercial banking industry unites in opposition.

The S&L industry is far more homogeneous. Like commercial banks, there is great diversity in the size distribution of associations, but functional diversity is not so closely related to size. The industry's interests are more readily defined, and therefore can be more easily unified on major legislative issues. Nevertheless, the large/small institution differences occasionally hamper the achievement of a legislative position held by the industry.

Commercial bankers often contend that S&L legislative efforts are extraordinarily successful. The S&L industry's trade associations are ably led, and the institutional homogeneity makes for clearer goals. Moreover, emphasis on housing has allied the S&L industry with the construction trade unions and homebuilders, both formidable lobbyists.

Short-Run v. Long-Run Views

In recent years, however, the alliance with the trade unions and homebuilders has subverted certain legislative goals of the S&L industry. The enforced specialization in housing remains a goal of the trade unions and homebuilders, but, as described above, specialization is the Achilles heel of the thrift industry.

When interest rates rise, savings flow to the S&Ls dries up and they cannot make mortgage commitments, even at high rates. This concerns the unions as well as the homebuilders. Broadened powers will probably improve the ability of S&Ls to compete for deposits and augment the flow of funds to the mortgage markets in periods of rising interest rates. But broadened powers may reduce mortgage availability during periods of monetary ease. This should not deter reform, since the industry's long-run viability is in jeopardy if its operating characteristics are not altered. However, the legislative program of the homebuilders and the building-trade unions have not demonstrated a willingness to chance the possible short-term loss of funds in order to secure the long-run health of the S&L industry.

This difference in the short- and long-term views is also crucial in another sense. Within the deposit intermediaries, the major characteristic determining the position of the institution on the question of change is the asset size of the institution. Through the 1960s and 1970s, large commercial banks have progressively moved closer to open-market prices in acquiring funds. They therefore have experienced an ever-decreasing advantage from deposit-interest restrictions. However, smaller banks continue to derive a large benefit from deposit-rate ceilings. This basic difference must be understood as short term; technology will ultimately cause banks of all sizes to be affected by these same forces. In addition, management of large banks feels more secure in its ability to provide services utilizing the new computer technology and in its ability to compete in a less-regulated environment.

Among S&Ls, the problem is mainly the industry's remarkable growth record of the past thirty years. In the last decade, major concerns have surfaced during periods of rising interest rates. But when interest rates receded, deposit inflows increased and S&Ls returned to a strongly profitable position. Support for reform requires understanding of the long-run implications of the depositor learning curve and the impact of the emerging electronic funds-transfer system. This demands managerial sophistication which is positively correlated with institution size. But, given the past growth record, it is easy for the management of smaller institutions to decry change and expect to ride out the storm. Moreover, as in the case of commercial banks, the management of larger institutions is more secure in its ability to offer competitive products in a less-regulated environment.

Other purveyors of financial services can be expected to oppose efforts to permit the regulated institutions to enlarge their operating powers. Such opposition has been most evident in the controversy surrounding the services permitted bank holding companies and S&L service corporations. Lobbying is to be expected, but two anomalies are noteworthy. First, there are examples where the service in question came into being in response to the inability of banks and S&Ls to adjust to market conditions because of regulatory constraints. Second, and perhaps more important, these nondeposit suppliers of financial services are expanding into the major

area where banks had recently been virtually the only
supplier—namely, third-party transfers. Because these
suppliers are new in the market, they are unregulated; they
therefore enjoy cost advantages in competing with commercial banks and S&Ls.

THE PATH TO DEREGULATION

Because my proposals for stimulating deregulation call for
some perseverance on the part of large commercial banks, we
should squarely face the impediments to reform. Reform has
been retarded by the visceral fear of change and by the relative prosperity of the smaller institutions—both commercial
banks and S&Ls. Another impediment has been pressure
groups interested in assuring a robust flow of funds to the
residential real estate markets.

Dealing with the last problem first, I see no alternative to
the Hunt Commission's proposal that any institution receiving
interest income on residential mortgages be permitted to de-
duct a portion of such receipts from gross taxable income.
The proportion could be temporarily progressive, to permit
large holders of such assets time to restructure their balance
sheets; but after some period the deduction should be propor-
tional. The deductible proportion could be varied over the
business cycle to adjust fund flows into this market.

This proposal flies in the face of the expressed desire of the
administration and tax experts to reduce the use of tax subsidies to encourage social-priority investment. But the
alternative—warping the financial system to augment real estate financing—contains even greater dangers. The present
system encourages residential financing by constraining
financial institutions to underpay the small savers. The system is thereby weakened and made more prone to failures,
and probably will not survive in the future without additional
governmental support and interference.

Unfortunately, there is no easy way to allay fear of the unknown. It is too early to forecast the impact of a fully implemented electronic funds-transfer system. But it seems clear that smaller institutions face a bleak future, given present regulations. Electronic funds-transfer will undermine the geographic isolation of markets, permitting larger deposit institutions to serve more distant customers conveniently. In addition, a wide array of nondeposit financial institutions, and even nonfinancial businesses, may compete with the deposit institutions in providing financial services to households.

This possible entry of nonfinancial businesses poses the greatest threat to the smaller deposit institutions. Potential competitors are essentially unregulated in terms of what they could pay for household funds, and they do not sustain other regulatory costs such as reserve requirements and examination fees. Nor are they burdened by geographic constraints on their activities. If the regulatory environment is not relaxed, deposit institutions will surely lose their market share to these other competitors, and the greatest losers will probably be the smaller institutions.

Proposals for Reform

I would first propose to permit thrift institutions to hold all assets and perform all services conducted by commercial banks. Second, I propose gradually to abolish all ceilings on interest payment on deposits, say, over five years. During the five-year adjustment period, institutions designated as "thrift banks" would be permitted to offer a rate one-quarter percent above that offered by commercial banks. Thrift banks would be defined to include deposit intermediaries with less than, say, 10 percent of their assets in the form of business loans. Thus, many small commercial banks might fall into this class. This latter possibility is an important aspect of the recommendation. First, these "new" thrift institutions will be permitted some additional powers which can be expected to improve the viability of small banks. Second, small commercial banks have been most vocal in arguing that thrift institutions have a major competitive advantage. This proposal would allow small banks to alter their status if they so desire. At the same time, the proposal would facilitate the transformation into commercial banks of the larger S&Ls and mutual savings banks if they desire.

Thrift institutions with a high proportion of their assets—say, 50 percent—invested in real estate would be eligible for membership in the Federal Home Loan Bank. The others would be members of the Federal Reserve. This recognizes the different type of borrowing facility that would be required by institutions whose assets are commercial or real-estate dominated. To maintain the competitive position of deposit institutions with the nonregulated sector that will supply financial services, the cost of reserve requirements will have to be reduced, either by a gradual reduction in required reserves or through some form of compensation on reserve holdings.

Thrift banks would be permitted to engage in both equity and debt brokerage and to be insurance agents, whereas commercial banks would be permitted the full range of investment banking powers.

Expected Benefits

Granting these new powers to deposit intermediaries could result in large social benefits. Because of the nature of the business, investment banks are few and spatially concentrated. Of the small number of existing investment bankers, only a small proportion are interested in underwriting securities for small enterprises. The broad geographic distribution of sizable commercial banks would encourage such business in all parts of the country. Because of their familiarity with small businesses, commercial banks would be able to advise and handle underwriting more inexpensively than outsiders, who would need to learn the business for this one transaction.

The distribution network for equity and corporate debt securities is more extensive than the number of investment banks. The addition of the broad coverage implied by permitting thrift banks to perform this function will greatly increase the proportion of the population with ready access to investment advice regarding corporate securities. The local focus of thrift banks will again enhance the financing ability of small businesses.

This large, highly localized system should also improve the distribution of insurance. Although the existing insurance distribution network is substantially more extensive than the security underwriting and brokerage systems, there is still reason to believe that the enhanced counseling capability will produce greater information to consumers and an increase in competition which should lower the price of these services.

Commercial banks were excluded from the investment banking business to reduce the riskiness of commercial banking. It is now understood it was not the banking system, but rather the general economic instability, which caused banking failures. The major problem internal to the banking system was contagion of deposit withdrawals, a problem which was cured by deposit insurance.

A second concern arose from widely publicized examples of self-dealing in the investment banking activities of a few commercial banks. Banks now operate subject to the close scrutiny of examination procedures. Moreover, availability of machine-readable data allows increasingly close surveillance of these institutions.

This proposal separates the underwriting from the secondary distribution of securities. Rather than completely excluding commercial banks from the secondary distribution business, it would be desirable to allow the individual bank to choose in which part of the business it will engage. Moreover, these rules should be reviewed after, say, five years, to determine if they should be eased.

Both commercial banks and thrift banks could engage in a wide array of services which would improve financial markets. Many such opportunities stem from improved technology. Methods must be developed to permit timely reassessment of these opportunities. A possible way to do this would be for the Congress to empower a federal banking authority—the Federal Deposit Insurance Corporation, the Comptroller of the Currency, or the Federal Home Loan Bank Board—to authorize new services that are in the public interest. The Congress could reserve the right to negate this authority by requiring a ninety-day notice before any new service authorization is implemented. The history of banking legislation suggests the necessity for such a delegation of authority. The ability of coalitions of interest groups to frustrate reform has been demonstrated over the past three decades.

This proposal recognizes that a major impediment to regulatory reform is concern over the viability of the small and medium-sized institution. It attempts to give some comfort to the management of those institutions. At the same time, the proposal would greatly improve the social efficiency of the system and make it less vulnerable to crisis.

COMMENT

RICHARD GILBERT
President, Citizens' Savings Association, Canton, Ohio
Former President, United States League of Savings Associations
In my judgment we are already an overregulated society. Often the intended benefits are not forthcoming, and the cost of the regulations is generally expensive. Many regulations are counterproductive. . . .

I agree with Dr. Jacobs . . . that unless the regulatory framework is changed for regulated depository institutions, . . . the nonregulated sector may well take over. For the regulated sector, the outlook is bleak . . . most specifically, for the savings and loan business. However, as we . . . search for ways to begin deregulation . . . we should recall that the greatest number of existing savings and loan executives have never been off the government regulation, and it has been pleasant and profitable. It has provided good jobs, and good salaries, and stature in the community, and being part of the second largest set of financial intermediaries. So if the present life is good, partly because of and in spite of regulations—and it is—then threatening to kick the crutch out from under the person who has never walked without it is bound to bring about adverse reaction. . . .

I question that there is anything like the monolithic savings and loan business . . . [just] described. When I . . . headed our major trade association, I often looked for just one little bit of unity about which we might rally, and didn't find it. I question that there is . . . polarization . . . in our business around large and small. . . . Some of the innovations have come elsewhere, but generally it is not around large and small. . . . One reason that we have been effective [at lobbying] . . . is that basically we have been against change. It is much easier to kill legislation than it is to foster and pass it. . . .

Only a few people . . . desire substituting the unknown for the known. . . . If we are going to begin the process of . . . deregulation, we should begin with some knowns, and aim at the pocketbook. For example, the mortgage interest tax credit has the greatest potential for beginning to free up our business from mortgage investment. . . . I believe that at the outset it should be made optional for savings and loan, and I think you will attract a number—and perhaps the majority—by saying, "Look, try it. I think you'll like it.". . .

Regulation Q . . . has been around for half a century, and it hasn't done all that badly over time. It is beginning to cause some real problems since the late 1960s and early 1970s, but . . . [most] savings and loan executives . . . don't view it as having caused any major disallocation. . . . In their minds, discomfort was generally caused by deregulation. . . . They felt that deregulation heightened the problems, and that regulation . . . alleviated them. . . . With our failures in attempting to start the process of deregulation, I think . . . a new approach might well be taken. . . . We might give primary attention to both method and timing. Instead of setting the date for the funeral of Regulation Q, we might begin the evolutionary process and pay strict attention to time. . . . To effect changes in Q, I think the changes should be effected when the ceilings are not the floor. . . . A flexible Q at the outset might well be developed, . . . [one] that could be more responsive to the market, yet would eliminate the fear of unbridled competition. . . . Specialization would be specialization of choice, not government regulation.

JOHN H. PERKINS
President, Continental Illinois National Bank
and Trust Company of Chicago
It is hard for those who haven't been involved day to day in the
regulatory and governmental process, the legislative process, to
realize the explosive growth of legislation for various social and
related purposes . . . in the late 1960s and early 1970s . . .
[leading] in the early and middle 1970s to an absolutely explosive
growth in the regulatory output. . . . I would agree that the spread
of powers to more properly broaden the powers of thrifts and other
institutions [is] a very proper public policy aim, providing . . .
these powers are spread by the equalization of responsibilities
and [of] our ability to compete. . . .

The commercial banking system, by law, now is not able to pay
a competitive rate for the savings of individuals which does, . . . in
effect, penalize by edict 94 million savers in commercial
banks. . . . Your . . . conclusion about the thrift bank idea for the
banks in real estate bothers me. . . . The growth of [special mis-
sion] institutions has resulted in problems which we now have to
cure, and for which we have had these disintermediation periods
and other problems. To develop another special class of special
institutions . . . [may] not solve the problem, but rather will create
additional problems, . . . more regulation, . . . special size rules,
special power rules, and all the rest. I worry, too, about the kind of
given . . . that there is a public good to be served by credit allocation . . . either directly or indirectly toward real estate . . . specifically . . toward residential mortgages. . . . I think the diversity
of this country, the institutions, and the needs of the people, are so
great, and the needs differ so widely, that I am not willing to accept
the fact that it is [good] public policy to concentrate this way on
real estate. . . . [In] a lot of areas . . . the farmers are the principal
customers . . . and the small farmer looks to the small thrift institution to take care of him. . . . A lot of small institutions finance a lot
of jobs in small town America, and . . . in large city and suburban
America with smaller business. . . .

A tax deduction for mortgages . . . leads to a credit allocation
process. The end of the road on that is a political allocation of
credit and resources rather than a market allocation. . . .

The 1974 recession, accompanied by the long secular collapse of
the real estate markets, . . . led to a couple of highly publicized
bank failures. I am not sure they were regulatory failures at all. No
depositors were hurt. . . . [No] law ever guaranteed that stockholders should be protected from risk, as indeed the stockholders

were the ones that were hurt. . . . The reaction . . . in our congressional atmosphere . . . and our highly publicized approach to public policy, has led to a call for more and more regulation. . . . This process . . . has led the regulators, in my judgment, to go into . . . overreaction, legislative regulatory overkill. . . . This, to me, is our problem. . . . We probably ought to get on with fair restructuring of the financial mechanism where it is needed in the public interest.

3

ALFRED E. KAHN

Deregulation of Air Transportation—Getting from Here to There

CAB regulation of the airline industry. Suggested methods of transition to deregulation and increased competition. Free market entry. Price regulation: discount fares and the adjustment of airline revenues. The elasticity of industry demands. Scheduled v. standby service. Price discriminatory practices—discount and standby rates.

This paper will report on a fascinating venture in applied economics—the current efforts at the Civil Aeronautics Board (CAB) to deregulate the airline industry and to restore it as much as possible to the rule of competition. My emphasis will not be on the case for and against deregulation, but rather on the problems of transition, especially on the problem of getting a clear intellectual grasp of what a rational policy for the transition would be. Yet I must begin with the case for deregulation, since it has a strong bearing on the course we are following.

THE CASE FOR DEREGULATION, AND A FIRST AREA OF UNCERTAINTY

Fundamentally, this industry is structurally suited to effective competition. Economies of scale are evidently quite limited, and—but for the Federal Aviation Act and the CAB itself—barriers to entry are relatively low. This is true of entry into the industry itself *de novo,* but even more of the entry by existing carriers into new markets, since the principal physical plant is itself mobile.

A second strand in the case for deregulation is that there is no reason to fear that competition in this industry would be destructive. Most city pair markets will support only one carrier, and most of the traffic is concentrated in markets that will support only a few, so oligopolistic restraint is far more likely than cutthroat price rivalry.

The prime requisite for destructive competition is that capital, once sunk in an industry, be immobile, so that under intense rivalry it may have to remain in a depressed industry, while earning subnormal returns for long periods of time. But in this respect the airline industry is almost unique, in that its physical plant, which is only moderately long-lived, can move from one market to another, including to an active second-hand market.

With relatively easy entry, relatively small economies of scale, and mobility of its capital equipment, the technology of aviation seems ideally suited to exactly the flexible adaptation of supply to dynamic market conditions that a market system, if unimpeded by government restrictions, can efficiently accomplish.

There are also the familiar defects of regulation as practiced in the last four years: its heavily protectionist character, the tight limitations on entry, the clogged lineup of applicants for new entry, the restrictions on carrier operations and price competiton. And while it would be quite wrong not to appreciate the quality of service that the airline industry provides, it is possible to see in its performance the consequences of this governmentally imposed cartelization: the tendency for service—and especially scheduling—competition to adjust costs upward to meet the price rather than the reverse, the limited availability of low price and cost options to travelers and shippers, and the inefficiencies and inflexibilities forced on carriers by the persuasive, protectionist restrictions to which they are subject.

My major residual uncertainty concerns the phenomenon of scheduled service. The untutored observer may think that what the airlines provide is simply seats on moving objects, and that one seat is pretty much the same as any other. But an important aspect of the service is availability—the reasonable probability that a passenger can get a ticket by a simple telephone call, on relatively short notice, and for a conveniently scheduled flight, with no penalty if he fails to show up at the flight time. Thus, when average load factors begin to get above 60 or 65 percent, the quality of that particular service begins to deteriorate markedly.

This means that the equilibrium price for this particular, regularly scheduled service has to be high enough to cover unit costs with planes less than, say, 65 percent full; and that means, in turn, that the typical situation is one in which the short-run marginal costs of taking on additional passengers is less than average total costs.

The implications of this are not entirely clear. When marginal costs are close to zero, destructive competition becomes

possible because of the strong temptation for sellers to compete in trying to fill those seats at prices far below average
cost.

This situation suggests the desirability of a complicated,
differentiated scheme of different prices for different
packages or kinds of service associated with a seat on a
plane. The most obvious, of course, is standby service; but
other variations are conceivable, such as truly firm
reservations—at some sort of premium, particularly as long
as penalties for no-shows are infeasible. Other possibilities
include conditional reservations, to account for the necessity
of deliberate overbooking in order to maintain load factors
and the consequent probability of having to bump overbooked
passengers, and various possible auction schemes to
minimize the social costs of overbooking by ensuring that
passengers who are bumped accept that fate voluntarily because they are suitably compensated. A variety of peak-load
pricing schemes is also possible, with standbys being only
one kind; other kinds would involve probabilistic calculations
in advance of the relationship of demand to capacity at different times and on different flights, along with suitable variations in price (this is the purported basis for such discount
fares as Super-Saver, Budget, Apex, and Super-Apex); yet
another variation is charter service, with restrictions—
advance ticket purchases, cancellation penalties, and accep-
tance of the risk that the flight will be cancelled if too few
seats are subscribed—designed to assure the high load factors
that are essential to the economics of the charter operation.

It would seem that the optimum competitive solution
would be to offer these various packages of services with
only such restrictions on each as are required to make certain
that its price is related to the cost of providing it, permitting
travelers a free choice among them. While this is indeed my
disposition, I confess to a lingering uncertainty about the beneficial effects of the outcome—again, because of the peculiar nature of scheduled service.[1]

THE PROBLEMS OF GRADUALISM

There are really two possible approaches to the goal of transferring this industry from governance by the CAB to the
competitive market. One, which is intellectually attractive, is
the big-bang method: total freedom of entry and total freedom
of pricing at some pre-announced time in the future. That is
one that I can genuinely understand, and a reasonably well-
developed body of economic theory exists to predict its consequences.

But there is no realistic hope of getting such an act of faith
by Congress, and it is impossible to be convinced of its desirability. This is an industry that has grown up in a
hothouse, that gives good service, and that has to be finan-
cially healthy if it is to continue to give good service in the
future. Yet this industry, exposed as it is to critical fluctua-
tions, has one of the highest debt-to-equity ratios in the
economy, has only a 2.6 times coverage of its fixed charges,
and earned only about 11 percent on equity last year on its
trunk lines. Investors obviously agree, since market values of
airline equities are averaging only about two-thirds of book
value.

So we are inevitably committed to gradualism —
necessarily, if there is no change in the statute, but almost
certainly even if there is. The problem, however, is that there
really is no blueprint for a gradual transition, no organized
body of theory by which to plan and monitor it.

Second-Best Options

On the contrary, we are left with the theory of second best.
This theory tells us that if we want to go from point A, which
is here, to point C, which is there, it is not necessarily socially efficient to go part way in that direction, from A to B.

One lesson we have learned from the history of airlines is
that, in the absence of price competition, rivalry among car-

riers tends to take the form instead of costly improvements in service. And the evidence seems quite clear that an increase in the number of carriers in a particular market appears to be correlated with a decline in load factors—an increase, in other words, in cost-inflating service rivalry.

These applications, therefore, confront me regularly with the vexing question of whether in fact I want to substitute a less efficient duopoly or oligopoly for a more efficient monopoly. This is not to deprecate the value of service competition: in view of the kinds of needs that scheduled service is intended to satisfy, load factors can be too high as well as too low. The difficulty is that if passengers are presented with no alternative, higher load factor/lower fare options, there is no effective market determination of whether service is too good, in a sense of being costlier than consumers would be willing to accept if given a choice.

Although, therefore, two sellers are closer than is one seller to many, and the change may increase the likelihood of effective competition in second-best terms, going part way (or, in the more familiar application of second best, all the way in one part of the economy) may be worse than not moving at all.

I am reasonably persuaded that if we are to make genuine progress toward effective competition, we have to institute some system of automatic, discretionary entry into markets—some reliable promise to all the carriers that they will at some certain date, or according to some predetermined time schedule, be free to start entering new markets, and, by the same token, be subject to penetration of their markets by others, without CAB permission.

The virtue of such an arrangement is that it will force each of the carriers to start figuring out now what services it can provide best, and what kinds it had better leave to its competitors; to start planning a rationalization of its route structures in order to improve its ability to compete; to start examining the services it now offers and effecting such improvements as it can, with an eye to forestalling competitive entry.

But if the process—of entry, rationalization, and exit—is to be gradual and limited, we have reason to be worried about the beneficence and effectiveness of the competition that is likely to ensue.

It is unlikely that the resulting competition can be on the basis of relative efficiency alone. From past practice, the main determinant of relative carrier costs is not the quality of management, but the route structures—long haul or short, in thin markets or thick. The ability of carrier A to compete successfully over a particular route with carrier B will be heavily influenced not by its efficiency, but by the nature of the carriers' respective feed-in and beyond routes. Competition is based on whether business goes to seller A in preference to seller B because A has customers available from its own feeder routes, or because it has rights to routes beyond that enable only A to offer single-plane service to travelers to these beyond points.

This last distortion raises questions about the ultimate feasibility of competition in this industry, not simply about the feasibility of a gradual transition. I am, I regret to say, unable as yet to assess its significance. In part, it seems to describe a genuine service advantage of integration, to the extent that multistop carriage by a single airline reduces the need to change planes. But where transfer between planes is involved, the advantage enjoyed by a single airline is merely tactical: if a single carrier handled all the traffic in and out of O'Hare airport, it is difficult to see how the average walk between planes could be reduced, unless the monopolist reduced flight schedules.

My tentative resolution of these dilemmas—the danger of transforming efficient monopolies into inefficient duopolies, competing only in cost-inflating services, and the dangers of unequal competition because of differential route restrictions and handicaps—is along the following lines:

First, we must be as receptive and as liberal as possible in permitting existing carriers to realign their routes and to slough off the restrictions that limit their operating flexibility and force inefficiencies on them.

Second, more and more of the certificated authority that we grant must be made *permissive* and *nonexclusive*. If two carriers are applying for a particular route—the traffic on which appears to be large enough to justify only one—I suggest that we should carefully consider *permitting both* but *requiring neither*. At present, applications are too often essentially preclusive in their motivation: a carrier applies for a certificate for a particular market because it wants to prevent a competitor from getting the award, and because also, since the license is exclusive, it is salable. These considerations, it may feel, are valuable enough to justify its undertaking the minimum service required to keep the authority, even if it is uneconomic.

Making the grants nonexclusive and permissive in these circumstances should:

(a) cut down on the applications that are justified only on the expectation that the certificates granted will be few, and that if X gets it, Y will not;
(b) cut down on the offer of uneconomic service, merely in order to hold an authority;
(c) keep a competitor or competitors with unexercised authority standing by at the edge of the market and in a position to enter without further permission from us, if service is too poor or rates too high;
(d) and so, perhaps, put a limit on cost-inflating, nonprice competition.

Third, we should be particularly receptive to proposed new services with a low price dimension. I refer here not to the mere verbal promises of low fares, but to the offer of a plan that backs up that promise with a credible expectation of low-cost operations with high break-even load factors. Such entry is the most effective device for holding cost-inflating service rivalry in check.

And fourth, we must extend freedom of entry as widely as possible. This, paradoxically, is the only answer I can think of to the contention that free entry will permit the bigger airlines, with ample feeder and beyond operations, to funnel intermediate traffic into its own aircraft, making it impossible for smaller, more specialized carriers to compete. For if there are either genuine economies or merely tactical advantages of linking routes together in this way, there are also powerful economies of specialization.

So far as I know there is no objective basis for deciding where the integrated, typically larger carrier can out-compete more specialized rivals, and where the specialized carrier will have a clear advantage. Since there will undoubtedly be situations of both kinds, we may conclude that under a competitive regime these various market situations will sift themselves out automatically, with various kinds of suppliers emerging successful on the basis of their respective advantages and handicaps in each kind of market situation. Hence my prescription of free entry.

PRICING

The task of trying to regulate price in a period of transition is proving even more difficult than regulating entry.

Price Ceilings

First is the question of whether carriers should be free to raise their rates. In principle, obviously they should: the introduction of more competition surely means that some prices will have to go up just as others will go down.

But there is still a great deal of monopoly power in this industry. To extend to carriers the freedom to increase prices more rapidly than the increase in effective competition is to assure exploitation of customers. Introduction of the former must be synchronized with the latter, and specifically with freedom of entry, if we are not going to follow the big-bang approach.

So I don't see how we can soon give up control over rate levels or cease to set rate ceilings. In fact, we have scarcely begun to confront the question of whether we can ever totally deregulate price in the majority of markets that can support only a single carrier.

Rate Reductions

The question of whether we need to limit the freedom to cut prices, and if so, how, is the most complicated of all.

At first blush, it would seem that we must be able to set price floors so long as we must also fix ceilings. In a system that is part competitive and part monopolistic, price reductions are likely to be selective and discriminatory—directed at particular markets or at particular categories of travelers, and framed to deny the benefits to customers whose demands are comparatively inelastic. This is not necessarily bad in a situation in which marginal costs are below average, and in which, therefore, the cost of picking up additional customers may be very low. But in contrast with the regulation of traditional public utilities, where, at least in principle, the regulatory commission can permit such selective price reductions only when they produce additional net revenues which can be passed on to all customers, there is no way the CAB can permit unrestricted price competition and have that kind of assurance. On the contrary, if we do not intervene in one way or another, the clear danger is that selective price reductions producing declines in net revenues will lead automatically to requests for general rate increases—with the probable result of accenting the discrimination between the customers who get the cuts and the ones who are forced to bear the increases.

In regulated markets, there is ordinarily no reason for concern about this kind of recoupment: there is usually no reason why a price cut in one market would change the profit-maximizing price in another. But if price regulation is at all effective, it prevents the full exploitation of monopoly power, so that recoupment of net revenue losses is not only possible but, in a sense, obligatory under the 5th and 14th amendments to the Constitution!

Partly for this reason, the CAB has typically judged proposed discount fares in terms of whether they would be mainly "diversionary" or "generative" of new traffic. In so doing, the board was actually deciding whether the reduction was in the interest of the carrier that proposed it. But the board also seems to have attempted to serve as a grand monopolist, permitting only price decreases that would be profitable for the industry as a whole. So, for example, it traditionally opposed rate cuts by small suppliers, on the ground that the increased sales would be mainly at the expense of their competitors. Of course, it is precisely the greater elasticity in the demand for the services of the individual competitor—and particularly the individual competitor with a small stake in the market—that of the market as a whole that makes competition work; and it is precisely in the nature of a monopoly or an effective cartel to permit only price decreases that are justified in terms of the elasticity of total industry demand.

It is not clear to me, however, that this kind of close CAB scrutiny of proposed discount fares is necessary to protect regular fare-paying customers from the burden of recoupment. We make our calculations of industry cost of service, and therefore of the presence or absence of revenue deficiencies such as are required to justify general rate increases, on an industry-wide basis; and, even more pertinent, for the last several years we have, in making these calculations, applied an adjustment of industry revenues for the traffic moving under discount fares. The purpose of this adjustment is to assure that revenue deficiencies resulting from discount fares do not in fact justify fare increases.

To understand this discount fare adjustment, one must begin with the board's decision in the early 1970s, in its Domestic Passenger Fare Investigation, to establish a load factor standard—which it set at 55 percent—in order to shelter passengers from having to bear the costs of excessive unused capacity. Under that adjustment, when the carriers come to us with a request for fare increases, we remove from consideration a share of capacity-related costs equivalent to the number of percentage points by which the percentage of seats occupied falls short of the standard. In principle, this adjustment makes 55 percent the break-even load factor for the industry as a whole. If the companies acquire equipment and schedule flights beyond the levels that will permit a 55 percent use of capacity, they will earn less than their nominally permitted rate of return.

But this adjustment alone does not say anything about how those permitted revenues will be obtained from the various classes of customers; specifically, it does not protect the regular fare-paying customer from the burdens of nonremunerative discount fares. The more the 55 percent standard load factor is achieved with discount-fare passengers, the higher the regular fares will have to be. For this reason, the board has introduced its discount fare adjustment, the essential purpose and consequence of which is to set the fares for regular service at the *average* cost of service with the standard load factor.

This means that if carriers charge some passengers less than this fare, they will either suffer shortfalls in their rate of return *or* will have to operate at a higher than 55 percent load factor. The adjustment, therefore, increases the break-even load factor above 55 percent in proportion to the discount fares offered. Thus, the carriers as a group will be motivated on the one hand to control their scheduling, and on the other to offer only such discount fares as generate enough additional traffic to compensate for the reduced average yield.

I began this discussion by expressing doubt that, in view of the discount fare adjustment, it is necessary for the CAB to evaluate and consider disallowing proposed discount fares in order to protect regular fare-paying customers from having their rates increased to compensate for any resultant net revenue deficiencies. There might, however, be three residual bases to justify the CAB continuing to pass on discount offerings. First, they might be predatory. Second is the possibility that competition in the industry, in price and/or scheduling, tends to be destructive—i.e., tends chronically to induce companies to offer discounts that cover marginal but not average costs and that generate insufficient additional traffic to compensate for the reduced yields; and/or to schedule flights in such volume as to make the industry as a whole fail to achieve its break-even load factor. These fears are not necessarily ridiculous, when the typical situation is one in which (a) flights go out with large numbers of empty seats, and (b) seats are not auctioned off to the highest bidders when the demand for reservations exceeds the number available, but must instead be sold at average costs.

The third possible reason for CAB review of proposed price cuts would be a desire to protect the regular fare-paying customer, the threat to whom is not only that his fares may be raised—something that the discount adjustment presumably prevents—but that the quality of the service provided may deteriorate. If the various discount fares have the effect of filling planes, they clearly could diminish the ability of regular fare-paying customers to make reservations on flights of their choice on relatively short notice. Such customers can obviously be injured just as much by increases in load factors above 55 percent—with a consequent decline in the quality of the service they get, while continuing to pay fares set at the cost of giving them 55 percent load factor service—as by having the fares themselves increased to recover net revenue losses from discount fares. I am told it was Louis Engman who coined the aphorism that the businessman who has an empty seat next to him to put his hat on would probably be less pleased if he realized he was paying the fare for the hat too; but he would presumably be even less pleased if he continued to pay for the hat, but the empty seat was now filled with a discount fare-paying passenger!

The Question of Discrimination

As this last consideration suggests, we cannot ignore the question of whether discount fares of various kinds are, as the statute puts it, unduly discriminatory.

The first question is, are they discriminatory? The answer is neither obvious nor simple.

A reduced fare for genuine standby service is obviously in itself not discriminatory: the passenger is buying a distinct (and inferior) service, with a marginal cost anywhere down from the regular fare to zero.[2]

But, you may remonstrate, if a plane would otherwise go out with seats empty, isn't the marginal cost below the regular fare for all the passengers, rather than just for those who happened to opt for standby service? Wouldn't the only non-discriminatory price be the one that cleared the entire market—i.e., equated the total number of seats on the plane with the number demanded—on every flight just before departure time?

One answer is that the regular passenger buys an advance assurance of a seat, at a fixed price, as well as some reasonable possibility of being able to make reservations in advance on a flight of his choice; he is also paying for the privilege of not having to pay a penalty if he does not show up at flight time. All of these aspects of the service have a higher marginal cost than does standby service. Scheduled service is marginally responsible for a carrier's incurring capacity costs; standby, which corresponds to sales of gas or electricity on an incompatible basis, is not.

Lower rates for charters, similarly, are not in themselves discriminatory. In charter service, the unit of sale is the entire plane, at an implicit price per seat equal to the average total cost of a flight 100 percent full. The risk of a lower load factor is transferred to the tour operator, and through him, in large measure, to the ultimate passenger; the latter bears the burden of guaranteeing the operator a sale in advance, with a heavy penalty for no-shows, and a risk that if the load factor falls far enough below 100 percent, the plane will not depart. Both the short-run and the long-run marginal cost of this kind of service is clearly far below that of regular scheduled service.

On the other hand, there can be no question that many of the restrictions imposed on charter flights go far beyond what is necessary to assure the kind of risk shifting I have just described and the low marginal costs it entails, and are therefore clearly discriminatory. The most obvious case is the historic attempt to confine the privilege of flying on charters to affinity groups. But also the long advance-purchase requirements, the minimum stay (this blatant discrimination obviously prevails on scheduled service as well: there is absolutely no inherent reason why the marginal or average cost of providing service to travelers who stay, say, 22 to 45 days is in any way less than for passengers whose trips must be much briefer); the prohibition of fill-ups (which, in fact, contribute positively to the likelihood of securing the high load factors that make charters cost-justified); the requirement that the traveler purchase various ground packages; the minimum group sizes; the limits on the substitution; and the obligation to return with the group. All of these restrictions were clearly designed for protectionist reasons, to confine these lower fares to the presumably demand-elastic customers, to prevent leakage into that market of the demand-inelastic customers, and to protect the scheduled carriers against excessive loss of traffic. They are, in short, designed to effect the separation of markets that is necessary for price discrimination to be practiced; in the process, they clearly harass and confuse passengers, and unnecessarily degrade the quality of service they receive.

The most interesting and difficult cases are the discount fares that we have been receiving in great profusion during the last year from the scheduled carriers. These provide advance reservation of guaranteed seats on regularly scheduled flights at low rates, subject to such restrictions as the need for advance reservation, advance ticket purchase, a penalty for no-shows or cancellations, and minimum stay requirements. In the case of Budget fares, some uncertainty about the particular day and time of departure exists until as little as a week before flight time; in the case of part charters and charter transfers, the same restrictions are applied as those of the charters themselves, with the transfer being at the option of the carrier; and, in all cases, a carrier sets limits, varying with the day of the week and season of the year, on the number of seats made available at these rates.

The theory is, of course, that these fares will be used only to fill seats that would otherwise go empty. They therefore represent a form of peak-load pricing, and—paradoxically, in view of the fact that the reservation must be made many weeks in advance—they partake of the character of standbys, anticipatory standbys, as it were, with the carriers estimating the number of seats that they can safely offer at these low rates. The carriers say they can make these advance commitments without later having to deny regular fare-paying customers reservations because of the accuracy of their forecasting techniques and their conservation in determining the number of seats they will offer at these fares.

In many ways, therefore, the marginal costs of this business, both long- and short-run—including the opportunity cost of denying places to other passengers—is less than those of regular service, for the same reasons as apply to standbys: these are off-peak rates, and the limitation on the number of seats made available at these low prices is a form of interruptibility, such as is frequently practiced in the distribution of gas and electricity. The passenger who calls for a regular reservation has a greater likelihood of obtaining a seat; the greater that likelihood, the more it costs in the long run to provide. The purchaser of the Super-Apex stands a greater chance of being told that the number of seats available has been exhausted.

But, in contrast with ordinary standbys, these fares also embody very substantial elements of discrimination. Many of the restrictions on their availability, closely resembling the ones imposed on charter passengers, are clearly aimed at confining them to demand-elastic customers. Indeed, the discrimination is even more blatant here than in the case of charters, since these tickets are on regularly scheduled flights, and since—apart from the rather mild penalty for cancellation (and some of the timing uncertainties of Budget service)—the customer gets the same assured reservation, far in advance, as the normal fare-payer.

Moreover, if the availability of seats is correctly calculated so that these are truly anticipatory standbys, with the result that the short-run marginal cost is very low, then it is just as clearly very low for the regular fare-payer, who may call on the very same day to make a reservation on the very same flight but, if he fails to utter the magic words "Super-Apex," pays twice as much.

The question of whether these fares—and particularly the last group—are discriminatory is thus a fairly easy one. But an affirmative answer to that question is not a sufficient basis for prohibiting this kind of pricing on either economic or legal grounds. The economic case for price discrimination in situations in which the marginal costs are below average is a familiar one: so long as the lower-fare traffic covers its marginal cost, it is economically efficient to take it on; and so long as the demand for the lower-fare services is sufficiently elastic that the discounts will bring in additional net revenues, the customers discriminated against cannot be injured and may actually be benefited. How do these fares measure up against these two conditions?

Do These Fares Cover Marginal Costs?

There are three dimensions or components of the short-run marginal cost (SRMC) of a service like Super-Saver or Super-Apex.

1. One is the costs, such as ticketing, check-ins, baggage handling, and meals, that vary with the number of customers. If the only seats made available are seats that would otherwise go out empty, these would be the only marginal costs imposed on the supplier.
2. Since the number of seats made available at the discount fares is restricted, there is a possibility that the supply on a particular profit will fall short of the number demanded, with the rationing accomplished on a first-come-first-served basis. In these circumstances, the measure of SRMC would be the opportunity cost involved in A getting the seat in preference to B—specifically, the value of the trip to the one who would have been the highest unsuccessful bidder if the seats had been auctioned off.
3. Finally, there are what we might regard as the external costs— the effect of filling these seats in advance on the ability of regular fare-paying customers to get reservations, and the diminution in the comfort those customers experience when planes are fuller than the 55 percent load factor, the average cost of which their fares are intended to cover.

I do not see any reason to believe the carriers would ordinarily set these fares below SRMC, measured in any of these ways, except possibly for predatory reasons.

For the first component, it would clearly be irrational for them not to cover the out-of-pocket customer costs. As for the second aspect, it is difficult to see why the carriers would intentionally set the prices of the restricted number of seats they offer at a level below what would clear the particular market. On the contrary, one would expect them to try to maximize their net return over customer costs, even if that meant letting some of the seats remain empty. In point of fact, their range of discretion is probably quite limited. These fares are set within range of such alternatives as charters and the Laker Skytrain, with adjustments for differences in the quality of service; because of the expected high cross-elasticity of demand among these competing services, there seems little reason to expect carriers to set these fares significantly below their short-run marginal opportunity costs, as I have defined them. The main purposes of the capacity limitations would seem not so much to ration demand at prices below the market-clearing levels as to minimize the adverse impact on the availability of reservations for regular service, and to placate regulatory authorities who may be concerned about an impact.

This is *not* to say it would be reasonable to expect the third component of marginal cost—the value of these seats to any would-be normal fare-paying customers foreclosed from getting them by the discount traffic (and the marginal discomfort imposed because of the congestion they cause)—to be held to zero. On the contrary, I would expect carriers, if they were free to pursue their interests, to offer these discount seats up to the point at which their marginal costs, measured in this way, equal the fares. It would pay a carrier to offer these seats at, say, $100 (above customer costs) until the point that the expected loss of passengers at the normal fare of $200 (above customer costs) reached 0.5. What I would *not* expect them to do would be to charge *less* than those short-run marginal opportunity costs—i.e., the value of the seats to the displaced regular fare-paying customers, multiplied by the probability of such displacement at the margin. There is no reason to expect a carrier to take on a $100 discount customer when there is *more* than 0.5 probability of displacing a $200 one—i.e., when the mean expected result would be to lose $101.

So, still confining our attention to SRMC (and ignoring the possibility of predatory motives), I believe these fares are probably economically efficient. If a carrier prefers to take on two discount customers at $100 each (above customer costs) at a mean expected loss of one regular fare at $198, that is

socially efficient: the value of the service to the marginal customer who travels is $100, the marginal social opportunity
cost $99.

Long-Run Incremental Costs (LRIC)

The Civil Aeronautics Board has objected in the past to discount fares, however—only a few years ago, in its Discount
Passenger Fares Investigation (DPFI), it adopted the rule that
it would permit them only temporarily, and in times of general excess capacity—on the ground that in the long run the
marginal cost of discount traffic is no less than that of regular
traffic.

There were two bases for this conclusion: first, the apparent absence of economies of scale in the airline industry, and
second, the belief that additional discount traffic in the long
run leads to additional scheduling in the same way as regular
traffic. These two premises, taken together, compel the conclusion that any additional traffic generated by discount fares
has the same LRIC as regular traffic, with both being equal
to average, fully allocated costs.

The second of these assumptions is, I think, incredible, in
the presence of the board's discount fare adjustment. It would
be irrational for a carrier to count a half-fare paying passenger more than half as much as a full-fare customer (as
always, I refer to fares in excess of customer costs) in induc-
ing it to acquire additional planes or to schedule additional
flights. The break-even load factor—which is the point at
which adding capacity becomes marginally profitable—of a
plane with a large number of discount customers will obviously be higher than if all paid the full fare.

This would not be so in the absence of the discount fare
adjustment. If a carrier can recoup any net revenue losses
from discount traffic by raising regular fares, with the result
that its *average* net yield per passenger is unchanged, the
break-even load factor and the point of adding capacity would

obviously remain constant. This is perhaps part of the explanation of the historical stability of load factors in the face of
spreading discount fares in the past to which opponents of
these fares have often pointed.

This reasoning has the interesting consequences of making
the LRIC of a particular class of customers dependent on the
price they are charged—the lower the fare, the less the individual sale contributes causally to additional scheduling. But
of course it is rational for a supplier to vary output so as to
equate marginal cost with prices; and that is what I am pre-
dicting here.[3]

In short, then, I see these troublesome fares as almost certainly covering both their SRMC and LRIC; in these circumstances, it seems it would almost always be economically
efficient to permit them.

The Impact on the Regular Fare-Payer

There is a strong regulatory tradition, however, that discriminatory discounts should be permitted to certain classes of customers only up to the point that maximizes the benefit to the
customers discriminated against; that tradition would not contemplate with equanimity an actual injury to the latter. But,
although our discount fare adjustment protects regular fare-
paying customers from recoupment in the form of higher
money prices, it does not protect them against an effective
increase in price when the quality of service declines.

Increasing the average load factor to, say, 75 percent by
the sale of "anticipatory standbys" does not necessarily diminish the ability of regular fare-paying customers to get
reservations. If carriers had perfect foresight, they could
theoretically get even 100 percent load factors without having
that effect. But, as I have already observed, it appears carriers would have to go beyond 75 percent, because two birds
in hand at half fare are worth up to one in the bush at full
fare, even though the telephone call from the one in the bush

were 100 percent predictable. And there remains the fact also that a full plane is less comfortable to ride in than one that is half full.

The regulator under injunction to avoid "undue discrimination" will continue to be uneasy with discriminatory discounts, therefore, even if persuaded they are economically efficient, until he can figure out some way of having the regular fare-paying customer get some benefit from them as well. Perhaps they do benefit automatically. The possibility of scheduled carriers offering these special rates to fill empty seats improves the financial viability of their service—recall my earlier expression of concern about the possible attrition of scheduled service if travelers have free access to low-cost charters, and my suggestion that one way of preserving the former option is to encourage the scheduled carriers to offer a variety of price/quality options in order to fill more of their seats. Indeed, the additional traffic they are able to attract in this way could justify additional scheduling, and in this way confer positive benefits on their regular fare-paying patrons.

It is worth considering the possibility of a direct recompense as well. Possibly regular fare-paying customers should be entitled to rebates when load factors on a particular flight get above a certain level—forcing the carriers to share with them some of the benefits from the higher load factors that also adulterate the quality of the service they receive. One drawback of such a scheme would be that the rebates would go partially to the wrong people—to the ones who get on the high load factor flights rather than to those who call vainly for reservations on them.

THE PROPER FOCUS OF
REGULATORY CONCERN

Although we spend a great deal of time evaluating these special rates and trying to devise standards by which to judge them, the overriding responsibility and concern of regulators must ultimately be to preserve and accentuate the competitiveness of this industry's market structure as the principal means of protecting the interest of passengers. This means not only that we must be alert to possibly predatory price cuts—to which I have alluded only in passing—as we obviously were in dealing with the transatlantic fares that purported to be responses to the Laker Skytrain. Much more important, we must liberalize the conditions of entry and exit, leaving those decisions to the unfettered discretion of management. This is the best possible protection for passengers, regular fare-payers, and discount passengers alike.

This means, among other things, that we should be constantly considering how we can loosen the fetters we now impose upon different segments of the industry. Here, as in the case of entry, if we are not to take the big-bang approach, we must try to introduce the liberalizations as much in step as possible, in the interest of preserving equality of competitive opportunities—loosening the restrictions on the incumbents as well as new entrants, on supplementals, tour operators, and the scheduled carriers, on the combination carriers of freight and the all-cargo carriers, on the airlines traditionally restricted to international traffic as well as to domestic routes, and to foreign carriers as well as to domestic.

During the next several years—in a regime less hostile to rate cuts, selective or general, and more hospitable to entry—I look to a more variegated airline industry structure, in which the traditional rigid geographic and functional boundaries between different carriers and categories become blurred and governmentally protected spheres of influence less distinct, a structure that offers the maximum possible assurance of continuation of the competitive spur and that offers exciting new opportunities for managerial enterprise. And I look for a corresponding and increasingly variegated set of price and service options, competitively offered to passengers and shippers.

COMMENT

RAYMOND F. O'BRIEN
President, Consolidated Freightways, Inc.
The two basic regulatory features which are the chief targets of the
[motor carrier] deregulators are control of entry and collective
ratemaking. Congress believed these provisions were necessary to
ensure a healthy and stable transportation industry. Those who advocate removal or substantial weakening of those provisions believe
it would mean more competition, lower rates, and presumably, better service.

The trucking industry—or most of it—thinks it would result in
rate and service discrimination against small shippers and small
towns, a deterioration in the quality of service, and general distress,
if not chaos, in much of the industry—all without accomplishing
the stated goals except for a few big shippers. . . .

Judging by the nervousness of . . . lenders and investors, the
current pressure for deregulation seems to be a bit stronger than in
the past. . . . [It] also reflects the growing public distrust of both
big government and big business, and the popularity of words like
"reform.". . . If you're going to reform something, you have to
change it. Governmentally speaking, that generally translates into
more regulation of what is perceived as too free, and more freedom
for what seems too regulated. Some of the same people who advocate deregulating the trucking industry to provide more competition
and lower prices seem to think we should regulate the oil industry
to provide more competition and lower prices. . . .

The director of the ICC's Bureau of Economics, Ernest R. Ol-
son, recently commented on the lack of adequate information. He
said the ICC knows little about such problems as traffic flow, commodities hauled, authorities used, industry structure, service factors, and the infrastructure of trucking. If this makes it hard to
regulate, it should also make us leery of academics who claim to
have all the answers. So my first question is: What is the problem? . . . There are remarkably few facts on which there is any
general agreement. Most of the statements are made by people who
really know very little about the trucking business, or about any
business, for that matter. . . .

When I hear someone say there should be more competition, I
think they must be talking about some other business. Investors in
some of the well-known companies which have gone bankrupt in
the past few years . . . would have to laugh at that idea if it didn't
hurt so much. A Department of Transportation study found that 85

percent of shippers surveyed thought there was enough competition in trucking. That's about as close to a consensus as you're likely to get on any subject. . . .

Who wants a change? . . . We find a strong push coming from educators, economists, and government officials, many of whom consider themselves spokesmen for and defenders of the public interest. They deal mainly in theories, and they have plenty of colleagues who disagree on all counts. I, for one, do not agree that Ralph Nader and his associates necessarily represent the public interest 100 percent of the time.

Another group which generally favors partial or total deregulation is the independent operator, the man who owns his own truck and either operates under lease to a certified carrier or handles unregulated commodities. Either way, he often has difficulty lining up return loads, and assumes that he could do better if he were permitted to haul anything for anybody. I agree that he has problems, stemming largely from the steep rise in fuel costs and the 55-mile speed limit. But letting him haul common carrier freight would only shift the problem, not cure it. . . . Deregulation would not create any new freight to haul. It would only redistribute it somewhat.

Why do they want a change? . . . The world is full of people who want to change things, and other people who want to leave things as they are. Some feel a need to justify their education by tinkering with the system. They are full of solutions and looking for problems.

It is often charged that the regulators have become more concerned with the well-being of those they are regulating than with the public interest . . . but after all, the National Transportation Policy as enacted by Congress clearly requires the regulators to "foster sound economic conditions in . . . and among the several carriers." Regulatory tradition calls for an adversary relationship, but a realistic view of the problems of large portions of our transportation system indicates that a cooperative approach may be needed. . . .

Suppose we allow freedom of entry. As Mr. Kahn has stated, effective competition and simple equity would require that carriers be given freedom of exit as well as entry. When I count the number of motor carriers with whom we compete in every sizable market, I feel we already have all the freedom of entry we need. . . . In California, which has an easy entry policy, the "in and out" turnover rate is already estimated at 2,500 small carriers per year. It's hard to see how such a situation can result in the kind of stability needed to foster sound business relationships.

Finally . . . from a purely selfish standpoint, Consolidated Freightways should probably favor total deregulation of trucking. I believe we would eventually operate more profitably, and that we have little to fear. . . . The fact that there is no regulation of an industry does not mean there is complete freedom of entry. In today's world, most industries require substantial capital investment to compete successfully, let alone start from scratch. There are many fields in which there is seldom if ever a new competitor to contend with, yet there is generally plenty of competition.

I recently read a letter to the chairman of the Interstate Commerce Commission, Dan O'Neal, from John Wagner, president of the Local and Short Haul Carriers National Conference . . . outlining the serious effects which commission actions and proposals have had and would have on members of the conference. His letter makes the following statement: "Deregulation—by big government action—is, after all, really pro-big business. Easier entry into trucking, for example, is ultimately a hollow thing, an empty promise, because the economic forces are already so heavily weighted in favor of existing big carriers." I think Mr. Wagner has a point, and that there are economies of scale in trucking despite Mr. Shenefield's contrary opinion. . . .

The need to assure efficient service to the public at reasonable rates, and without discrimination as to people or places, is what tips the scales in favor of ICC-type regulation, in our opinion.

To close with another quotation, the report on National Transportation Policy prepared in 1961 for the Senate Committee on Interstate and Foreign Commerce remarked that, "There appears to be no chance of unregulated competition operating in the national interest until the Golden Rule becomes the universally accepted law of business relations." It would seem a lot of people think the millenium is already upon us.

JORDAN JAY HILLMAN
Professor of Law, Northwestern University

Having made room for the future in our total calculus, we have to shift our mental gears again by recognizing that an established system of regulation inevitably engenders its own adaptive responses and nurtured expectations. We simply can't sweep away the investments which have been made under the rules as they are known today, whether those rules be economically rational or not. . . .

Like any broker representing all parties to a transaction, who would like to continue in the job, Congress often finds equivocation a prudent substitute for clear-cut decisions. . . . In the Transportation Act of 1958 . . . Congress provided a first-rate demonstration of how to make major changes in the language of the law while keeping its substance intact. I note the possibility of a similar occurrence in the 1976 Quad-R Act. While seeming to establish the reasonableness of competitive rates productive of revenues in excess of relevant variable costs, Congress nevertheless declared as unlawful, not only any competitive practice which is "unfair, destructive or predatory," but also those which "otherwise undermine competition which is necessary in the public interest." The opportunity to find rates illegal on the basis of this amorphous phrase again gives to a regulatory agency which remains hostile to the basic statutory standard a potentially powerful weapon with which to subvert that standard. . . .

It is not hard to entice Congress into using boards and commissions as dumping grounds for hard decisions. It is an especially dangerous practice, however, when the effort is to force new rules and the administrative agency, in its heart, remains wedded to the old rules.

4

V. KERRY SMITH

Regulating Energy: Indicative Planning or Creeping Nationalization*

Rationale for government intervention. Efficiency motives—micro and macro. The three Ps of regulation: principles, procedures, and practice. Private market allocation of exhaustible resources. The old policy and the NEP. Price control inefficiencies. NEP misconceptions and implications for the future.

INTRODUCTION

The president's recent energy proposals are based on the premise that energy is a unique resource, requiring continu-

*Thanks are due J. Alterman, E. N. Castle, R. Kopp, M. Russell, E. Seskin, S. P. Smith, and P. Smith for most helpful discussions of these issues. The views expressed, however, are entirely those of the author.

ous governmental regulation.[1] The allocation of energy resources therefore offers an appropriate case study for those
interested in the uses and abuses of regulation. Moreover, our
newly formulated National Energy Plan (NEP) is an excellent
starting point. It proposes national consumption goals, out-
lines government policies which are admittedly incapable of
achievement without complementary efforts, acknowledges
that further mandatory controls will be undertaken if these
goals are not realized, and extols the virtues of voluntary private market solutions to the energy problem.

Large-scale government intervention in the extractive sector does not begin with the proposed NEP. Its origins can be
found in the 1913 provisions of early income tax legislation.
Differential treatment of these industries has increased historically, partly by accident, partly by design. In this paper,
however, I will argue that our current policy proposals represent a new, potentially ill-fated approach to remedy problems
induced, in part, by the failures of past government intervention.[2] Assuming that "a price is enough," current proposals
seek simultaneously to: (a) achieve the microefficiency goals
traditionally associated with regulatory programs, (b) "do no
harm" to the overall economy, and (c) determine the quantity, mix, and ultimate consumers of our energy resources—
all under the banner of "indicative planning."[3]

While this appraisal may seem too roughshod and therefore
unfair, the history of intervention in this area suggests that
our current energy problems are closely linked to the failures
of government policies, particularly since 1973. Rather than
reform the process of intervention completely, the newly
proposed measures merely "add on" further controls, potentially compounding past errors.

Let's begin by considering whether our energy problems
are the direct result of OAPEC actions in 1973.[4] In my judgment, the dramatic increase in world prices that occurred at
that time only accentuated a process initiated by earlier regulation of the industry. The most basic problem is that regulation has served to give *different* signals to consumers and

producers of energy resources, with corresponding differences in their responses.

Figure 1: Real Price Trends for Energy to Consumers

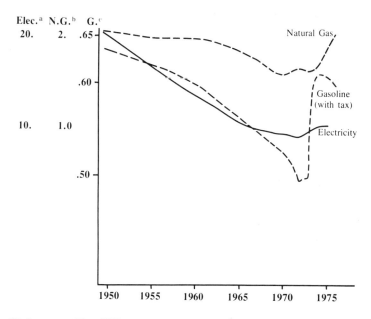

aDollars per million BTU.
aDollars per million BTU.
cCents per gallon.

Source: Russell 1977*a*

Figure 1 illustrates the movements in the real prices of three primary sources of energy for U.S. consumers from 1950 to 1976. In all cases the prices, in constant dollars, are lower in 1976 than they were twenty-five years earlier. The unsurprising result was the substantial increase in energy consumption.[5] At the same time, however, the real prices received by producers remained relatively stable until 1973, and the additions to domestic energy resources (oil and natural gas) have fallen behind the growth in demand.[6]

Thus the events of 1973 merely accentuated a process whose origins lie in the structure of regulations. The governmental response attempted to insulate American consumers from the cost increases, and the result has been an increased discrepancy between the relative prices of energy compared to other resources as perceived by consumers and producers.

With this indictment of what Schultze (1977) designated in his Godkin lectures as the "command-and-control" approach to intervention, it would seem reasonable to inquire why the government gets involved in the first place. The next section of this paper reviews the objectives of government regulation. It is followed by a discussion of the economics of the allocation process for an exhaustible resource, by a description of the pattern of past government regulation and the proposed efforts of the NEP, and, finally, by consideration of the outlook for energy regulation and prospects for the use of private markets in the future allocation of energy resources.

WHY REGULATE?

Under ideal conditions, private markets represent a rather unique form of social interaction. Through the process of exchange, those who demand products and those who supply them reveal their respective marginal valuations and costs, and this interaction assures that resources are allocated to their highest valued uses. Unfortunately, these circumstances are idealized, and there are a number of cases when the production or consumption of a good or service has special attributes not reflected by market prices.[7] Therefore, if these characteristics affect resource allocation, intervention is often warranted on grounds of efficiency.

In discussing efficiency as a motive for intervention, it is important to distinguish the concepts of micro and macro efficiency. The former relates to the allocation of resources to their highest valued uses—in general terms, a gauge of the manner in which an allocation process meets the material needs of consumers. Macro efficiency relates to stabilization policy, to the overall use of society's resources, and thus to the aggregate outcomes of micro processes, such as unemployment and price stability.

Within the general category of micro efficiency, it is possible to identify the source of resource misallocations to be corrected through intervention. In most cases these are associated with impediments to the process of market-based social interaction. For example, ownership rights for the resources exchanged must be clearly defined. In addition, if there are side effects of the production or use of the goods involved whose implications are not, or cannot be, adequately reflected in the transactions, then the idealized conditions for efficient interaction are violated.[8] Finally, the transaction costs and/or informational requirements for the functioning of a market may be prohibitive. The most apparent examples of this last problem can be found in the issue of the safety of a wide array of consumer products. It would seem to be impossible (certainly very costly) for an individual to acquire the information required to appreciate the full effects of all the goods and services he may utilize. Regulations offer one means of conveying this information.

Apart from efficiency objectives, social intervention is also motivated by the desire to assure a certain threshold level of access to all, or to a particular subset of material goods and services by all individuals. While we can logically distinguish efficiency and equity objectives, all resolutions of efficiency-related problems have corresponding equity implications. In fact, several prominent economists contend that failure of the economics profession to promote effective intervention processes can be tied to their unwillingness to deal, in a substantive way, with the equity implications of policies designed to promote efficiency.[9]

All of these concepts relate to the first of the three Ps of regulation, namely the *principles* that form the initial rationale for intervention.[10] In evaluating existing regulations such as our national energy policies, it is necessary also to consider the *procedures* used to redress apparent inefficiencies (or inequities in resource allocations), and ultimately the actual *practice* of intervention. Schultze focuses on procedures, and calls for marketlike incentives rather than the command-and-control approach to achieve policy objectives.[11] Evaluation of intervention programs requires consideration of all dimensions of regulation; therefore it would be incomplete to concentrate on any one aspect—principles, procedures, or practice.[12] Energy policies are particularly difficult to evaluate within this framework, since they have been designed to respond to multiple objectives, including several we have not considered. With this limitation in mind, we will discuss the general principles for private market allocation of an exhaustible resource as a means of identifying the conventional motives for intervening in the allocation of energy resources.

PRIVATE MARKET ALLOCATION OF EXHAUSTIBLE RESOURCES

One of the central propositions underlying the National Energy Plan is that the world is running out of crude oil and natural gas. Despite the incomplete evidence available, policymakers have chosen to assume that world production of these resources will peak before the end of this century, and then decline. If this assumption is correct, the principle of micro efficiency as discussed in the previous section leaves no role for social intervention. Referring to issues paralleling this case, Stiglitz (1978:25) recently observed that:

the existence of a natural resource problem has no immediate impli-cations:it is neither a necessary nor a sufficient condition for gov-ernmental intervention in the markets for natural resources. The market could be doing as well as could be done—and the economy could still be facing a doomsday; and the market could be doing a quite bad job of resource allocation and yet there might be no doomsday in store. . . . A pattern of growth which left our grand-children with few resources might be efficient, yet very undesir-able.

The prospects of exhaustion for a particular natural resource do not in themselves imply micro inefficiency in allocation among economic agents at either a given point of time or over time.[13] Stiglitz suggests, rather, that these resources or their existing markets may have characteristics which would warrant government intervention on the grounds of micro efficiency.

For exhaustible resources, four attributes of their allocation process have been suggested as grounds for intervention to improve efficiency of allocation, aside from the existing pat-tern of government policy. They are (a) structure of the mar-ket, (b) absence of futures markets, (c) absence of risk mar-kets, and (d) common property problems. The first issue, which concerns the possibility of monopoly power, has re-ceived great attention in regulatory literature. In the case of exhaustible energy resources, market structure is not neces-sarily sufficient to change extraction patterns over time. Competitive firms and a monopoly may yield identical pat-terns of extraction.[14] Moreover, this has *not* been the basis for past or current energy policies concerning petroleum or natural gas. Despite some debate over monopoly control and market power of the major oil companies, most policymakers seem to agree that there is "workable competition."[15] For this reason policies have not been designed to reduce the market position of energy firms (particularly the large pe-troleum firms).

On the remaining issues there is scope for judgment. Organized futures markets for future delivery of resources do not exist.[16] The same is true for risk markets. The question is whether their absence is important to resource allocation. Regarding futures markets, the issue is whether investors can make systematic, persistent errors in guessing future prices. While market incentives exist to discover such systematic mistakes, great variation in expectations can nonetheless cause market instability.[17] Similar difficulties arise from the absence of insurance (risk) markets, as owners of the exhaustible resource must bear all risks arising with price instability, new technologies, and other unforeseen events.

Different analysts evaluate these imperfections with different conclusions. Stiglitz observed that, without futures markets, indicative planning may be a useful role for government as an aid to forecasting demand and supplies, but that it should avoid direct allocation of resources themselves. Regarding risk markets, he is less convinced (Stiglitz 1978:35):

> Uncertainty undoubtedly has an effect on the intertemporal allocation, but for some purposes this is not as important as the question of what policy implication this has. . . . The risks associated with uncertain future supplies and demands borne by private individuals in imperfect risk markets are real "costs"; and the fact that under some idealized world in which these risks are not borne by these individuals the intertemporal allocation of oil would be different is of interest, but of no direct policy import. An appropriate question to ask, for instance, is whether a Pareto optimal improvement could be made within our market structure by taxing or subsidizing the return to holding oil; . . . The answer, in general is no.

In contrast, William Nordhaus (a current member of the Council of Economic Advisors), in a paper published shortly after the OPEC cartel's 1973 actions, concluded that the market mechanism in the U.S. was an "unreliable means of pricing and allocating exhaustible appropriable natural resources," with energy serving as his prime example (Nordhaus (1973:537). He urged the use of indicative planning as a policy alternative.[18] Under this approach, the government would determine a complete set of spot and future prices implied by an efficient allocation of energy resources (Nordhaus 1973:538).

The last problem—the common property or common pool nature of oil and natural gas—yields more consistent recommendations on the appropriate intervention. Difficulties arise when one or more independent producers simultaneously seek to extract resources (i.e., oil) from a common pool. Under a single producer (i.e., where the property rights are clearly defined), individuals can forego consumption today and know that it will be available in the future. But when many producers have access to the same source, these circumstances are not maintained; therefore a decision by a producer not to extract today offers no guarantee of future availability. Since other producers may extract it, there are incentives for an excessively rapid extraction.[19] One way to avoid this problem is to establish a single managerial unit for the pool. Compulsory field unitization accomplishes this.

Macro-Efficiency Motives

Turning to the equity and macro-efficiency motives for intervention, the arguments are again not clear-cut. The crux of the debate on equity concerns the treatment of future generations. When judging how a particular extraction pattern for an exhaustible resource affects different generations, most analysts urge that consideration be given to the levels of technology and physical capital that are transferred to future generations.[20] Of course, their conclusions assume that the resource in question has ready substitutes, and that its production and consumption do not result in harm to environmental common property.[21] In any case, current policy does not seem to have intertemporal equity objectives.[22]

This discussion suggests that, based on the principles stated earlier, there may be a place for government involvement in the allocation of energy resources. But the rationale does not arise from the exhaustibility of energy. It comes, rather, from the market failures we noted at the outset *and* their importance to efficient allocations in markets for exhaustible resources.[23]

These conclusions do not necessarily imply that regulatory intervention will improve (in a Pareto sense) the allocation of oil or natural gas. In fact, Stiglitz's views may be interpreted as a judgment on the ability of conventional *procedures* for intervention to achieve such an improvement.[24]

The question of macro efficiency has not been considered in theoretical models for the allocation patterns of exhaustible resources. It has, however, played an important role in much current and proposed energy regulation, and for that reason I will now discuss the problem, along with a review and evaluation of past interventions in the market allocation of oil and the NEP in terms of the criteria we have discussed.

ENERGY POLICY: THE OLD AND THE NEW

Any brief summary of sixty years of government intervention in a market is bound to be oversimplified, and the present account is no exception. To keep manageable the scope of our inquiry, we will focus on crude oil to highlight the relationship, if any, between past policies, the general goals of regulation, and the special features of the markets for exhaustible resources.

The Old

The first column of Table 1 summarizes the primary components of past intervention in the domestic crude-oil market. It is clear that the effects on prices and on incentives for new supplies are quite mixed. The percentage depletion allowance and favorable treatment of intangible costs both promote investment into oil (and gas) exploration and production, since the former is similar to a negative excise tax, and the latter directly reduces tax liability. In the absence of constraints on entry of foreign crude to the United States, the third policy would also encourage exploration to other parts of the world. Thus, on balance, we would expect the first three actions to reduce prices. The next two measures, however, seem to move in the opposite direction. Both prorationing[25] and the oil import-quota system tend to increase prices by restricting the supply of oil.

None of these measures can be related directly to the objectives of intervention, and they cast doubt on the prospects for any well-designed intervention in this sector. This view is supported by Walter Mead (1977:341), who recently concluded: "This record does not lead one to be confident that the public interest will be served by additional government intervention. This record should surprise no one. Congress and the Administration must respond to dominant organized pressures." These comments may be more relevant to the pre-1971 period than to more recent government policies. Items 6 through 8 in Table 1 do seem to serve, at least in part, the objectives of macro efficiency and intratemporal equity.

In hopes of controlling inflationary price increases, Phase IV of the Nixon administration's Economic Stabilization Program and the Emergency Petroleum Allocation Act of 1973 introduced extensive price controls which finally produced a two-tier price system for domestic crude oil. Oil produced from a property at roughly 1972 levels or less was "old" (first tier) oil, with prices controlled at slightly above pre-embargo domestic wellhead levels. Production above these levels from the same property was "new" oil, and its price was uncontrolled. In addition, each barrel of "new" oil produced released one barrel of "old" oil from price controls — thus giving those refineries with greatest access to "old" oil a definite cost advantage. The price of "old" oil averaged

Table 1

Overview of Government Regulation of Petroleum[a]

Past Intervention	NEP[b]
1. Percentage depletion allowance at a rate of 27.5 percent (from 1926 to 1969)	1. Crude-oil equalization tax to bring prices to world levels in 1980
2. Favorable treatment of intangibles (i.e., non-salvageable drilling costs)	2. Price of newly discovered oil to rise to 1977 world price (adjusted for inflation) in three years; newly covered > 2.5 miles from onshore well or 1,000 ft. deeper, and offshore oil discovered after 20 May 1977
3. Foreign tax credit	
4. Market demand prorationing: producers permitted to produce only at a specified percentage of maximum efficient rate (ended in 1972)	3. Users' tax beginning at $0.50 per barrel in 1979, rising to $3.00 per barrel in 1985 for industrial users; utilities taxed at $1.50 per barrel beginning in 1983; exemption for consumption under 90,000 barrels per year, and for fertilizer manufacturers and certain agricultural uses
5. Mandatory Oil Import Quota System: limit amount of crude oil and petroleum products to enter U.S. (ended in 1973)	

4. Tax rebates equal to year's oil or gas tax for investment in coal conversion
5. No new gas-burning boilers; possible prohibition of oil-burning if capable of burning coal
6. Best available technology for all coal-burning plants; scrubbers mandatory regardless of coal type burned
7. Eliminate entitlements program
8. Liberalize tax treatment of intangibles
9. Expansion of strategic petroleum reserve

6. Phase IV of Economic Stabilization Program and Emergency Petroleum Allocation Act (1973):
   a. Crude oil price controls (two-tier pricing)
   b. Crude oil cost equalization (entitlements) program
   c. Petroleum product price controls
   d. Mandatory petroleum product allocation program
7. Energy Policy and Conservation Act of 1975: continued price controls for crude and petroleum products (phased out controls on latter except gasoline and jet fuel in 1976)
8. Energy Conservation and Production Act (1976): oil-pricing policy changed to reflect reassessment of macroeconomic conditions; greater increases in crude prices to allow for tertiary recovery

---

[a] Summary based on discussion in Congressional Budget Office (1977), Zarb and MacAvoy (1976), Mead (1977), and Montgomery (1977).

[b] The ''gas-guzzler'' and standby gasoline taxes have been ignored, since legislative action on them was unclear at the time this paper was prepared.

about $5.00 a barrel, while the uncontrolled price was about
$12.00 a barrel after the OAPEC price increases.

To insure that all U.S. refineries paid the same average
cost for crude oil, the cost equalization or entitlements program was instituted, giving monthly entitlements to each refiner, based on the national proportion of "old" oil to total
domestic production. For each refiner, entitlements to use
price-controlled oil must equal the quantities of "old" oil in
production—and therefore individual refiners would buy or
sell entitlements to maintain the balance. This practice is a
rationing scheme, which gives each producer equal access to
a scarce commodity—oil with a controlled price.

In addition, price controls and allocation schemes were
imposed on refinery products, and they remain in effect on
gasoline and jet fuel. These actions imposed direct control
over the markets, maintaining artificially low prices below
world levels, and constraining market adjustments.[26]

Do these actions bear any relation to the objectives discussed earlier? Montgomery (1977:25) notes that two reasons
were cited for the price controls in the discussion that accompanies the Energy Policy and Conservation Act (EPCA) of
1975: ". . . protection of low and middle income consumers
from the impact of energy price increases and mitigation of
the macro economic impact of a sudden increase in energy
prices." EPCA thus kept upper-tier ("new") oil below the
world price, with entitlements allocating both first-tier
("old") and second-tier ("new") oil—again requiring that
the average cost of crude to refiners, including imported oil,
be equalized. The EPCA of 1976 continued controls, but
permitted greater domestic crude-oil price increases than
under the earlier legislation.

The net result of the price controls was to prevent the
domestic market for crude oil from reaching equilibrium. At
the controlled prices, the quantity demanded would always
exceed domestic production. Without the ability to import,
rationing would have been essential; imports allowed the

market to clear. Unfortunately, the policy effects do not end with this imbalance; the dynamic incentives that result are at least as important as the static consequences.

Government policies since 1973 may be explained with the use of a stylized example. Consider the implications of holding the market price below equilibrium (i.e., below the point at which demand would equal supply). In equilibrium, the last unit of demand is priced at the willingness-to-pay for that unit—which, in turn, exactly equals the marginal cost of providing it. When price is maintained artificially below that point, demand will exceed supply. Without an external supply source (in addition to the market supply schedule) to meet this excess demand, the available supply must be rationed in some way among users. (For a more technical discussion of these arguments, see Appendix.) These conditions are important for two reasons. First, price controls introduce inefficiencies in resource allocation at the time when they are imposed. Second, and equally important, they can accentuate the imbalance in demand and supply over time by influencing expectations. This example is one simple way of understanding both the effects of the price controls initiated under the Economic Stabilization Program and the role of imports of crude oil since 1973. This foreign supply has served the role of meeting a growing excess of U.S. domestic demand over domestic supply at controlled prices.

Table 2 lists the individual regulatory programs in the Federal Energy Administration's (FEA) Office of Regulatory Programs. Private compliance with these mandates required an estimated 200,976 forms per year for the FEA to evaluate (Zarb and MacAvoy 1976: Appendix L, p. 2). The public cost of overseeing these programs in the FEA Office of Regulatory Programs and the General Counsel's Office will amount to an estimated $47 million in FY 1977.[27] Thus it is not surprising that the Presidential Task Force on Reform of Federal Energy Administration Regulations concluded (Zarb and MacAvoy 1976:20):

The cost of current FEA regulations outweighs their benefits.

a. FEA product pricing and allocation regulations, the crude oil buy/sell program and supplier/purchaser freeze are unnecessary in present supply conditions.

b. The current regulatory structure will not work in a future shortage.

c. FEA regulations impose substantial costs on the business community, taxpayers, and consumers.

d. Continuation of present controls will result in long-run inefficiencies.

Table 2

Regulatory Functions of FEA's
Office of Regulatory Programs

Program	Status
Crude Oil Entitlements Program	Current
Domestic Crude Oil Allocation Program (buy/sell)	Current
Canadian Crude Oil Allocation Program	Current
Refinery Yield Program	Current
Mandatory Oil Imports Program	Current
Propane/Butane and Other Products Allocation Program	Current
Motor Gasoline Allocation Program	Phase out under EPCA
Middle Distillate Allocation Program	Phase out under EPCA
Aviation Fuels Allocation Program	Phase out under EPCA
Residual Fuels Allocation Program (utilities)	Phase out under EPCA
Residual Fuels Allocation Program (nonutilities)	Phase out under EPCA
Regional Assistance Program	Phase out under EPCA

Source: Zarb and MacAvoy (1976).

Faced with these conclusions, the regulatory response which emerges in our new energy plan is an *increase* in the scope of control on the allocation of energy resources.

The National Energy Plan

The second column of Table 1 highlights principal aspects of the proposed National Energy Plan (NEP),[28] a dominant feature of which seeks to curtail the growth of domestic consumption of oil (and natural gas). This objective rests on two assumptions. The first is that domestic petroleum production will not greatly increase, regardless of price increases. Further increases in consumption thus will increase U.S. vulnerability to foreign supply interruptions, since most of the increased demand for crude oil must be met with imports. The second assumption is that world production of petroleum will decline before the end of this century; therefore, a beginning must be made to adjust to the end of crude oil as a dominant energy source. Curiously, the plan attempts to command and control the character of responses to these factors rather than to permit market adjustment.

In principle, it is possible to classify the impact of past regulations on the supply of crude oil and its domestic price. Problems arose, in large part, because demand factors were free to respond to the perceived opportunity costs for petroleum—that is, its value in alternative uses. And the result was a pattern of progressive increases in excess demand for crude oil and corresponding increases in imports, from 6.3 million barrels per day in 1973 to an estimated 9 million in 1977.

It seems reasonable to assume that meeting domestic demand for crude from domestic sources of supply alone would require a price in excess of the current world price. Thus, price adjustment to the world price levels will reduce but not eliminate the excess domestic demand (i.e., the difference between domestic demand and domestic supply). The NEP assumes that (a) complete price adjustment to achieve zero excess domestic demand is not feasible for policy purposes; and therefore, (b) excess demand must be reduced so that imports and consumption correspond to predefined targets at the plan's posted prices. Within our simple diagram, the only option available to achieve these targets, given the imposed constraints, is further control on the market by restrictions on *demand*. Thus, items 3 through 5 in Table 1 may be interpreted as direct attempts to control the derived demand for crude oil by the manufacturing sector and public utilities.[29]

The NEP does nothing to change regulatory control over supply. Prices are proposed to rise to the current world prices of crude oil (in real terms) by 1980. However, the complex and arbitrary pricing tiers for "old," "new" (designated "previously discovered oil"), and yet another category— "newly discovered oil"—are retained, with taxes raising the effective costs to refiners to the world price level. By equalizing the average costs of crude to all refiners, these taxes eliminate the need for the entitlements program. While it is apparently assumed that these prices will induce efficient responses by demanders and suppliers, a price in itself will not assure this response. Free adjustment must be permitted. Moreover, the price must result from the interaction of all economic agents. Even Meade's (1972) indicative planning called for a balancing of demands and supplies. If regulatory measures establish a single price, without controls both demanders and suppliers can be expected to respond to it efficiently. This efficient response must be interpreted as conditional to the established price. That is, it is possible that the reshuffling of resources which would arise from the imposition of a new price would yield an improvement in the well-being of all involved.

Thus, on efficiency grounds, it is difficult to justify the users' tax on petroleum, initiated at different times for different types of users, and with built-in exceptions for a consumption of less than 90,000 barrels of oil.[30] Moreover, restrictions on the use of multiple fuel boilers, and the acquisition of boilers designed for specific fuels (petroleum and natural gas), restrict the nature and timing of private sector responses. Finally, the mandates of BAT air pollution control technology, regardless of the sulphur content of the coal used, eliminates yet another avenue for adjustment. All these aspects of the plan seem to represent attempts to "second guess" market adjustment processes. Similar observations could be made on the pricing provisions, users' taxes, and boiler restrictions imposed on consumers of natural gas.

For these reasons, the NEP does not correspond to either the Stiglitz or Nordhaus conception of indicative planning. It assumes that prices and adjustment controls can direct economic behavior as a market would. More specifically, the NEP document observed that (Executive Office of the President 1977:93):

Achievements of the goals and strategy of the National Energy Plan could demonstrate the benefits of indicative planning. If private decision makers voluntarily act within the framework proposed in the plan, the United States could achieve its energy and economic goals with relatively little direct Government regulation of economic activity.

Unfortunately, little discretion is left for voluntarism; intervention is both direct and comprehensive.

The post-1971 pattern of intervention into energy markets appears to be based in concerns for equity and macro efficiency (i.e., price stabilization). These objectives were achieved at the cost of substantial losses in micro efficiency and in the resulting misallocation of energy resources. By contrast, the NEP proposes to achieve arbitrarily defined levels of consumption of energy resources while "doing no harm" to existing equity and macro-efficiency considerations. Energy resources thus are to be effectively removed from the market, and the micro efficiency of the resulting allocation pattern is ignored.

IMPLICATIONS

Most analysts of the NEP have argued that the proposed targets for the domestic consumption of crude oil, natural gas, and coal, as well as for the imports of oil, are unrealistic.[31] In all cases, the targets reflect an optimistic appraisal of outcomes which cannot be expected on the basis of the plan's incentive structure *alone*. The prospects for further controls thus seem assured, if the targets are to be maintained.

It seems logical, then, to ask why. Why must the rate of domestic consumption of crude oil and natural gas, imports of oil, and use of coal correspond to the specified mandates? The expanded Strategic Petroleum Reserve is designed to insure against the threat of supply interruptions, so that insecurity of supply from foreign sources cannot be the sole basis. One reason might be that policymakers feel we cannot afford the reserves required by an effective insurance program. It seems reasonable, however, that those responsible for imposing the risk of disruption should bear the costs of adequate insurance, and that the prices paid for crude oil should include the costs of this insurance.

An alternative justification for the plan's artificial limitations stems from the need to speed the process of adjustment to new energy sources. Past policies, however, provide ample evidence that intervention can retard adjustment mechanisms, and this is particularly true of the post-1973 policies. On the other hand, imposed adjustments can also come too quickly. Nordhaus's empirical demonstration of the role of his brand of indicative planning for energy resources, while admittedly a numerical exercise to illustrate the outcomes dictated under "efficient" allocation programs, concludes that (Nordhaus 1973:567):

As a long-run policy it would be unwise to jack up the prices of energy products in the interests of preserving energy resources. Nor does a more drastic policy of permanent rationing of energy make sense. As long as investment yields about 10 percent, it seems best to use the cheap resources now and to put the real resources thereby saved to work on producing synthetic fuels later.

Several years and a direct role in policymaking have intervened since he made these observations. The overall intent of the recommendation, however, is to call for energy use patterns that reflect relative costs of the resources involved as well as the costs of adjustment, and not for a mandated schedule of fuel switching.

Of course, Nordhaus's simplified schedules assume that smooth substitutions are fully possible. New energy sources must be available as the price rises with the exhaustion of the type in use. The circumstances are not so clear-cut today. The NEP recognizes some of these uncertainties in formulating its policies toward nuclear power, but not for increased coal production. Increases in coal use may *not* be possible in the presence of an effective BAT pollution-control policy. Moreover, some pollutants which are not currently subject to control, such as carbon dioxide, have been ignored; yet they have the potential for serious climatological impacts. Finally, international wealth transfers may be the central concern for some policy measures, but these cannot be the sole basis for domestic energy policies.

The National Energy Plan set forth policies which will effectively remove energy resources from the market allocation process in order to achieve mandated price *and* quantity targets simultaneously. These policies are in direct opposition to the principles outlined early in this paper. In part, this policy drift results from failures in the procedures and practices of past regulations. In part, the trend reflects an increase in the number of objectives to be subjected to control. Since no basis exists for accepting all of these objectives, we must conclude that the policies are misdirected.[32]

APPENDIX

Consider a simple demand and supply diagram as given in Figure 1A.

Figure 1A: Effects of price regulation on excess demand.

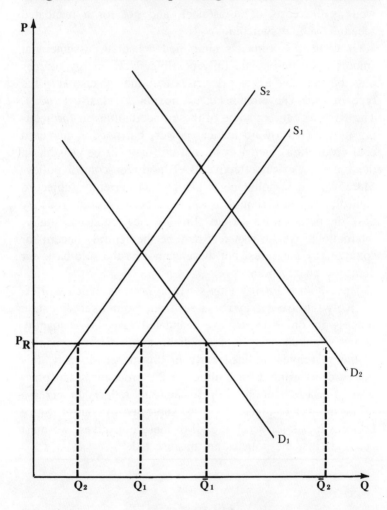

D_1 is the demand in period one and S_1 the domestic supply of crude oil. The government policies since 1973 have served to maintain prices at P_R—below the market equilibrium for domestic demand and supply, with an excess demand of

$Q_1\overline{Q}_1$. This excess demand was met through petroleum imports at world prices. Since domestic producers faced controlled prices for domestically produced oil and uncertainty as to whether (if ever) the government would allow them to rise to world prices, it seems reasonable to assert that there would be reduced incentives for additions to domestic supplies. To illustrate these effects, suppose supply in period two is S_2. Domestic demand also responds to an artificially low price by shifting to D_2 in period two (through consumers' choices of energy-using durables). The result is an increase in the extent of excess demand to $Q_2\overline{Q}_2$. Though obviously simple, this diagram serves to illustrate the incentive structure. In order to maintain the artificial condition in the markets for both crude and refinery products, government allocation schemes (see Table 2 in the text for a listing) were necessary. These measures serve to reduce the adjustments possible underlying a market supply relation, and *ceteris paribus* decrease its elasticity.

COMMENT

ERIC R. ZAUSNER
Senior Vice President-Energy, Booz, Allen & Hamilton
Former Deputy Administrator, Federal Energy Administration
In the three or four years I spent in the government working on the energy problem, I guess I came into Washington as more of a regulator than I left Washington. . . . There are several problems. . . . Perhaps the most important . . . is what I will call the law of averages. . . . When you deal with a very complicated industry, you can't set a regulation for all 22,000 oil producers or all 220,000 gasoline stations. Regulations are developed on average. They are averages of what you expect to happen.[Like the] statistician with his head in the oven and his behind in the icebox, . . . on average he is very comfortable. . . .

On any regulation, you set it on the average and what you hear about is the extremes. . . . The result is either a system that is

tremendously . . . punitive, or a windfall . . . or a never-ending bat-
tle to set up exceptions and more complicated processes to deal
with the extremes and thereby make the average viable. . . . When
you look at [average] gasoline use, . . . in Wyoming you find four
times that use, and on the east coast and in Washington you find a
third of the average.

The second problem, and it seems like it infects all regulators
. . . is what I will call the "We're smarter than they are" syn-
drome. That manifests itself in several ways. One is that every new
regulator thinks he is smarter than the last regulator, and that he can
design a better system. And secondly, and as important, he thinks
he is smarter than the marketplace, that he can . . . perceive all the
complex signals that go on in the marketplace, and . . . can develop a program to harness those perfectly for all those hundreds of
thousands of people who operate in that marketplace. . . . All I
found when I was in government was . . . examples of things that
didn't work. . . . During the heat of the embargo, I remember
. . . struggling over those very long gasoline lines, and we were
very much concerned that the gasoline prices would skyrock-
et . . . out of control. . . . The lawyers wrote this regulation
which put a cap on gasoline at about sixty cents a gallon. . . . We
put it out at about ten o'clock at night, and on the eleven o'clock
news they were filming a picture of a gasoline station in Chicago
where the guy was selling rabbits' feet for a dollar, and with each
rabbit's foot you got a gallon of gasoline free. It turns out that was
legal under the regulations we wrote. But just to show you how
regulation works, we arrested the guy anyway just for the moral
value of the thing, and he got off later. . . . There are lots of other
examples of how we are not smarter than they are. . . .

The political process is not set up to deal with [long-term] planning. Energy regulations are designed for the short term. [Most]
actions . . . to affect supply and demand often have five- and ten-
year payoffs, and most congressmen run every two years. So when
one proposes, for example, natural gas deregulation, and you tell a
congressman with a straight face . . . [that] it's going to double the
prices in his district over the next three or four years, but in 1985 it
is going to make our supply situation a lot better, he looks at you
like you are crazy. There is no way, in a practical sense, that Congress readily can pass programs where the impact is today, and the
benefits are five or ten years away.

The other practical problem with regulation . . . [is that] people
look to it for a free lunch. The reality is that almost any program

one looks at today to either increase supply or cut demand costs . . . and that cost is often very painful, be it higher prices to produce more costly supplies, be it more environmental damage to mine and burn coal or produce offshore oil, or be it major regional impacts.

People tend to talk about the energy situation as a national problem with national solutions. But national solutions rapidly turn into regional, and massive regional development questions. If you want more oil, you don't produce it out of all fifty states. You are going to do it in Alaska and off the west and . . . the east coast. If you want more coal production, there are a very limited number of places that can sustain a doubling of coal production. If you want more electric power and nuclear power plants, that . . . [doesn't mean] everybody with little plants . . . [but] a hundred or two hundred massive nuclear facilities in a particular county at a particular address. And energy, in a way, is like garbage: everybody wants it picked up and nobody wants it put down. . . . Everybody wants to use energy, but nobody wants what are obviously the impacts of energy facilities. So, regardless of whether you look at price or environmental impact or regional impact, there is a cost to an affirmative program. . . . People look to regulation . . . as a way to not have to resolve conflicting goals. On coals conversion, for example, we can both have a Clean Air Act that says if you burn coal you are out of compliance with [it] . . . [and] a Coal Conversion Act which says that all those plants that were forced to convert from coal to oil five or ten years ago must now convert back. . . . Those conflicting goals rapidly translate into uncertainty, and I can give you an example of how that works in our regulatory environment.

One of my clients is an electric utility in the northeast, and it is planning to build two nuclear units which are going to cost about $3 billion. They have had that plant under design and development for . . . three or four years . . . and they have paid the up-front money to buy the long lead time—very expensive items—the nuclear containment vessels and a number of other things. They have recently received a letter from the EPA . . . which informed them that . . . this plant was sited . . . below a dam . . . [and] that the water which is [discharged] from the power plant . . . would impact some snubnosed sturgeon . . . an endangered species. . . . Under the Endangered Species Act, they could not discharge this water at all. . . . They were therefore directed to move the water discharge system above the dam where . . . these snubnosed sturgeon couldn't get because the dam was there. This would be about a $300 million modification, and would take about three or four years.

They started the redesign efforts, and then they got a letter from the state fish and wildlife service which ordered them to build a fish ladder . . . to allow fish to migrate upstream . . . [which] would mean that the snubnosed sturgeon could get above the dam. . . . On a $3 billion investment one has to be prudent, so they wrote back to the EPA . . . [who] replied: ". . . We'll have to shut you down, because you can't discharge there either.". . . They took another tack, and said: ". . . Maybe they're so endangered that they're already gone. Which means we could probably go ahead." So they tried to find out what a snubnosed sturgeon was. Well, it turns out that while there are very few snubnosed sturgeon, there are hundreds of millions of Atlantic sturgeon, and the difference between an Atlantic sturgeon and a snubnosed sturgeon is that its peritoneum, which, as I understand it, is one of the things that covers the internal organs, is black instead of transparent, and that is the only difference. And of course, the only way you can tell is by catching them and cutting them open. Which, needless to say, is also against the regulations of the endangered species.

To make a long story short, they are wondering whether they ought to build a nuclear power plant. And the moral of this story, if you will, is that, while in theory regulations . . . set rational goals and tradeoffs, and set a new envelope in which industry works, the reality is that regulations are often broad and conflicting, and when investments are very large and take ten or twenty or even thirty years to pay off, the uncertainty brought about by regulation and the way it is administered . . . is so great that often many of these massive investments can't be prudently justified. . . .

The Carter energy program attempts basically to deal with the difficult tradeoffs by one focusing on conservation, and the president calls it the keystone of his program in proposing mandatory standards to try to cut the rate of growth from something like the 4 percent historical rate to a 2 percent rate between now and 1985. His program is likely to work in that regard if it would pass. Although the reality is that even the conservation measures are politically unpalatable, and suffer from many of the same problems that the supply side suffers from. But the crux of the weakness in the program is what he does to stimulate supply. . . .

In reality, if you want to increase supply you must do it with conventional technology, and we only have [four] . . . choices for that . . . oil, gas, coal, and nuclear power. And the reality is that producing more oil and gas, using more coal, or building more nuclear power plants all involve very difficult tradeoffs in terms of increased prices, environmental damage, and regional development. And a program of energy regulation which promises to take care of all those problems and not cause price increases, environmental damage, or regional impact simply can't deliver the supply. . . . There is no free lunch. . . . Regulation doesn't, in fact, offer one, and the costs of a regulatory program are much larger than they seem on the surface. . . . The fallacy is very straightforward. Unfortunately, it is easy to hide it in the rhetoric.

CLAUDE S. BRINEGAR
Director and Senior Vice President, Union Oil Company of California
Former U.S. Secretary of Transportation

President Carter's energy plan is now having problems in the Senate, . . . not because of the "excessive power of the oil lobby," as he said in his press conference. . . . Repeatedly, the oil industry has lost issue after issue. . . . Rather, . . . [it is due to] growing public awareness that the president's plan is largely a huge tax proposal . . . and that it all ignores this real issue of where are the long-term energy supplies going to come from? . . .

[Carter's staff] became convinced at the start that most of the nation's oil and gas has already been found. . . . And consequently the market system has a very limited role to play in the future of allocating this already known resource. No amount of evidence about the nation's remaining undiscovered oil and gas resources . . . could cause them ever to doubt the validity of their assumption, . . . [or] the risk of taking such a narrow assumption in national policymaking. I might just note that this remaining resource base of oil certainly exceeds the amount that we have produced thus far, something far in excess, in my judgment, of [the] 150 billion barrels . . . which we produced since 1860. Certainly it is very large, and very worthwhile going after. . . .

With a very few possible exceptions . . . the oil companies of America are not awash with cash. . . . Nor will you find any large unused borrowing capacity. Thus, these producers, the ones who are liquidating old oil, find themselves in the position of the merchant who is selling his product for $2.00 and paying the wholesaler hopefully $3.00 to replace it. . . . Not even volume will overcome that headache. . . .

The industry's real problem in this program . . . is not long-term incentive. The $14.00 a barrel that they hold down the road is fine. Rather it . . . is the issue of [whether we] can really trust Washington to leave these long-term incentives alone as we work to get there. We have had repeatedly something held out and then suddenly taken away because the politics suggest it isn't all really that attractive. . . .

What is really at stake . . . is the nature of the transition process as America inevitably moves over the next two or three decades . . . away from the era of heavy reliance on oil and gas and into the era of heavy usage of other energy sources, as we must. Particularly coal and uranium and commercialization of new energy sources—oil shale, geothermal, solar, wind, or what have you. . . . We don't face an energy shortage in America per se. These other sources could be or are available in enormous quantities. What we really face is a shortage of oil and gas and a shortage of process—namely, the reliance on the market forces—to make a smooth transition from one era to another. Because we lack that process, we are beginning to face some very tough . . . political issues. . . .

A big argument will be . . . [over] the nature of the energy industry when this transition ends. Will it be nationalized . . . or simply heavily regulated, far more so than it is now? . . . I must note that I learned something in my Washington career that kind of saddened me about regulations. It is really appalling how quickly an industry, or at least its top executives, adapt themselves to a regulated environment. As a member of the oil industry, I now find myself fighting hard to eliminate regulations that we think are inadequate, inept, inefficient. But as Secretary of Transportation, I found myself fighting transportation industry executives who, almost without exception, felt they couldn't survive without regulations. I suspect . . . the next generation of oil men could be fighting to keep regulations, because they have learned that that is the way they survive. So maybe we have a kind of a crucial period here, where we can hopefully move to a more efficient system. But I am not optimistic.

5

PENNY HOLLANDER FELDMAN

RICHARD J. ZECKHAUSER

Some Sober Thoughts on Health Care Regulation

The objectives of health care regulation: cost, quality, availability. Lack of market control. Misallocation problems within the health care system. Compensation for regulatory distortions. State and federal funding programs and controls. Failures in regulation: ambivalence, compromise, fragmentation. Difficulties of reform.

INTRODUCTION

Health care is a major industry and a growth industry. It consumes more than 8 percent of the United States GNP in comparison to 4.5 percent twenty years ago (Worthington 1976; Gibson and Mueller 1977). Regulatory activities are burgeoning as well. Major efforts are under way at both state and federal levels to influence or control the costs and prices of service, the quality of services delivered, capital investments in facilities, and the production and location of health manpower. These activities are intended to improve the allocation of health resources, that is, to help assure that appropriate individuals receive appropriate services at appropriate times.

This essay reviews the causes and justifications for such regulation, its performance to date, explanations for its failures, and prospects for its future. Attention is focused on hospitals, and within the hospital sector on capital expenditure controls, efforts to contain costs and prices, and utilization and quality review mechanisms. Many other regulatory activities such as efforts to regulate manpower, medical devices, food and drugs, product safety and lifestyles, also impinge significantly on health care and/or health.

Rationale for Health Care Regulation

Recent health care regulation grew out of the widespread feeling within government that the rapid escalation of public expenditures on health care in the 1960s and 1970s had not yielded commensurate benefits. The regulatory objective was never in question: we should seek simultaneously to hold down costs and to enhance medical care delivered. The intention, using the language of the economist, was to push outwards the production-possibility frontier. Such expansion was thought possible for two reasons. First, the new entitlement and resource-providing policies had not produced the expected results, in terms of the costs, benefits, and availability of health care. Indeed, prominent academics and others argued that in some absolute efficiency sense the medical care sector was performing less well than it had a decade before (see, for example, Fuchs 1974). Second, specific sources of inefficiency could be identified, including excess hospital beds, duplicative surgical facilities, and wasteful—or indeed, harmful—modes of treatment. Less dramatically, inappropriate patterns of resource allocation, which failed to maximize health care output per dollar of expenditure, were apparent. It was shown, for example, that physicians tended to cluster in urban and suburban locations, away from inner city and rural areas where need seemed to be greatest. Regulation, it was thought, could quite simply reallocate resources in a more efficient manner.[1]

Why was it believed that market forces did not offer a reliable way of allocating health resources? First and foremost, the conditions for a competitive market are not met. Health is not a neatly divisible commodity produced by large numbers of competitors all adjusting prices and input mixes to maximize profits. Doctors and hospitals have predominantly captive clienteles, and may exercise substantial market power. Few appendicitis victims can be trusted to shop around for the most economical hospital or surgeon.

Information problems also plague the health sector; the most significant may be the problems of identifying benefits. The ill-defined relationship between health care and health, and the probabilistic nature of outcomes, make it difficult even for physicians—much less patients—to determine what the delivery of medical services in particular contexts will accomplish. Studies in the past six months have shown, for instance, that death rates from heart attacks and strokes are down significantly, yet the causal factor(s) remain unidentified (Walker 1977). Much of what determines health remains a mystery.

It is not surprising that in many traditional societies health care and religion are dispensed by the same individual, nor that many Westerners treat doctors as if they were vested with spiritual powers. Given their aura and their professional monopoly, it is hardly startling that physicians have generally taken over decision-making roles from the patient-consumer.

Yet the physician is not his agent in the traditional sense of that term, since the patient does not pay the full cost of the services that he receives.

A most significant distinguishing characteristic of health care is that, at the time of purchase, others share in its cost. For most individuals on most occasions, health care is a subsidized commodity. The subsidy may take the form of government support for the construction of facilities, purchase of equipment, or training of manpower. Sometimes the government pays directly for care, as with Medicare and Medicaid; in other cases, subsidy takes the form of tax deductions for health insurance premiums. For tens of millions of Americans, the major source of the subsidy is fellow insureds participating in some collective health plan.

This web of subsidies, we shall argue, is a primary source of misallocation problems within the health care system, and thus, although not always fully recognized, the principle motivating force for our present system of regulation. Why should these subsidies exist? Why should individuals not pay the full cost of the services they receive, as they do when purchasing haircuts, movie tickets, or carrots? First, medical care can be an exceedingly high cost item for an individual or family in a particular year. Certain types of medical services are low-probability, high-cost events, the type of contingency against which we normally carry insurance.[2] Second, health services have achieved a somewhat exalted position in our society. Large numbers of citizens, and a no smaller proportion of politicians, no longer view health care as a normal consumption item. Rather, health care is identified as a necessity, which in turn suggests that collective provision might be appropriate. To attempt to reenforce market discipline, say, through expanding coinsurance payments or deductible limits, would be working against the basic premise for collective provision of a necessity.[3]

Once price is eliminated, or at least debilitated, as a means of limiting demand, some other force must emerge in its place. In this industry, with the asymmetry of information, the producer rather than the consumer tends to determine what kind and how much care will be delivered. We might rely on the professional ethics of the physician to allocate resources efficiently: "Only deliver the care that is appropriate." However, as long as a doctor's reimbursement increases with the services delivered, his natural incentives to boost his income and simultaneously provide the highest quality care will defeat attempts to limit the consumption of medical services. Regulation is—or seemed to be—the only alternative.

We argue, then, that regulation in the health care sector exists primarily because we have chosen a system that does not permit individuals to pay anything close to the full costs of the care they receive. Regulation is intended to deal with three inevitably resulting classes of problems: (1) There is excess demand for care, since, in violation of the fundamental condition of economic efficiency, price is not set equal to marginal cost. (2) Quality levels may be inappropriate. There will be incentives for excessive quality if reimbursement is based on cost. Every hospital wants a CAT (computerized axial tomography) scanner. However, if reimbursement is made per unit of output—e.g., per day in a nursing home or per appendectomy—quality may well suffer. The so-called Medicaid mills provide a dramatic example. (3) Regulatory impositions introduce new distortions and inefficiencies of their own. For example, if hospitals are limited in their expenditures on new beds, they may compensate by spending more on equipment. If per-diem rates are limited, forgone revenues may be recouped through longer stays. We shall see that regulation-induced inefficiencies have been significant in limiting the effectiveness of health care regulation.

Health Care Regulation and the Regulatory Reform Movement

This volume is intended to provide an overview of regulation controversies in a range of policy areas. The implicit hope is

that lessons learned in one field, say, trucking, will turn out
to be applicable to other areas, perhaps airlines. Unfortunately, however, extrapolation from other areas to health regulation has only a limited value.

Clearly, some lessons on regulation are generic. They may
relate to the inevitable difficulties in drafting regulations,
monitoring the compliance of regulated parties, or imposing
sanctions. The problems to which regulation is directed,
however, may well be specific to particular industry structures. Although trucking and airline problems have common
elements, as do electric utility and telephone regulation, the
characteristics of the health care industry that are most significant as motives for regulation are not found elsewhere.
The critical elements are the prevalence of third-party payment for services, and the fact that the producer, the physician, acts as the decision-maker.

Because health care is a $150 billion industry, regulation in
this area is a problem of substantial importance, although one
that is not closely analogous to more traditional forms of regulation. The health care field does, however, share at least
one significant problem with other areas; that is, the
phenomenon of relying on regulation as a means of dealing
with problems created by previous interventions. When we
put emission control devices on cars, we may have to impose
additional regulations to make sure that people do not tamper
with them. The enactment of housing subsidies carries with it
the subsequent need for rules to determine eligibility for
housing (elderly, poor, family of a certain size), and for programs to inspect the housing to prevent its deterioration and
abandonment. Indeed, entitlement programs frequently call
for regulation to control utilization. The regulation is thus a
follow-on part of a process of pyramiding intervention. This
phenomenon is particularly striking in health care, as we
demonstrate below.

Let us foreshadow our findings at the outset. No new forms
of health care regulation seem likely to improve performance
dramatically, either in terms of holding down costs or en-

hancing the quantity or quality of services delivered for a given cost. Nor does deregulation seem particularly promising. There is apparently no regulatory policy that will push the production-possibility frontier noticeably outward. It would, however, be possible to shift our location along that frontier significantly—to reduce costs at the expense of services, or to increase services while incurring greater costs—through different financing policies. Whether a radically different financing policy should or will be adopted is primarily a political question with which we shall not grapple here. However, the prospects for significant change in the near future seem dim, and regulation will apparently continue to be with us in its various forms for some time to come.

Despite, or perhaps because of, these rather negative conclusions, we think that a thorough review of regulatory performance in the health care area is worthwhile. First, the research effort would be repaid by even a very small percentage improvement in performance, because of the sheer size of the health care industry. Second, if the limitations of regulatory activities in this area are better understood, less effort will be wasted on exhausting struggles for one kind of control or another, since it will be recognized that only limited results can be expected in any case. Third, we may save ourselves from some new policies whose effectiveness would depend on an already overburdened regulatory system. Each new program of entitlements, for example, will carry with it the need for regulatory efforts to control costs and utilization. And regulatory efforts themselves, in the process we have called pyramiding intervention, call for further regulation. Fourth, if it is well understood that costs and services must be traded off against one another, we may be able to focus political and intellectual energies on the tough choices and nonregulatory alternatives. Perhaps we would then devote more effort to determine what is and is not sacred about health care. We might be encouraged to explore the consequences of making deductibles and coinsurance rates significant, or the effects of a comprehensive government financing scheme offering varying service packages with varying degrees of consumer liability. As long as the promise of substantial improvement through regulation remains unexamined, we will not undertake or even consider more fundamental actions to improve outcomes.

In the sections that follow, we first outline the major forms of health regulation and their effects. We then turn to explain the "failures" of health care regulation, and finally to our conclusions.

MAJOR FORMS OF HEALTH REGULATION AND THEIR EFFECTS

Federal and state efforts to control expenditures within the health care sector have focused on hospital costs. Four kinds of programs have been employed. Three—entry controls, price controls, and quality regulation—fall into the classic regulatory mode. The fourth represents an attempt to foster more cost-effective modes of treatment—so-called health maintenance organizations (HMOs)—through the government's traditional grant mechanism.

Entry controls have long been used in the health care system, although not primarily as a governmental means of controlling cost. Licensure of doctors and hospitals has been justified, and predominantly perceived by the public, as a means for protecting consumers from unqualified practitioners or inferior institutions. (It limits competition as well, of course.) Moreover, the power to license has generally been delegated by government to the medical profession. Only in the last decade have Congress and the state legislatures attempted to impose public entry controls, most notably on the growth of hospitals and their acquisition of costly equipment, but also on the supply and geographic distribution of physicians.

State programs to control hospital investment—commonly called certificate of need (CON) programs—began to multiply in the late 1960s. New York enacted the nation's first such program in 1964. By 1975, twenty-nine states had enacted some form of CON legislation (Stiles and Johnson 1976). The National Health Planning and Resources Development Act of 1974 further institutionalized capital expenditure controls; it requires participating states to adopt not only CON controls, but also a rather elaborate state and local health planning process.

CON programs are based on the premise that excess hospital capacity generates unnecessary medical services whose costs are borne by unsuspecting consumers, by government, and, ultimately and inevitably, by taxpayers. If capital investment controls can prevent hospitals from expanding services and purchasing costly, unnecessary, or duplicative equipment, health care costs can be constrained. This method of control is thought to work first, by reducing capital costs, and second, by reducing utilization and operating costs caused by supply-induced demand.

Certificate of need controls are justified by the argument that hospital beds tend to be filled once they are built. Similarly, controls on the supply and distribution of physicians reflect the view that doctors tend to find procedures to perform once they are in practice. Thus, federal health manpower legislation enacted in 1976 seeks to control the entry of foreign medical graduates into practice in the United States, and to impose requirements on medical schools as to the numbers of graduates they can train in various specialties, limiting the number of surgeons produced, for example, and promoting family practitioners. In addition, federal and state governments have begun to curtail capitation grants and other subsidies to independent and state medical schools, grants which in an earlier period were used to stimulate the production of doctors.

Price regulation, long familiar in the public utilities field, has only recently been used in health care. Cost-based reimbursement mechanisms, traditionally employed by Medicare and Medicaid as well as by Blue Cross and other health care insurers, provide little or no incentive for hospitals to control costs or even to allocate their resources efficiently. Whatever costs are incurred have traditionally been reimbursed fully and after the fact. In contrast, some states have experimented recently with setting rates of payment in advance of the incurrence of costs, and holding hospitals responsible for any and all costs in excess of those rates. The National Economic Stabilization Program, in force between December 1971 and April 1974, and the Carter Hospital Cost Control Bill, still buried in the congressional labyrinth, are both variants of classic public utility rate regulation. The traditional justification for such regulation is monopoly or market power; here it is that consumers are paying less than the marginal costs of received services, and therefore have incentives to purchase too much. This problem is exacerbated in the sector because producers, the doctors, make most consumption decisions.

Excessive utilization has also been the motivation for recent product quality regulation in the health care sector. (Hospital audits have been required for accreditation for many years.) In the late 1960s, Medicare, Medicaid, and private insurers began to adopt "utilization review" programs to monitor the appropriateness of hospital admissions and lengths of stay. Such activities were further institutionalized when the federal government mandated a national network of Professional Standards Review Organizations (PSROs) in 1972.

Although utilization controls are motivated largely by economic concerns, they are commonly justified on quality grounds. Excessive hospitalization, unnecessary laboratory tests, and surgery that is not mandated, for example, not only maintain medical costs at an artificially high level but—it can be argued—constitute inferior or inappropriate treatment for the affected individual patients (Stuart and Stockton 1973). Thus, prior screening of patients to justify hospitalization, concurrent (in-hospital) review of hospitalization and treatment, and retrospective review, have all been employed for the related, although frequently conflicting, purposes of guaranteeing the quality of medical services and controlling their costs.

Finally, the federal government has attempted to promote "alternate" health care delivery systems, or HMOs. HMOs are financed by capitation payments for individuals or families, and their physicians are salaried. Providers thus are discouraged from offering medical care of doubtful or marginal value, and are encouraged to supply more cost-effective care. We do not explore the growing literature on the performance of HMOs here. Nevertheless, it is worth noting that while HMO financing schemes have been able to alter patterns of health care delivery and costs, the federal government's attempts to promote HMOs have suffered from a characteristic problem of interventions: the basic tension between developing innovative programs and regulating them to ensure appropriate quality.

The Performance of Entry, Price, and Quality Controls

In the discussion that follows, we survey available evidence on the effects of entry, price, and quality controls in the health sector, and offer some explanation for their relatively unimpressive performance.

Entry Controls. Capital expenditure or certificate of need (CON) controls have been part of health care regulation for little more than a decade, and manpower controls are even more recent—indeed, hardly in place. Therefore, we restrict our survey to data on the effects of hospital investment regulation.

Recent studies of the impact of capital expenditure controls on hospital investment and expansion have produced data on total hospital investment, on hospital investment in beds and plant, and on per capita hospital costs. Some of the studies are based on aggregate data, while others look at the impact of programs in particular states or groups of states.

These outcome studies show that CON controls have been significantly associated with lower overall growth in hospital beds (Salkever and Bice 1976a, 1976b). However, the impact of CON programs has varied among states. A critical question is how health care administrators and institutions respond in other areas of expenditure when bed construction is restricted. In some states, reductions in bed investment have been offset by increased investment in medical equipment, while in other states they have not (Salkever and Bice 1976a, 1976b; also Cohodes 1976). In California, for example, growth in bed investment fell 33 percent between the pre-CON period (1963-1968) and the post-CON period (1969-1974), but growth in investment in equipment rose 60 percent between the same periods. In rosy contrast, Connecticut experienced reduced growth in both bed (39.2 percent) and equipment (19.2 percent) investment (Cohodes 1976).

Mindful of other areas where regulation has fostered anticompetitive activities, critics of hospital entry controls have predicted that CON programs would serve the interests of hospitals that are already large and capital-intensive and impede innovations in medical care delivery systems. Evidence from Massachusetts, for example, supports this hypothesis: large urban teaching hospitals have evidently fared better in the application-approval process than smaller and poorer community hospitals (Britton 1975). Furthermore, a recent study of some forty-one states with capital expenditure controls found that states tended to discriminate against proprietary hospitals, whose denial rates were seven times higher than those of nonprofit institutions. The study did not, however, find evidence that states actively tried to block health maintenance organizations or other ambulatory care facilities through the certificate of need process (Lewin et al. 1975).

What has been the impact of these activities on per-capita hospital costs? Given interstate variations, the answer to this question is not unambiguous. Salkever and Bice (1976a, 1976b), analyzing hospital investment patterns and hospital costs in forty-eight states for the period January 1969 through

December 1972, did not find that CON controls had a significant effect—negative or positive—on per-capita hospital costs. On the other hand, in a follow-up study for the period 1971-1974, they focused on the five states in which CON programs had been in effect the longest, and found hospital expenditures may have been somewhat lower (about 3 percent) than they would have been otherwise.

How are we to account for the small and quite variable impact of certificate of need controls? In general, CON programs require health care facilities to obtain state approval for investments in plant and equipment that exceed a given dollar threshold or substantially alter the services provided by the facility. States differ significantly in the comprehensiveness and vigor of their programs. There is wide variation in the scope of investment decisions covered, the dollar thresholds employed, the thoroughness of review procedures, the use of monitoring mechanisms to determine whether a facility complies with a particular CON decision, and the imposition of sanctions on noncompliant institutions. Even more significant, however, states vary in the nature of the criteria they use to make their decisions and in the consistency with which they apply those criteria.

The disappointing performance of CON controls reflects the inability of regulators to arrive at definitions of "need" that are both limiting and defensible. If the criteria for making certificate of need decisions are not limiting, institutions will have no reason to alter their investment patterns in anticipation of regulatory decisions. If CON criteria are not defensible, providers will have strong incentives to appeal adverse regulatory decisions in the courts or even in the state legislatures, which have been known to override CON authorities.

One reason why criteria cannot be made too restrictive is that the state-of-the-art of assessing health care resource needs is really quite primitive. Essentially, there are three ways of assessing needs, none of which is particularly satisfactory (Correia 1975).

Current use patterns can be projected into the future. These projections are valid guidelines for decisions only if current practices are accepted as desirable. If available beds and services create their own demand, so to speak, and if current demand is viewed as excessive, then projection from current practice is hardly satisfactory. Moreover, the rapid pace of health technology development means that in many cases there will not be adequate current use data from which to extrapolate.

Alternatively, needs can be assessed by drawing on the experience of institutions or systems with a record or reputation of "good performance." Thus, for example, the reference point used in deciding whether a particular expansion or change of service is justified might be the bed/population ratio characteristic of Great Britain, Kaiser, or the Harvard Community Health Plan. Such criteria will often prove to be limiting. Whether they are defensible depends to some extent on how closely the characteristics of the community match those of the model. Unquestionably, however, this approach has some utility. For example, across the United States, areas with relatively similar populations show a three-to-one variation in hospital beds per capita (HEW 1976:Table 12). Reference to a "good performance" standard would clearly suggest beds should be curtailed in high-endowment areas.

The third method for assessing need is to determine some optimal—as distinct from an empirically derived—distribution of resources. The problem with this approach is that from a medical-economic standpoint it is virtually impossible to determine what comprises an "optimal" supply of hospital or nursing home beds, much less an optimal distribution of open-heart surgery facilities, CAT scanners, or angiography units. We know very little about the efficacy of many medical services and procedures; what we do know is often not helpful in enabling us to determine at precisely what point money spent for one purpose would yield greater returns if invested elsewhere. And from the political standpoint, we lack consensus on what is a just and equitable distribution of health care resources.

Given the lack of an intellectually sound and politically acceptable means for defining need, it is not surprising that CON authorities in different institutional and political contexts apply different regulatory standards and achieve different results.

Price Controls. Price control programs in the health care sector vary along a number of dimensions, principally the mechanism by which rates are determined, the proportion of participating hospitals, and the number of third-party payers covered. Existing studies on the effects of such programs suggest that controls based on reviews of individual hospital budgets are relatively ineffective in constraining costs; that formula-based controls may constrain price increases — though reduced growth in average hospital *costs* may be less than proportionate; and that decreased growth in *average* unit hospital costs — per patient/day, for instance — may not necessarily yield decreased growth in *total* hospital costs.

Hellinger (1976) has analyzed budget-based programs in Rhode Island, Western Pennsylvania, and New Jersey through 1973. In the limited Western Pennsylvania experiment, five (self-selected) hospitals participated in a combination budget review and formula reimbursement system. Their inpatient costs increased 8 percent between 1971 and 1974, while those of a control group of hospitals in the same area increased 12 percent. Savings were primarily due to reductions in the growth rates of housekeeping and general service costs. The results for New Jersey and Rhode Island, based on regression analysis, are less impressive. Hellinger concluded that prospective rate systems, with rates set through a hospital-by-hospital budget review, were ineffective in controlling hospital costs.

In contrast, there is evidence that formula-based price controls can mitigate hospital costs. Data on Phase II of the National Economic Stabilization Program suggest that it had a moderating impact on average hospital costs, albeit one that was less than proportionate to its impact on prices. The rate of increase in hospital room and board rates during the thirteen-month period of Phase II declined by about one-half, from roughly 12 percent to roughly 6 percent. However, increases in costs per adjusted patient day and costs per adjusted hospital admission declined by only about one-quarter.

Evaluation of New York's rate-setting program also attests to the possible moderating effects of a formula-based system. Between 1965 and 1970, before its formula system went into effect, New York's hospitals compared unfavorably with those of New England, Ohio, and the U.S. as a whole on virtually all counts: percentage increases in revenue per patient day and per admission, average costs per patient day and admission, and personnel and real inputs per patient day and admission. In contrast, between 1970 and 1973, under a formula program, New York's rates of increase were actually lower in half of twenty-eight comparisons (Berry 1976).

However, although formula reimbursement in New York has somewhat moderated the rates of increase in prices and average unit costs, it has apparently also led to some increase in average lengths of stay and occupancy rates. The net result may have been an increase in total hospital costs (Berry 1976). Moreover, some New York hospitals have run consistent deficits since the introduction of formula reimbursement. While over the long run such deficits may lead to constrained investment (and to obvious difficulties as well), over the short run they evidently have not. And if hospitals can survive deficits over the short run, the cost increases represented by those deficits may ultimately be institutionalized in the reimbursement formula.

The relatively poor performance of price controls based on hospital-by-hospital budget review is explained in part by the nature of the bargaining process in which regulators must engage when the system requires them to deal with institutions on an individual basis. Individual hospitals know far more about their own financial situation than outside reviewers. If reviewers consume too much time scrutinizing the budgets of individual hospitals or disallow too many items, they are liable to create regulatory delays and generate numerous appeals as well as noisy protests from the industry. On the other hand, it is rather easy to justify exceptions in individual cases; they rarely appear to undermine the regulatory process to the degree that delays and appeals might. Hence, when rate-setters negotiate rates with individual hospitals, they will be under a great deal of pressure to accept the hospital's cost figures and set rates accordingly.

Formula approaches to rate-setting overcome some of these obstacles, but encounter a new set of their own. Decision criteria embodied in formulas are necessarily more explicit than those applied in case-by-case negotiations, and the implications of departing from them are more severe. Moreover, in committing themselves to a particular formula, regulators limit their discretion to deal with institutions as "unique" or "exceptional" cases. The problem with such a system, of course, is that it is only as good as the formula on which it depends, and its decisions, even more than those in hospital-by-hospital regulation, are always vulnerable to appeal.

Formulas may be deficient for several reasons. First, their provisions may be subject to a good deal of bargaining between regulators and providers. Providers will naturally attempt to influence the formula adopted, and the result may be decision criteria that, while lucid and unambiguous, are insufficiently limiting. Second, like all regulatory standards, formulas are likely to focus on dimensions of provider behavior that are observable and enforceable, even if they are not precisely the most relevant dimensions from the standpoint of program objectives. In the case of hospital reimbursement, for instance, formulas based on cost per case or cost per diagnosis may be preferable to those based on cost per day, from the point of view of holding down total costs. Yet cost per day is what is used, because it is easier to administer. Formula systems, then, provide far from a fail-safe mechanism for setting appropriate hospital rates.

Quality Controls.   Quality controls in health regulation can take a variety of forms. Medical care audits or "medical care evaluation studies," which are required by the Joint Commission on Accreditation of Hospitals and by PSROs, respectively, are principally directed at assuring patients a minimum quality of care. Usually they provide that committees of doctors specify the elements of appropriate medical management for a particular diagnosis, disease, or group of patients; identify cases of deficient management; prescribe remedial action, and monitor follow-up on that action. They are essentially educational rather than regulatory in nature, based on the assumption that physicians and institutions will correct deficient behavior once they are made aware of it. In contrast, utilization review activities are directed at preventing unnecessary or excessive hospitalization and are more explicitly regulatory in nature, since they are usually tied to reimbursement sanctions. Under Medicare and Medicaid (and most health insurance plans), if a patient's hospitalization is found to be unnecessary or excessive by a peer review committee, the hospital is denied payment for the patient's total stay or for days in excess of what is deemed appropriate.

There have been few outcome studies that indicate the effectiveness of such activities. The Institute of Medicine (1976) undertook an evaluation of the evidence on quality assurance programs, and reported that "the kinds of quality improvement said to derive from medical care evaluation studies can be described anecdotally. Whether the improvements are causally associated with the imposition of a review program or other factors is a matter of conjecture."

Data on the effects of utilization review *per se* are somewhat better, but inconsistent. Evaluations of concurrent (in-hospital) review programs in Utah (Bonner 1976) and New Mexico (Brook and Williams 1976) found no evidence of reduction in hospital admissions or lengths of stay. On the other hand, evaluation of the "Certified Hospital Admission Program" (CHAP) in Sacramento found reductions in both length of stay and hospitalization rates, leading to an overall decline in total hospitalization for the Medicare population covered by the CHAP review mechanism (Kolins and Baugh 1976). The CHAP program, unlike the Utah and New Mexico programs, provided for pre-admission screening of all elective admissions *prior* to hospitalization.

If the Sacramento data suggest that pre-admission review programs may be more effective over the long run than concurrent review programs, data from Pennsylvania suggest that differences between concurrent and retrospective review programs may be insignificant. Lave and Leinhardt (1976) analyzed the effects of a voluntary concurrent review program in Western Pennsylvania, and found that average lengths of stay, adjusted for case mix, were no lower for Medicaid patients in hospitals with concurrent review than they were for Medicaid patients in hospitals with a retrospective review system. They also found that adjusted patient days fell more for Medicaid Patients (where reimbursement was tied to review) than for Blue Cross in both types of hospitals. They conclude that "both length of stay review programs, post-discharge and predischarge, were effective."

These studies and others evaluate a variety of programs implemented in a variety of ways in quite different settings. They seem to suggest that monitoring hospitalization before a patient enters the hospital, or tying control to public reimbursement (as with Medicaid), may be more effective than waiting for patients to enter the hospital before monitoring their care or monitoring it only perfunctorily, as many health insurers do. On the whole, however, there is little evidence that such programs can significantly constrain hospital costs.

As in the case of certificate of need controls, the limited effectiveness of quality regulation seems to derive from the fundamental problem of defining what is medically necessary or appropriate. Such definitions are highly judgmental and potentially controversial, and when applied to individual physicians and individual patients—as they are in this regulatory mode—they are particularly threatening to the doctor-patient relationship. The medical profession has responded by generally opposing nationally determined standards of medical practice, preferring to define appropriate care in terms of typical patterns of local practice. But if typical patterns of local practice are enshrined in regulation, we can expect little change in providers' behavior.

EXPLAINING THE "FAILURES" OF HEALTH CARE REGULATION

The two most popular explanations for regulatory "failure" are: (1) regulated institutions have "captured" the regulatory machinery and converted it to their own ends, and (2) the regulations themselves have been poorly designed or improperly carried out. Instances of both industry capture and regulatory incompetence may be found in the health sector, but they do not account, we believe, for the basic failure of health care regulation to achieve its purposes.

Successful health care regulation, like all regulation, must produce appropriate behavior in those who are regulated, in this case the providers of health care. For the most part, in the health sector, this requires their active cooperation.[4] The level and disposition of resources are ultimately controlled by doctors and hospitals, not by certificate of need agencies, rate-setting bodies, or utilization review organizations. In part, this is because no single governmental unit—indeed, not government itself—is the sole source of health care financing. Hospitals and doctors, therefore, can usually find a way of paying for equipment or services which are not approved by regulatory agencies, or at least of securing reimbursement for compensatory types of expenditures. Once installed, moreover, capacity can—by and large—generate its own demand, independent of the regulatory process.

Health care regulators, even more than regulators in other areas, must depend on providers, since it is extremely difficult for outsiders to make informed and accepted judgments about the industry. Hospital entry and investment controls, as well as utilization controls, are tied to the determination of medical need. Even rate-setting programs, ostensibly concerned with the price of care rather than its necessity, are predicated on the assumption that what is medically necessary will be included in the prenegotiated rate. But medical need is a vague and indeterminate concept whose definition is generally believed to be the legitimate domain of health care professionals, not of public officials. Lacking strong evidence on which to base their decisions, and operating in a consumer climate in which "more and better" health care is usually equated with "more and better" health, regulators are on weak ground when they try to disapprove medical expenditures, particularly in the vast majority of cases where expert and political consensus is lacking. There is also a strong tradition of deferring to the judgment of professionals in medical matters.

In the United States today, there is little consensus—expert or otherwise—on appropriate standards to govern the purchase and use of medical services, equipment, or technology. Patterns of medical practice—ranging from the propensity to perform tonsillectomies to the use of fetal heart monitors or the more costly CAT scanners—vary widely, even among immediately contiguous areas, for no apparently objective reason (see Wennberg and Gittelsohn 1973). And neither the medical profession nor the hospital industry moves quickly to lessen such disparities unless it is demonstrably to its advantage to do so.

All these problems are complicated by the lack of data persuasively linking particular modes of practice to positive health outcomes. (It is unclear, for example, to what degree the reported reductions in fatal heart attacks and strokes cited earlier are attributable to changes in medical practice, as distinct from changes in Americans' diet and smoking habits. Hence, the resource allocation implications of the observation are also unclear.) Even where data on the efficacy of particular medical procedures are available—as with coronary-artery

bypass surgery, for example—they are often subject to
conflicting interpretations and numerous qualifications which
make it difficult for regulators to base decisions on them.[5]

Regulation in the health sector is severely hampered by the
inability to anticipate the variety of responses which providers can fashion to virtually any government initiative. Experience gained from certificate of need regulation may suggest
that hospitals will divert resources from beds to services and
technology, but experience cannot indicate which new services or technologies may be emphasized (and thus, perhaps,
merit control). Similarly, experience with rate-setting programs may suggest that hospitals will push up lengths of stay
and occupancy rates when they are reimbursed on a per-diem
basis and penalized for empty beds. It is not necessarily a
good predictor, however, of responses to reimbursement on a
cost-per-case or cost-per-diagnosis basis. It is difficult, indeed, to anticipate how doctors might alter their labeling of
symptoms or their selection of procedures under a per-case or
per-diagnosis system. In short, regulators face formidable obstacles in trying to constrain health care costs by controlling
the composition and quality of medical services.

As if these problems were not enough, health care regulation is carried out in an organizational and political environment that would hamper even programs based on sounder
scientific evidence and greater technical experience and expertise. At the state level, hospital entry, price, and utilization controls are administered by different organizations; the
lack of coordination can undermine the effectiveness of any
one program. If a lenient rate-setting body includes in its
rates the costs of capital investments not approved by a CON
agency, the actions of the latter are almost certain to be com-
promised. If, on the other hand, a lenient CON agency ap-
proves capital expenditures that rate regulators do not wish to
reimburse, their ability to deny payment is likely to be com-
promised by the CON agency's finding of medical need.

At the federal level, congressional ambivalence and political compromise have produced a network of consumer-

oriented agencies (HSAs) to regulate capital investment in health care resources, and a separate network of provider-controlled organizations (PSROs) to regulate the quality and use of those resources. Rational health care regulation, assuming such to be possible, would require that resource allocation decisions reflect judgments about efficacy and quality in relation to costs. Yet Congress has entrusted utilization and quality control to doctors' organizations, which have little interest in cost, and even less incentive to share their judgments with the consumer majorities who, by law, govern HSAs.

Fragmentation, of course, reflects the underlying political source of regulation. Regulation and regulatory agencies are the products of legislatures, which are themselves characterized by fragmented power and responsiveness to multiple diverse interests. It is not merely the influence of organized interests, however, that causes legislatures to hedge the powers of health regulators. Like other consumers of health care, legislators are apparently unwilling or unable to resolve their fundamental ambivalence about the goals of health regulation. Insofar as the public and its elected representatives continue to believe that more and more sophisticated health services will enhance the health of the American people, and that any increment in health is desirable, regardless of the cost of producing it, our political system is unlikely to grapple with difficult tradeoffs between the cost and availability of medical services.

PROGNOSIS

Three factors constrain effective health care regulation: conceptual clarity, administrative feasibility, and political will. The traditional concept of the role of regulation is simply not relevant in health care, an industry where most of the conditions for a market are not met. The traditional objectives of regulation are to shore up, facilitate, or simulate the function of a market; here, however, the goal has been to induce the nonmarket system for allocating health care to function more effectively along a variety of dimensions. At best, then, regulatory reformers might hope to reintroduce some elements of the market system. For example, efforts could be made to restore financial incentives as a means of limiting demand.

Administrative feasibility is the ability to put a chosen system into practice. We have argued that health care regulatory programs are generally poorly conceived from the perspective of implementation. They seek to reallocate resources by intervening more or less directly in hospital investment decisions and budget processes, and in physician decision-making. Such interventions, however, depend heavily on judgments of medical necessity and appropriateness— judgments which regulators are ill-equipped to make.

Traditional economic theory suggests that cutbacks in expenditure should begin in those areas where benefits are the smallest. Thus, for example, we are frequently told how much could be saved by eliminating unnecessary surgical procedures. The implication is that a 10 percent cut in expenditure level would entail much less than a 10 percent sacrifice in the real value of health services delivered. However, since producers can significantly, indeed, predominantly, influence not only the quantity but the composition of services delivered, they can direct intended cutbacks towards society's high priority areas, making matters almost impossible for economy-minded regulators.

Regulation is intended to reshape the health care sector into more productive form. The industry, however, is highly resilient, and versatile enough to rearrange itself under pressure. It might be thought of as a partially filled balloon—squeeze it at one end and all the air goes to the other, but nothing is lost from the system. For example, our review of the cost-control literature indicates that when certain types of expenditures— say, the number of hospital beds—are limited, other expenditures, in this instance capital equipment per bed, may be expanded. In the absence of price competition, we should expect that every effort to intervene in one area of the health care system will tend to introduce new inefficiencies in other areas. Therefore, a major lesson of our experience with health care regulation is that no policy should be formulated without investigation of how it is likely to be implemented, how effective it will prove, and how its impact may be offset by new developments.

Experience also suggests that, except for minor effects, only sweeping reforms have the potential to alter the system significantly. Regulation of the health care system should have two objectives. First, to help define appropriate levels of expenditures. Second, to achieve maximum health benefits for whatever level of expenditure is undertaken. Many academics and policymakers believe that expenditure control could be achieved through major structural reform. Britain's experience suggests that universal, closed-end financing of health care can set limits to expenditures. The significant point about the British experience, however, is that the political system has made a commitment to living within these limits. It has accepted the consequences in terms of the quantity and quality of health services delivered, and the nonmonetary prices exacted for health care—primarily, accessibility and waiting time. (Queuing time, unlike a monetary price, represents a deadweight loss; it cannot be put to another productive use in society.) The American political system, however, has not made a similar commitment to trade off quality and access against expenditure control.

Conventional measures are frequently employed to suggest that we are spending too much on medical care. We now devote well over 8 percent of GNP to this purpose, compared to only 6 percent a decade ago. Health status indices have not shown commensurate improvement. Moreover, there is widespread sentiment that other variables, principally changes in lifestyle, could make much more significant contributions to physical wellbeing than another 1 percent of GNP spent on health care (see Fuchs 1974).

Why is 8 percent the right amount to spend on medical care? Why not 11 percent? Traditional spending patterns or cross-national comparisons count little when one's health is, or is thought to be, at stake. And since most spending decisions are substantially removed from the consumer, the dollar amounts do not register heavily. Consider the difference between a $100 rise in the cost of one's company-paid health plan and an equivalent increase in fuel costs. The former expenditure is almost invisible to the worker, showing up perhaps at a distance when labor negotiations are under way. Fuel costs, however, are a direct out-of-pocket expenditure. The political pressures to contain fuel costs will be many times greater. And while the costs of health care may be obscured, hence undercounted, the benefits are likely to be overestimated. Although the experts may agree that many health encounters accomplish little, few citizens would prefer to sacrifice, say, $50 of health resource consumption rather than $50 of fuel use. With benefits overweighted and costs underweighted, it is no surprise that we lack the political will to constrain medical expenditures stringently.

Assume, for purposes of argument, that the electorate, hence our politicians, were sufficiently aroused to undertake the considerable structural reforms necessary to contain health care expenditures. What would be the prospects for maximizing the efficacy of those expenditures? The U.S. experience with quality controls on health care is not very promising. Neither the health care professions nor the research establishment now possess the requisite knowledge about the efficacy of basic medical practices and technologies to allow effective quality regulation. Nor has the British system, despite its effective control over expenditures, been able to ensure maximum health benefits for the levels of expenditure it has undertaken. In England, as here, the knowledge for making effective tradeoff decisions is thought to be the domain of the medical profession, but that profession has hardly engaged in substantial and systematic assessment of the most cost/effective practice in medicine.

Our conclusions are mostly pessimistic. Present knowledge of which sweeping reforms would accomplish which purposes, with what deleterious consequences, is purely theoretical. But since they have not been tried, we cannot rule out their potential. Nevertheless, given political realities, we believe that current forms of health care regulation are likely to persist. Moreover, given regulatory capabilities, those efforts are unlikely to significantly constrain costs or enhance efficacy. Taking as a given our current system of financing with substantial third-party payment, there is an inevitable tension between cost control and efficiency.

Our view of health care regulation, then, is a sober one. This is not the area in which the deregulation movement should expend its fervor—unlike airlines, where dramatic changes and, we would argue, predominantly benefits, can be achieved with a stroke of the deregulatory pen. Nor are efforts to improve methods of regulation likely to accomplish much in health care, in contrast, say, to the environmental area, where incentive or pricing approaches might well prove substantially superior to the present command and control approach. Health care is not the disaster area of occupational safety and health regulation, where no attempt is made to examine the consequences of regulatory imposition, and where a little rationality could both improve protection and conserve resources. No, health care regulation is an area where hard study and diligent effort might improve matters a little—and since the sector is vast, it may be worth making the effort to achieve even a small percentage gain. A more important benefit may come from the study of health care regulation. We may be able to formulate new policies, particularly those offering health care entitlements, with an awareness of the inherent weakness of our regulatory capabilities.

Confronted with this dour situation, politicians and analysts frequently conclude that something dramatically new is needed. National health insurance is the most frequently cited solution. If the federal government assumes primary responsibility for both financing health care and regulating its delivery, it will be a more comprehensive, and perhaps a more comprehensible, system. But that in itself will be an irrelevant accomplishment unless national health insurance addresses the major source of our current difficulties—the fact that neither government nor consumers make tough resource allocation decisions in the context of financial responsibility. Moreover, our experience with the inadequacies of our present regulation system suggests that we should always be reluctant to increase the regulatory tasks of government.

Let us conclude with a metaphor. Health care regulation is intended to direct the resources that flow in and out of the sector, with regulatory bodies functioning as gatekeepers and switchmen. Our observation of the scene suggests that things are not working that way. For the most part, the regulators stand by the whirring turnstiles, perhaps blocking one or another, only to watch the resources flow through one that is adjacent.

COMMENT

HARRY SCHWARTZ
Member, Editorial Board, **The New York Times**
In the early and mid-1960s . . . we were constantly being told how dreadful the American medical system was and how nobody could get a doctor. . . . [Yet] what we were being promised was Nirvana; . . . the dominant political environment . . . [was] promising the people of the United States that they were going to get everything free, and particularly health care. And Medicare and Medicaid were the products of that environment. . . .

[Those] who saw that this was going to lead to a series of later disasters and . . . tried to warn about it . . . were either fired like Dr. Myers [the actuary of the Social Security System] . . . or they were dismissed as being animated by partisan interest or by self-serving interest. [This] may have been in some cases, but it turned out they were right in the long run. . . .

Powell's Law says . . . that the demand for free medical care is essentially infinite. We'll exhaust all resources that can possibly be provided for it. And that is really where we are. . . . Washington opened the floodgates and now they are trying to set up . . . dikes to contain [the flood]. . . . The problem was caused in Washington . . . [with] help from the union leaders and the insurance industry, both Blue Cross and commercial insurance people. . . .

We've heard talk about . . . [the] tremendous difference in beds and doctors and nurses without any differences in mortality or morbidity statistics. But that misses the point. . . . People don't go to the doctor usually because they are terribly, dreadfully ill, or because they are about to die. People go to the doctor a very large percent of the time because they are unhappy. The medical care system in this age of widespread disbelief has become the surrogate for the church, and you go to the doctor because you have had a fight with your husband or wife or your boss is about to fire you . . . for all the infinite number of reasons that people get unhappy. . . . You know, most ambulatory medicine is psychiatry. . . . And how do you measure the reassurance, the psychiatric support, which is the product of most medical encounters? . . .

If medical care is going to be free—and that's . . . what it is increasingly coming to be . . . there is no end to the demand. . . . Have you ever noticed how the advocates of cost containment lose all sight of that noble goal when they are sick? . . . I want to report a story about Mr. Califano, and my source is the *Wall Street Journal*. . . . You know that Mr. Califano . . . considers the American medical system obese. . . . But one thing he apparently insists on is that the people who are associates of his in HEW . . . keep a central point informed so that they can be reached at any hour of the day or night. Apparently some high muck-a-muck doctor in HEW finally got permission to go on vacation, and he was barreling along in his automobile . . . [and] had reached the New Jersey/New York border . . . [when] somehow or other word was gotten to him, "The Chief wants you." So, his vacation plans disrupted, . . . he got back to Washington . . . and went to see Mr. Califano. What great policy issue had arisen? . . . According to the *Wall Street Journal,* Mr. Califano said, "Hey, look, Joe, I got this tennis elbow. What can you do for me?" You see, cost containment is for the other guy. . . . The regulations, etc., are in there for the other guy. . . .

I don't think there are any politically feasible solutions. We are stuck with a slogan that health care is a right, nobody wanting to spell out what we mean by health care, so why shouldn't I have that psychoanalysis I'd love to have and some of you think I probably need? But I am just too tight to pay for it. We are ruled by slogans; we're ruled by cynical calculations of political advantage. . . .

Most people, the overwhelming majority of Americans, can pay for the medical care they need during the year—normal medical care. One, two, three, maybe four visits to the doctor. No problem. The real problem comes when you get a catastrophic illness. . . . [We should] set up a system of catastrophic medical insurance . . . defining catastrophic in terms of percentage of income so those who are completely destitute will be taken care of too.

WALTER McNERNY
President, Blue Cross Association
There is no question that the problem of cost is deeply related to the fact that the individual doesn't pay the full cost at the time of the transaction for his illness, nor does the doctor know much about . . . the full cost of the illness or the services. I agree, the cost is very definitely related to the fact that this is not a normal consumption item; that the whole issue of health service is deeply embedded in a community ethic. . . . Regulation reflects a concern with the quality and quantity of service not being justified by the cost. . . . The high costs of health care are not only unevenly distributed across the population . . . but they are unrelated to income. . . . The individual and the family are peculiarly vulnerable. . . . Care is a necessity. . . .

Let's experience-rate individuals; those who smoke and those who debauch and so forth should pay a high premium. Wonderful idea, except when you begin to moralize against a one-person family—father not home . . . four kids, and a level of despondency that translates itself to drugs and other problems. By charging a higher premium, you run smack . . . [against] social justice. How about experience-rating providers—put them in nice little clusters, give them an incentive to compete against one another? When you think of the logistic problems . . . it is sobering. . . . [To] come down hard on regulation and then begin to examine the alternatives, it . . . doesn't take a genius to conclude that you have to work pretty hard on both. . . .

There is something about new directions that deserves a quick point. . . . Keep people well instead of get them well, and put a regular burden on the individual to accept responsibility for his own welfare through moderation in drinking, smoking, exercise, etc. . . . There is widespread agreement about this direction as a way to go. . . . [But] the establishment is geared against [these ideas], and they are going to come very hard. . . . It is nonsense to expect people to do better just because somebody tells them to. . . . There is resistance on the part of industry and others to the cost implications of a better environment. . . . The going is rough indeed. . . .

You are not going to get good regulation . . . unless it's seen as a strengthening from the bottom up rather than the top down. . . . There must be a strengthening of the market, or an excessive burden will be put on regulation which it can't stand. . . . The critical ideas are incentive reimbursement, . . . with some market innovations having to do with freeing up the options—not only HMOs, but other choices . . .[including] an option of going in *and* out of the system or systems on a periodic option basis, so it is the individual employee who animates the system.

6

RICHARD H. HOLTON

Advancing the Backward Art of Spending Money

The consumer and the industrial purchaser: the mutual search for quality and economy. Information acquisition and processing problems: advertising, consumer reports, government publications, product promotion. The rise in consumer activism. Time and experience factors in purchasing patterns. Agency regulation of products, promotion, marketing, manufacture, buyer protection. Federal Trade Commission; Truth-in-Lending legislation; unit pricing and performance levels.

A full discussion of government regulation of markets and marketing would cover not only the marketing of consumer goods and services, but of raw materials, intermediate products, and capital equipment as well. Interesting as these other

125

markets might be from a regulatory point of view, because of space limitations I will concentrate on certain aspects of the marketing of consumer goods and services.

The consumer movement, and with it the public's interest in the performance of the market for consumer goods and services, was revitalized in the mid-1960s. Several developments accounted for this revival, or at least were of major influence. Ralph Nader's book on automobile safety, *Unsafe at Any Speed,* appeared. In response, President Johnson appointed Esther Peterson as Special Assistant for Consumer Affairs, a newly created position in the White House. The administration's "War on Poverty" focused attention on the poor, including the special problems which face the poor as consumers. Congressmen and Senators found it as easy to be for the "consumer" as for motherhood and the flag; and no doubt the anti-establishment sentiments among the young on the campuses in the late 1960s fueled this revival as well.

Now, a decade later, consumer legislation continues to be popular on Capitol Hill. It appears that any moves toward less regulation are not likely to mean more freedom for the marketers of consumer goods. As debates about new or revised consumer legislation and regulation continue, our sense of priorities can be enhanced if we keep in mind the fundamental problem in the markets for consumer goods and services. The problem, in essence, is that the consumer does not have the time and knowledge to become an expert buyer of everything. This basic problem has important implications for public policy.

THE INDUSTRIAL BUYER AND CONSUMER CONTRASTED

Although we will concentrate on the consumer as a buyer, it is illuminating to reflect on the industrial purchasing agent as a buyer, since the contrast with the consumer is great, and for reasons which can help us understand the consumer's problem.

Most obvious, perhaps, is the sheer magnitude of the task of intelligent buying which the consumer faces, compared with that of the industrial purchasing agent. The household, as a buying unit in the United States, faces a huge array of alternative uses for its money. Just within the supermarket today, the alternatives number in the thousands. In the model of the ideal competitive market, the buyers all possess complete and accurate information about all the alternatives in the market. The impossibility of any single consumer having such complete information is immediately apparent, especially when one considers the choices the consumer faces in an economy as rich and varied as ours. Even in 1912, Wesley Claire Mitchell (1912:269) recognized the housewife's problem:

She must buy milk and shoes, furniture and meat, magazines and fuel, hats and underwear, bedding and disinfectants, medical services and toys, rugs and candy. Surely no one can be expected to possess expert knowledge of the qualities and prices of such varied wares. The ease with which defects of materials or workmanship can be concealed in finishing many of these articles forces the purchaser often to judge quality by price, or to depend upon the interested assurances of advertisers and shopkeepers. The small scale on which many purchases are made precludes the opportunity of testing before buying, and many articles must be bought hurriedly wherever they are found at whatever price is asked.

For the consumer or the manufacturing firm (or any other buyer), rational search calls for continuing the search for the best value until the buyer's perceived probable gain from further search is no longer greater than the cost of further search (Stigler 1961). The buyer gains from further search if he finds a "better buy," i.e., an item which offers more quality, defined as the buyer wishes, for the money. The cost of search is measured in terms of the time, effort, and money required in the search process. The buyer extends the "shopping," i.e., the search, until he thinks further search is no longer "worth it."

The sheer scale of the manufacturer's individual purchases warrants the allocation of substantial staff time and money to the search process. The family man doing minor household repairs will not shop widely for a dozen one-inch, number eight, flathead wood screws. But the furniture manufacturer may make a single purchase of several hundred dollars' worth of such screws. Suppose both buyers think they might save 5 percent by careful shopping. Clearly, the furniture manufacturer will engage in the more extensive search.

The scale of the industrial buying process accounts for other significant contrasts with household buying as well. In part because of the size of the manufacturing operation, the company can bring different types of talents to bear on the purchasing decision. The design engineer, for example, or the plant superintendent or the foreman on the factory floor might affect significantly (and indeed, at times dictate) the decision actually implemented by the purchasing agent. Thus, several sets of expert skills and knowledge, generally not readily available to the consumer for his buying decisions, are commonly participating in industrial buying. Furthermore, the size of the purchase often warrants considerable testing before the purchase commitment is made. The testing is part of the search process; the probable gain from careful search, including testing in these cases, is considered greater than the cost of the testing, in part because of the large amount of money involved in the purchase.

The industrial buying decision benefits also from the quantity and quality of information which can economically be brought to bear, quite separately from the number of people and their expertise (or perhaps one should say that the quantity and quality of information reinforces the expertise). The company which owns its own fleet of trucks, for example, is likely to have at hand rather good information on the number of miles it can expect from the particular brand of tires it has been using; the individual buying a replacement tire for his own car has no comparable source of information. Again, the scale of purchasing, and the possible savings from wise purchasing, makes it worthwhile for the manufacturer to develop an information and reporting system to back up the buying process.

The industrial buyer engages in more careful search than does the consumer, in part because of the convention of the supply contract. The industrial buyer can sign a contract with a supplier for some minimum number of units of the item, to be delivered according to a certain schedule extending over several months or even years. The total value of the contract is such that careful search is justified. The consumer also uses the contract approach for some things, e.g., health insurance; but the supply contract is much more common for the industrial buyer than for the consumer, in large part because of the greater predictability of the industrial buyer's supply requirements. Since the supply contract involves a large dollar figure, the search for the best source will be a careful one.

The large size of the individual supply contract in many cases simplifies the search process for the buyer, because he can set the specifications for the item he wants, then ask suppliers to bid for the contract. The number of units involved is great enough to justify a vendor's producing to those specifications for that one customer. Thus in these cases the industrial buyer does not have to compare the features of the product as it is offered by suppliers; the buyer sets those features.

The larger size of the industrial purchase eases the search process in yet another way: the seller typically calls directly on the buyer, bringing the information to him. For most consumer goods and services, the individual purchase is so small that direct contact between the manufacturer and the final consumer is not economically feasible, so a retailer is used and the consumer shops among retailers. (Door-to-door selling and the life insurance industry are two of several exceptions to this.)

Concern for cost reduction and improved efficiency in the search process has led to the development of voluntary industry standards and to agreed definitions of terms. One effect of this is to reduce negotiating time, thus simplifying the search process.

A final difference of major consequence between industrial and consumer markets is that the industrial buyer is typically more interested in objectively observable quality and performance features than is the consumer. The consumer may be persuaded to buy something because it is "in style" or because the manufacturer, through advertising, has built up an aura of prestige around a particular brand. The industrial buyer is usually less susceptible to such considerations, and is more technically qualified than the clerk in the appliance store, which eases the search process for the industrial buyer.

These contrasts between the consumer and the industrial buyer in the search process do not always apply. When management redecorates the headquarters office, for example, style rather than functional performance may be the dominant consideration. And for smaller purchases, the company purchasing agent may engage in very limited search, as does the consumer.

PERCEPTIONS OF THE PROBLEM

To summarize to this point, in most industrial buying the economics of search causes the company to bring considerable professional expertise and information to bear on the purchasing decision. The family as a buying unit, by contrast, makes a host of relatively small buying decisions over the course of a year, and the economics of search dictates that its members cannot become professional, expert buyers of everything. Family members are not full-time buyers; they have other ways they want to (or must) spend their time. At the risk of oversimplification, we can say that in consumer markets the full-time professional seller faces the part-time amateur buyer. Industrial markets, on the other hand, are characterized usually by professionalism on both sides.

The fundamental difficulty in consumer markets is that the consumer faces a monumental information acquisition and processing problem. For larger purchases, the consumer may perceive that the probable gain from further search is worthwhile, i.e., he or she will consider doing additional homework or shopping because it might be worth the additional cost in terms of time and money and effort. But for the smaller purchases, becoming an expert buyer is viewed as not worth the candle. So the buying will be quite casual.

This general view is confirmed by public surveys, which reveal the extent of contrasts and similarities between the views of the total public, business executives, and consumer activists about certain key aspects of consumer markets.[1] As one would expect, 95 percent of the businessmen agreed with the statement that "Most companies do a good job of providing reasonable products at fair prices," but only 52 percent of the total public agreed with the statement. When presented with the statement, "Most companies are so concerned about making a profit, they don't care about quality," only 7 percent of the businessmen agreed, but 59 percent of the total public agreed. At the same time, the great majority of the total public—72 percent—agreed with the statement that "Competition among companies is the best way to ensure better quality products and services." Yet a little more than half of the total public agreed with the statement that "Most people's problems as consumers are among the most nagging and annoying of everyday life." It is interesting that almost one-third of the businessmen also agreed with that statement.

Thus it appears that although the public continues to hold a reassuring belief in competition, presumably rather than public regulation, as the "best way" to ensure quality products and services, there is still considerable unhappiness about how well the process is working. As one might expect, consumer activists are not so confident about the effectiveness of competition; only 53 percent, compared with 72 percent of the general public, agreed that competition is the best way to ensure quality products and services. The obverse of this is suggested in the response to the statement, "Consumers don't need any help in looking after their own interest; they are quite able to do it themselves." Only 24 percent of the total public agreed with that statement, and 8 percent of the consumer activists; but interestingly enough, among the businessmen only 28 percent agreed.

One can conclude from this that, although the American public still is prepared to rely primarily on competition to assure that consumer markets operate as we would like, they also recognize the need for some help in looking after their own interests. Presumably this means that they expect continuing help from government regulation. And even a majority of businessmen agree that consumers can't look after their own interests by themselves. This appears to be consistent with the argument here that the consumer cannot be expected to be a professional buyer of everything, even though nearly three-fourths of the public is content with the way competition works to ensure quality goods and services.

Given the consumer information processing problem, the professional consumer advocate misses the point when he argues that the consumer doesn't have enough information; and the businessman misses the point when he says the consumer doesn't use all the information he has. Both are right, but only in part. The consumer does not have enough time or expertise to gather and absorb the information which exists.

The consumer's problem of allocating time to buying goods and using them properly comes through in some of the responses to questions in the Harris-Marketing Science Institute poll referred to earlier. For example, 75 percent of the public agree with the statement, "If people are careful and use good judgment, they can still get good value for their money today." Sixty-nine percent agree that "Many of the mistakes consumers make are the result of their own carelessness." And 65 percent agree that "Most consumers do not use the information available about different products in order to decide to buy one of them." Fifty-eight percent agree that "There is generally enough information available for consumers to make sensible buying decisions." One interpretation one can give to all of this is that consumers can be wise buyers if they choose to devote enough time to the shopping process.

But the problem goes beyond that of the consumer not having enough *time* to become an expert buyer of everything. In some cases, he or she simply cannot be expected to have the technical expertise needed to judge a product, and technical experts to whom he might turn may disagree on certain points. And even if this problem does not exist, the consumer may find that the weights he gives to the different attributes of a product change after the product is purchased; for example, when buying an automobile, he may think certain features are very important to him, but two years later he may wish that he had given more attention to the probability that a particular feature might mean higher repair bills.

IS THE CONSUMER INFORMATION PROBLEM GROWING?

Over time, the consumer information problem may well be getting worse rather than better, largely because of the great success our economy has witnessed as incomes have increased and as the choice of goods and services has expanded. First, if one compares the economy at present with the situation in, say 1900 or 1920, it is apparent that the consumer has a much wider selection to consider in the marketplace. Second, the consumer has more income, and consequently can exercise more purchasing decisions in the course of a year than was possible a generation or two ago. Third, our advancing technology has developed more product features which are below the threshold of perception for the typical consumer, so he must turn to sources of information other than his own experience (or the experiences of his friends) to learn about those features. Vitamins and other food additives are a case in point, and some of the safety features of automobiles. Fourth, it has been argued that the rate of technological change is increasing, and the commercial life of new products is growing shorter. Consequently, the consumer's information about a product, once acquired, becomes obsolete sooner than was formerly the case. A possible fifth problem is that, at least for consumer durables, the cost of servicing the product relative to the original purchase price has risen, which gives rise to two difficulties. One cannot determine at the time of purchase just how much servicing the product is likely to require over its useful life, and the shopping for servicing itself is complex; the consumer can only hope that unnecessary repairs are not done, and that the price charged is reasonable.

Our great success in developing an economy in which well-to-do consumers face a large selection of goods and services has permitted us to enjoy a great many luxuries. One of these is the luxury of not bothering to shop carefully. We can afford to be careless. If this is true, then the consumer does not exert the competitive discipline on the marketplace to the extent that was characteristic of simpler times, when people were poorer.

Unfortunately for the business community, in the face of what I consider to be these growing difficulties the consumer faces in trying to buy wisely, our expectations about the performance of the system are probably rising. For example, the public's expectations about automobile safety were elevated, no doubt, after the publication of Nader's *Unsafe at Any Speed*. And a friend who heads a major consumer goods manufacturing company argues that advertising itself raises consumers' expectations about the performance of the system.[2] All this may be good, but it does mean that the performance of the business community must constantly improve if consumer confidence in the system is not to erode further.

ALTERNATIVE SOURCES OF INFORMATION

Our argument thus far is that markets for consumer goods do not function as well as we would like, in large part because the consumer cannot allocate enough time to the search process to become an expert buyer of everything; and for countless products and services, the consumer would not have the technical knowledge to assess some of the information, even if he had time to gather the information in the first place. This suggests that we should seek ways to make the search process more efficient, i.e., to permit the consumer to gain more information more easily. Before considering means by which this might be done, we can note the principal sources of information the consumer uses for the purchasing decision, and the nature of the inadequacies of those sources.

For a great many goods and services, one's own experience is a primary source of information. But the quality of this source varies considerably across the goods and services in the marketplace. It is a good source if (1) the item is one which the individual buys frequently; (2) its performance and quality characteristics are either apparent before one buys the item or quickly thereafter; (3) the rate of technological change is slow relative to the frequency of purchase; and (4) the terms of sale are relatively stable from one purchase to the next.

If the first condition is not met, i.e., if the item is infrequently purchased, then one simply does not gain much experience with alternative brands very quickly. Most household appliances prove a case in point. If the second condition is not met, then one's experience is not relevant; if I am not aware that the air conditioner I bought consumes twice as much electricity per unit of output as a competing brand, that difference is really not a part of my experience. Someone else, say, *Consumer Reports* or a competing manufacturer, might bring it to my attention, true, but that knowledge would not come to me through my own experimentation with competing brands. With rapid technological change relative to the frequency of purchase, the information generated from experience becomes obsolete faster than if the rate of technological change is slow. Similarly, the buyer's experience is made obsolete by changes in the terms of sale; the careful price comparisons of six months ago will not do today, if the relative prices of the brands have changed.

Razor blades and scouring powder might be illustrations of products for which one's own experience can provide reasonably complete and accurate information. The individual buys them frequently enough so that experimentation with different brands is feasible; the performance characteristics are fairly obvious; the rate of technological change relative to the frequency of purchase is low, so the information gained from one purchase is still relevant when the next is made. The terms of sale change, it is true, so even with these simple goods, one's experience can become obsolete with respect to relative prices.

At the other end of the spectrum are a variety of goods and services. Automobile tires are a good illustration: the individual who tries very hard to be a wise consumer is not likely to accumulate experience with competing brands of tires very quickly, simply because he doesn't buy them frequently. For most drivers, many of the quality and performance characteristics are not clear; did that replacement tire wear out quickly because it was subjected to some unusually bad road conditions at some time? And the rate of technological change and the terms of sale are such that little that one learns from one purchase is applicable to the next; one must begin the search process afresh.

Unfortunately, a large number of goods and services are bought under circumstances where the four conditions I have suggested are not met. In addition to tires, illustrations include automobiles themselves, appliances, pharmaceuticals, at least some clothing items, and many of the services — medical services, automobile repair, appliance repair, and casualty and life insurance.

Other sources of information, of course, are available to and used by the consumer. Friends and acquaintances are no doubt a primary source. But if your friend recommends Brand X tires because he has always used them and had good experience with them, one can ask, "good experience" relative to what? He is simply saying that in some generalized way he has not been unhappy with Brand X tires, but he really does not know *from his own experience* how other brands would have performed. He may have had "good experience" with his tires because his expectations were low, and so he was never motivated to try other brands. In such consumer markets, relying on the recommendations of friends and acquaintances is to rely on pooled ignorance. If the item is one with which friends have individually gained experience with competing brands, then the consumer's knowledge can be advanced by information from this source.

Advertising can be a source of information, of course, and if, for the sake of convenience, we include with advertising the information on the label or elsewhere at the point of sale, then this can be very helpful. But it is also self-serving, and even advertising which is legally not false or misleading can at the very least be incomplete. The recent move toward comparative advertising, in which an advertisement mentions competing brands by name, is helpful in this respect. But even the most complete information in advertising for some goods and services encounters the problem of relevant technical information which cannot be understood or properly assessed by many consumers.

Technically qualified third parties can provide useful information. *Consumer Reports* and government publications are perhaps the most obvious illustrations. But even here, one finds at least three sets of difficulties. First, weaknesses which appear only with time or extensive use might not be discerned when the product is rated. Thus, testing an automobile or an appliance might not provide any reliable indication about the repair bills the buyer can expect three and five years later. Second, a product might contain an ingredient or component which is dangerous, but the danger is simply not known when the product is produced and marketed. The errors that lead to automobile recalls and the cyclamate furor are illustrations. Finally, the two consumer rating services face the problem of assigning weights to the different attributes of the product. What may be a major design disadvantage for one consumer might not be for another; different segments of consumer markets apply different weights to the various attributes of products.

The retailer can be a major source of information for the consumer. Ideally, he serves as something of a purchasing agent for consumers, in selecting those few brands which he thinks are the best values for the customers he is trying to reach. The large retail chain carries this purchasing agent function one step further and arranges, directly with the manufacturers, to have items produced to the retailer's specifications and under the retailer's label. The retailer takes over the information problem, in a sense, and makes a selection which he thinks will appeal to the consumer.

How well the retailer plays the information-screening function varies widely from case to case. The retailer who advertises a great breadth of stock—i.e., many brands of each item—may have eliminated only a few items from the spectrum of the choice the consumer faces. At the other extreme is the retailer who handles one or more products on an exclusive basis; i.e., he has agreed with the manufacturer that he will sell only that one brand of the product. In this case, the retailer is probably viewed by the consumer as the local representative of the manufacturer; here the retailer, in his role as purchasing agent for the consumer, has narrowed the selection to the ultimate, and therefore throws the selection among brands back onto the consumer.

In perhaps the most common case, the retailer decides on a segment of the buying public to which he wishes to appeal, and then selects brands which he thinks this market segment would select if it were doing the screening process.[3] Clearly this can simplify the information processing problem the consumer faces. At the same time, this process can be distorted. The manufacturer with a second-rate product may have a set of policies, including pricing policies, which is very attractive to the retailer; so the retailer stocks the item and promotes it, not because he thinks it is the best for the customer, but because, for example, it carries a higher markup than other brands.

The well-trained retail clerk can be an excellent source of information for the consumer. An able clerk selling major appliances can advise the consumer about the alternative features to look for and how to evaluate them, thus helping the consumer to become a more "professional" buyer. However, one can expect the clerk to be biased toward the brands which he carries.

From this review, one can see that each of the major sources of consumer information—namely, one's own experience, one's friends and acquaintances, advertising, technically qualified third parties, and the retailer—is subject to inadequacies and bias.[4]

IMPLICATIONS FOR MARKETING PRACTICES AND REGULATORY PRIORITIES

Restating the argument, the fundamental problem in consumer markets is that the consumer does not have enough time or expertise to become a thoroughly knowledgeable buyer of everything. In deciding what goods and what brands to buy, he or she will push the search process out to the point where the probable gain from additional search is not worth the additional shopping effort. For major purchases, this calls for extensive shopping; but for a large number of items, namely, what marketing people know as convenience goods, the price is low enough, or the brands are considered sufficiently similar, that the probable gain from doing more homework is not considered worth the effort. The same rationale for the search process applies to industrial buying. But there the scale of purchasing and the company's ability to bring more talent to bear on the problem, combined with other features of industrial markets, lead to very knowledgeable buying of most of the company's requirements.

Although consumers are generally content with the way competition works to provide quality goods and services, a majority also consider many of the mistakes consumers make to be a result of their own carelessness, and that they do not use the information already available before they buy. Meanwhile, the problems of making consumer markets work well may be worsening, primarily because we have been so successful in developing a wide choice of goods and services, many with technically advanced features. The various sources of information on which the consumer can draw are all unsatisfactory in at least some respects. But even if they were not, the consumer would not have enough time to make use of the information available.

An ironic footnote here is that at least some of the erosion of the public's confidence in business may be attributed to our affluence, which permits us the luxury of not bothering to shop carefully. So we complain that business does not make our shopping easier.

How might this view of the problem apply to the question of regulatory priorities and marketing practices?

Much, but by no means all, of the existing regulation of marketing practices is designed to help the consumer make a more informed choice. My argument here is that, given the consumer's problem of coping with all the information which is or might conceivably be made available, we can judge much of the regulatory effort (existing as well as proposed) in terms of its impact on the *efficiency* of the consumer's information processing. Does the regulation permit the consumer to absorb more information (relevant information, we hope) in less time and in more readily usable form? Does it do this in a least-cost way? And finally, does the least-cost version yield social benefits which are greater than the costs?

Here we can at least begin to explore the application of this approach to the regulation of consumer goods markets. Most of the discussion concerns either the regulation of the product itself or what is said about the product in advertising, on labels and so forth.

The regulation of the physical product is usually motivated by concern for the public's health and safety. Public policy regarding unhealthful or unsafe products is that without regulation, the market would not function as we wish; either the buyers would not be sufficiently well informed to avoid the product, or they would not weight adequately the cost to society associated with the use of the product.

How should we regulate the unhealthful or unsafe product? One is tempted to let the experts decide if a product is unsafe, and if so, keep it off the market. But there are problems. Experts can disagree about whether a product is unsafe, and under what circumstances. The Food and Drug Administration, for example, faces the problem of assessing tests of pharmaceuticals. And the Consumer Products Safety Commission faces similar problems in evaluating design features and instructions for use.

The safety problem is enormously complex when we consider priorities of safety. Even a relatively simple and common product such as the kitchen range is unsafe if not used properly. At one end of the spectrum is the over-the-counter pharmaceutical product, for example, where the consumer can scarcely assess for himself whether the item is safe to use or not; at the other end is something like the skateboard, where little is demanded of one's intelligence to perceive that the product is inherently unsafe unless properly used. Reading and following instructions is part of the consumer's information processing problem if a product is to be purchased and used satisfactorily. It is widely recognized that many safety problems arise because people do not read instructions properly (80 percent of the "total public" agreed with this point in the Harris-MSI poll cited earlier).

A rational approach to the safety problem in consumer goods would be first to identify those products which show the highest accident cost, i.e., pain and suffering, lost income, medical expenses, and so on. *If* this could be satisfactorily accomplished, it would provide an array of problems to be attacked. The next step would be to find ways of reducing the accident cost; in an ideal world of perfect information, one could judge the gross social benefit from a proposed safety measure by multiplying the reduced probability of an accident by the cost of the average accident. If the social benefit exceeds the cost of instituting the safety measure, then it should be instituted.

Since consumers are not likely to inform themselves sufficiently to allow market forces alone to solve the health and safety problem, public regulation can, for example, (1) prohibit the manufacture, sale, or use of the product; (2) permit the sale, but mandate design specifications to reduce the danger, as with flammable fabrics; (3) require that sales be made only under certain conditions, as with prescription drugs; or (4) require published instructions and/or warnings. Although data on total accident cost for any given product are readily available, we do not have good data on the effect of any of these alternative proposals on the probability of accident or injury, and the social cost of instituting a particular measure is fuzzy at best.[5] So even though the rationale for handling the problem may be fairly clear, we cannot hope to have complete and unambiguous data to guide us to solutions.

Regardless of whether regulation concerns product design, instructions, terms of sale, or advertising, the regulators are likely to argue that those being regulated exaggerate the cost of compliance (and other costs) associated with the proposed regulations; and industry representatives often see the regulators as exaggerating the probable social benefits of the proposed regulations. Clearly such disagreements underlie much business criticism of the Consumer Products Safety Commission.

If we go beyond regulation of the physical product to regulation of information about the product, we face the array of problems in the regulation of advertising. One obvious way to maximize the efficiency of the consumer's information processing is to be sure the information received through advertising is reasonably accurate. Unfortunately, we cannot expect advertising to provide complete information as well; that simply is not feasible.

The Federal Trade Commission serves as our principal watchdog regarding false and misleading advertising. But its powers have been limited in many respects. For example, an objectionable advertising campaign might conclude before the legal process at the FTC could be adjudicated, and penalties for false and misleading advertising have been minimal.

The FTC's ability to stop false and misleading advertising has been substantially enhanced by the FTC Improvement Act of 1975. The commission can now move against practices "in or affecting commerce," not just those "in commerce" — which brings within the commission's reach cases which would earlier have been considered intrastate commerce. The commission's rulemaking authority, covering whole sets of industry practices, has been clarified. The commission can now fund the participation of consumer groups in FTC proceedings, and can levy fines for knowing violations of FTC rules or of a cease and desist order (formerly, only the latter was covered). In what may be one of the most important changes, the act provides that a cease and desist order, once obtained against a particular company for a particular act or practice, applies to anyone engaging in such acts or practices. Thus, a company which was not subject to the cease and desist order can now be fined for violating the order. This power can obviously have a substantial multiplier effect on the commission's cease and desist orders.

Of even greater consequence may be the FTC's new power to obtain equitable relief for consumers. Formerly a company could be subject to a cease and desist order without having to pay for its past sins, so to speak. Now the FTC can seek relief through recision or reformation of contracts, refund of money or return of property, payment of compensatory damages and public notification. Thus, the possible penalties for false and misleading advertising have been increased substantially.

The FTC's ability to require firms to engage in corrective advertising at this writing is still being subject to court test. The FTC determined in 1975 that the Warner-Lambert product, Listerine, does not prevent or cure colds, as had been advertised. The FTC ordered that Listerine advertisements in the future include the statement, "Contrary to prior advertising, Listerine will not prevent colds or sore throats or lessen their severity." A federal appeals court has upheld the FTC, but said that the statement, "Contrary to prior advertising," need not be included. Warner-Lambert says it will take the case to the Supreme Court. If the FTC is eventually upheld in this case, no doubt most advertisers will consider the corrective statements to be a rather severe penalty for false and misleading advertising.

A major but little-known private effort to minimize false and misleading advertising is that of the National Advertising Division of the Council of Better Business Bureaus. The NAD monitors advertising, investigates alleged abuses, and works with advertisers to gain voluntary corrections of claims. Over 1,100 cases have been brought before NAD since its inception in 1971, with 175 cases being presented in 1976 alone.[6] Of these, only 49 were still pending at the end of 1976. Since, in comparison with FTC procedures, the NAD operates in a very informal way, cases can be handled much more expeditiously by NAD. Indeed, advertising campaigns have been cancelled before completion because of NAD action.

Given the importance of advertising as a means by which the public gains information and impressions about products and services, it would seem that we should make every effort to hold false and misleading advertising to a minimum. The business community suffers from the lack of credibility many people find in advertising, and businessmen commonly agree that it is in the best interest of the business community to keep advertising honest.

The conflicts between the FTC and advertisers appear to turn largely on differences in estimates of the costs and benefits of certain FTC actions. The cost of substantiating an advertising claim, for example, can vary enormously, depending on the degree of certainty the FTC demands; but once that cost is identified, how can we estimate the benefits the public derives because the advertising claim is justified with more certainty than when less substantiation was required? A review of FTC activity regarding false and misleading advertising using a cost-benefit frame of reference might be quite revealing. However, the commission's staff presumably already thinks in terms of whether a particular policing effort is "worth it," a term which implies at least a crude cost-benefit approach.

The question of television advertising during children's viewing hours is a particularly troublesome aspect of any attempts to make the consumer's processing of information more efficient. The concern, of course, is that children are especially ill equipped to assess properly the information they receive through television commercials. So little seems to be known about the impact of advertising on children, that we must continue to give high priority to support for research on this topic. Meanwhile, certain obvious things might be done, whether by the networks or the individual stations or by the federal government, such as limiting, if not prohibiting, the advertising of over-the-counter drugs during children's viewing hours.

A major topic in discussions of public regulation of marketing practices in recent years has been the minimum disclosures that should be made in advertising, on labels and in other vehicles, such as point-of-sale material. An overwhelming majority, nearly 90 percent, of the executives covered in one large survey agree that "advertising should include adequate information for 'logical' buying decisions, whether or not consumers choose to use it" (Greyser and Diamond 1976:7). This would appear to be a reasonable standard, although the debate about how much information is required for a "logical" buying decision might well rival that surrounding the concept of the "prudent man" in the law. And one can scarcely expect the sixty-second television commercial for vegetable soup to list the ingredients in the detail provided on the label. Perhaps we should only ask that the information required for logical buying decisions be readily accessible, at least on the label if not in the advertising itself. The Truth-in-Lending legislation calls for disclosure of credit terms in considerable detail, and actually prohibits the advertising of credit terms unless all details are provided. One can well ask whether the net effect of that part of the legislation was in the community interest. The assumption was that the consumer would read and comprehend the full disclosure statement when it was encountered elsewhere than in the advertising. It is apparent that minimum disclosure is indeed a conceptual thicket.

Regardless of how much information is disclosed and by what means, the efficiency of the consumer's information processing can be improved by the use of standardized terminology.[7] In the case of automobile tires, for example, "first line" was used to suggest top quality, but just what this meant was by no means clear in terms of performance characteristics. The FTC's tire advertising and labeling guides have at least cleared the air to some extent. Recent efforts to standardize the terms used to describe the quality of fresh fruits and vegetables offer another illustration. The top grades applied through voluntary grade labeling have carried at least four different designations (U.S. Extra No. 1 for potatoes, U.S. Extra Fancy for apples, U.S. Fancy for oranges, and U.S. No. 1 for onions). Such variations in terminology complicate the consumer information process.

The move toward unit pricing is clearly one means of improving the efficiency with which the consumer can process the information available. At least some consumers are interested in the price per ounce or per pound. Given odd package sizes and weights, the consumer's ability to make price comparisons quickly is obviously enhanced by unit pricing.

Finally, the current Department of Commerce effort to encourage the use of performance labels on consumer goods is a step in the right direction. The efficiency of consumer information processing is improved if the relevant information needed for a logical buying decision is easily available. The consumer may not be sufficiently motivated to do detailed research on the objective performance of competing brands of automatic dishwashers, for example, but if that information is available at the point of sale, the shopper is more likely to see it and take it into account. Some companies are apparently resisting this, since the attributes of an appliance which can be objectively measured might not be the most important ones which an expert would consider in making the purchasing decision. Publicity about only the objective attributes might cause manufacturers to emphasize these, regardless of their importance. Despite this objection, point-of-sale performance information would appear to be a desirable means of improving the efficiency of the search process for the consumer.[8] And the cost to society would be minimal.

I recognize that my suggesting a way to think about at least one group of problems in the regulation of marketing practices does not lead to easy solutions. Our frustrations will no doubt persist as long as we lack unambiguous estimates of the social costs and benefits of particular regulatory programs. But at least our discussions of these problems might benefit if we know what questions to ask. If we do ask the right questions, we might provide the arguments for deregulation in some areas and for additional regulation in others.

I fear I must close with a rather pessimistic point. It is that since so many of the problems in consumer markets are there because of affluence and/or advanced technology, I doubt that, through public regulation, we can significantly advance the backward art of spending money. People simply do not have the time and technical background to buy everything expertly. So some purchases will continue to be made too hastily and without adequate information, and consumers too frequently will blame the business community for this, rather than themselves. I suggest that we keep in mind a thought well articulated by Charles J. Hitch (1977:7), president of Resources for the Future and former president of the University of California:

There is, I think, an American urge for answers to all our questions, for solutions to every problem that bedevils us. We tend to believe that given enough time and education and technology—and if we toss in enough money—somehow we will send voyagers to the planets or cure cancer or banish hunger. To the extent there are answers, this blend of optimism, skill and determination will find them. Unlike many of our predecessors, however, we are coming to recognize that perhaps every question does not have an answer, no matter how hard we try; we may even come to accept the fact that people have only limited dominion. To at least some extent, our task for the future will not be to realize paradise, but to make what we have better, more realistic, and more harmonious . . . to manage, not solve; to cope, not answer; to understand, not conquer.

COMMENT

JAMES W. BUTTON
Senior Executive Vice President-Marketing,
Sears Roebuck & Company
Regulations . . . have reached the point where they are an important factor in inflationary costs to the consumer, impacting on investments and stifling, in some instances, the very rights and free-

doms they purport to protect. The code of federal regulations alone contains over 72,000 pages. My company's five territorial offices now have forty-five attorneys on their staff to keep in touch with legislation and regulation that applies to our business, but only twenty-three merchants. Many of the bills and regulations are worthwhile—and . . . the public is supportive of some government regulation. However, the mass of the regulations poses a critical problem, since the regulations are economically out of context, compounding the cost of doing business.

In addition, . . . a direct cost imposed on business firms results . . . [from] governmental inspections and controls, including the expensive and time-consuming process of submitting reports, making applications, filling out questionnaires, replying to orders and directives, and appealing in the courts from other rulings and regulatory opinions. . . . As of 30 June 1974, according to the Office of Management and Budget, there were 5,146 different types of approved public-use forms, excluding all tax and banking forms. Individuals and business firms spend over 130 million man-hours a year filling out federal forms. . . .

Professor Holton is very aware that merchants and manufacturers survive by supplying the consuming public with their wants and needs. The sophistication of modern market research has brought the old art of the "intuitive" merchant to almost a science, enabling any supplier of goods to be responsive to consumer desires. . . . This statement as to the effectiveness of the market is supported by a 1976 Sears study of fifty-six durable, mechanical-type products offered by our competition. The study measured both consumer satisfaction and dissatisfaction on two levels of intensity. It found that:

—81 percent of the products had less than 5 percent dissatisfaction of any kind, or 95 percent satisfied users;
—55 percent had less than 3 percent dissatisfaction of any kind, or 97 percent satisfied users;
—-the worst item, with 6.1 percent "very dissatisfied," or a total 9.3 percent dissatisfaction, was a corn popper—still better than 90 percent satisfied users.

I cannot see that this record warrants new rules and regulations for information, performance, quality, design, and service for consumer goods imposing requirements other than those dictated by good marketing in the competitive marketplace. The cost-to-benefit of perfect consumer goods, or zero dissatisfaction, would be prohibitive and counterproductive.

The use of reliable market segmentation studies, and the development of merchandise to meet these segmented needs, is rapidly expanding in most industries. The manufacturer or merchant communicates new developments to the specific consumer segments in the market, using a variety of informational techniques. It is too costly and inefficient to market to an "average consumer" under these circumstances. The information in each instance is specific and recognizable by those interested. . . . Manufacturers and merchants have provided vast quantities of consumer literature over the years, only to experience a gross indifference on the part of the consumer.

Professor Greyser, who designed the Sentry (1977) study, said, upon the release of the results:

Even if the information environment were to be improved, the Sentry study data raise doubts in my own mind that people will want significant additional amounts of information, will use additional information if available, and (after the fact) will consider the costs of providing that additional information to have been worth it. . . .

Professor Holton . . . is persuasive, and has identified two regulatory priorities in some detail—namely, product safety, and the avoidance of false and misleading advertising. . . . There is a role for the regulatory process in these areas, particularly the involuntary risk to the young and [the] aged. In general, products should be safe for the purpose intended, without basically interfering with the quality of performance. However, in the light of the undesirable consequences emanating from an excessive resort to regulation, the real issues are what ought to be the scope of such regulations, who should determine the scope, and when should they be promulgated. . . . We need to identify the criteria that should be relied on to determine *when* regulation ought to be adopted, and *what* ought to be the sweep or coverage of the regulatory activity. . . .

A second criterion to be applied in determining whether to initiate regulatory action under an existing program, or whether to create a new program, is to consider whether the marketplace will self-correct and eliminate the perceived need for regulation. It's good business to satisfy customers. Regulation should be considered only as a last resort. If, in the relatively near term, the interplay of market forces will discipline marketers engaging in questionable practices, we should refrain from invoking any regulatory activity. A similar view was expressed by Charles Schultze, Chairman of the Council of Economic Advisers, . . . [who] advocated reliance upon financial incentives, rather than regulation, to produce desired social change.

He stated that the market mechanism often can achieve better results than the government, with less cost to society. . . .

Regulatory agencies should recognize their inability to ''fine tune'' the marketplace. Where advertisers in consumer markets are subjected to fine tuning, it appears that such programs are counterproductive. . . . In commenting on the consequences of the vigorous enforcement by the FTC of the ad-substantiation program, Robert Pitofsky (1977), former director of the FTC's Bureau of Consumer Protection, said that the program

might have less of a preclusive effect on false and deceptive advertising, which is already prohibited, *than on truthful claims that are too expensive to substantiate.* The greater the suppression of such claims, or suppression of informational advertising in favor of ''puffs'' not subject to the substantiation requirement, the more likely it is that the net effect of the requirement will be injurious to consumers.

It's amazing how understanding these people become when they are out of office. . . .

A fourth criterion to be considered . . . is an analysis which shows that the social benefits of the regulatory program outweigh the costs of the program. . . . The current attempt by Consumer Union for safety standards on lawn mowers, for example, is a disaster. This standard would have increased the cost of mowers 50 to 100 percent, while seriously impairing the mowers' performance in cutting grass. Fortunately, this proposed standard was adversely commented upon by the Council on Wage and Price Stability. . . .

In the light of the vast regulatory process that already enmeshes the marketplace, the regulatory activity ought not to be expanded, either through existing programs or new programs, unless the application of the foregoing criteria to the market situation under consideration demonstrates a clear and convincing need for a governmental presence. Avoid reaction to short-run phenomenon. Be sure there is a proper cost-benefit relationship, and a subsequent audit for effectiveness. If such a need is determined, the regulatory activity to be employed should be framed in a manner that interferes least with the free play of market forces.

MARY GARDINER JONES
Vice President-Consumer Affairs, Western Union Telegraph Corporation
Former Commissioner, Federal Trade Commission
Today's consumer concerns about health and safety issues in the marketplace places . . . in central focus the importance of informa-

tion if [consumers] are to deal in any respect with the proliferation of conflicting and controversial claims about the potential dangers to themselves or to the environment of an increasing number of products. . . . The issue . . . is essentially one of ensuring to individual citizens the freedom to choose and to live a lifestyle of his/her choice while not imposing counterproductive constraints on the business community or conferring unnecessary power on government. . . .

In many cases, the available product and service information provides either too little or too much detail to the consumer. . . . Consumers will typically not use unit pricing until they understand how it will help them. Nutritional information, unrelated to consumer health, can be noninformation to many consumers. A mere listing of chemical or other ingredients conveys little useful information to most consumers. . . . If information is to be of real value, . . . consumers must be able to locate it . . . when it is needed. Point of sale information . . . is seldom of the quality which enables most customers to perform the type of thoughtful, comparative evaluations which they need. . . . More objective and detailed information prepared by manufacturers or retailers . . . reflects the publisher's priorities, interests, or perceptions of important product categories or product features of interest to consumers. . . . Unless consumers know about these sources of information *and* have both a good memory and reliable filing system, putting their hands on the report or the data at the moment of decision is perhaps their most serious obstacle . . . at the moment of purchase. . . .

Information is a natural resource, comparable in importance and need to the vast outpouring of goods which has characterized our economy for the past hundred years. [If] access to information determines where the power in our society will reside, consumers have traditionally been at the lowest end of the power spectrum. . . . Today the technology exists to eliminate this disparity in power in the area of marketplace information. Yet . . . society must take affirmative steps to see . . . that consumer information data bases develop and . . . that the hardware is in place to enable consumers to have access to the telecommunications technology which is so rapidly emerging in the commercial world. . . .

I would like to offer up a few suggestions for approaching today's information problems as I see them, which go beyond Dr. Holton's proposals and which envisage a major governmental role in their design and implementation.

Americans today are living in an electronically based information society. Information, like any other product, is no better than its delivery systems and availability. . . . Unless we can develop national storage, retrieval, and delivery systems for the information and knowledge required by consumers and citizens to function in our society, we will perpetuate . . . the already serious power imbalances and injustices which exist throughout our society today between individuals and institutions as well as between rich and poor. . . . It is time we turned our attention to putting these technological advances to work for consumers. . . .

The interrelationship of computer, home terminal, and telecommunications network technologies opens up a vast area of memory storage and relay services for individuals.

III

General Issues

7

Regulation and Its Alternatives

The "public utility concept" of regulation. Economies of scale; cost/revenue issues; positive and negative externalities; public health and safety. The balance between social benefits and costs of regulation. Economic and social pricing system.

OLD SANFORD AND THE "PASSING OF THE PUBLIC UTILITY CONCEPT"

In 1940, Horace M. Gray analyzed the state of government regulation of business. He wrote optimistically of "the passing of the public utility concept" (Hoover and Dean

1949:280-303). The concept, Gray held, was rooted in the notion "that private privilege can be reconciled with public interest by the alchemy of public regulation" (Hoover and Dean 1949:281). Noting the spread of regulation to communications, electric power, motor transport, air transport, and natural gas, Gray condemned "the policy of state-created, state-protected monopoly [which has become] firmly established over a significant portion of the economy and . . . the keystone of modern public utility regulation" (Hoover and Dean 1949:283).

Regulation, Gray saw, was rationalized by some advocates because of alleged "natural monopoly" structural characteristics in many markets. Regulated firms were seen by their protagonists as "good" monopolies, entitled to a "fair return on a fair value." They were organized to produce efficiently, to utilize resources to the best advantage, to maintain high standards of service, to secure capital at least cost, to manage their affairs to the best interest of the public, and to prevent excessive charges and discriminations (Hoover and Dean 1949:284-85). But whatever the ostensibly beneficial reasons for their creation, it was observed by Gray that "protection of consumers" was subsequently superceded by "protection of property." Obsolete economic organizations were preserved by regulation, new types of businesses which offered competition to older, regulated firms were brought under the umbrella of regulation, and antisocial pricing practices prevailed. The public utility concept, as seen in practice, was a prime example of "institutional decadence" (Hoover and Dean 1949:286-95).[1]

Gray believed that "institutional inventiveness' would, of necessity, cause not just the end to the expansion of the application of the public utility concept to new industries and markets. "Like other outmoded institutions, [the concept] seems destined to decline in relative significance and ultimately be superceded by new and socially superior institutions" (Hoover and Dean 1949:302).[2]

The world has hardly moved in the directions that Gray predicted and desired. Indeed, while there has been continued discussion of deregulation,[3] and a few areas in which at least re-regulation is being attempted,[4] the nature and scope of regulation generally display remarkable resistance to change. A short story may make the point.

Not long ago, my wife and I had occasion to wander through New Market, a restored section of Philadelphia. There, harnessed to a renovated, four-wheeled Studebaker carriage, was a well-aged bay horse. Neatly lettered on the side of the carriage was "P.U.C. 3714." For a regulated price of $10, old Sanford, as the horse was called, takes passengers for a regulated ride of one-half hour.

Shortly after our ride with old Sanford, I had occasion to talk with Commissioner Helen O'Bannon of the Pennsylvania Public Utility Commission. "Why," I asked, after explaining the delights of travel with old Sanford, "is that business regulated?" Commissioner O'Bannon, a reform-oriented member of the commission, replied, "You know as well as I do. It started before there were automobiles in the taxi service, and no one has seriously pressed for deregulation. As a matter of fact, there is a filing now for a rate increase!"

The story of old Sanford has much to do with the topics covered in this volume on regulation. Whatever is the validity of arguments for deregulation, old Sanford is still there—and still regulated.

THE SCOPE OF REGULATORY CONCERN

It is possible that "entrenched property interests" are the sole reason for the retention of government regulation of business. These interests may, to this point in time, have been so pervasive and persuasive that "social inventiveness" has been unable to provide the supercession of regulatory regimes. Al-

ternatively, it is possible that, in spite of its critics, regulation
has some redeeming social value. In some market circumstances, with some social objectives, some types of regulation may be warranted.

Scale and Operating Economies

In economics, if not in law, the classic reason for regulation
is the existence of economies of scale.[5] Decreasing long-run
average costs for individual firms make competition impossible when they extend over the entire market.

A cursory examination of Sanford's operation would lead
one to suppose that economies of scale are insignificant now,
and were at the time regulation was inaugurated. The
facilities required for production come in small, indivisible,
and duplicable units, suggesting that *industry* long-run average costs would be constant, even though each production
unit might experience first decreasing and then increasing
costs with varying levels of output. Entry should be easy. At
first blush, it is hard to see a need for regulation.

A closer examination raises some problems about
economies, however. Sanford and other horses pulled carriages in a transportation network or, better perhaps, a maze.
The service being purchased by consumers was measured not
in just passenger miles, but also in terms of waiting times,
availability of service (even when none may have been actually demanded), travel time, and other qualitative aspects of
service. Moreover, the cost of providing the service—
especially if measured only in passenger miles supplied—
probably varied inversely with population density or, in modern terms, with load factors. Costs fall as the ratio of passenger miles demanded rises relative to seat miles supplied.

There are other problems, too. Ignoring the history of other
technologies, a dispatching system which coordinated the
movements of the several carriages between pickups at one
node, travel, and discharge at another node, might be more
efficient than uncoordinated moves. Empty hauls could be reduced, and additional passengers could be picked up and dis-

charged along routes reasonably proximate to the origin and destination route of the initial fare. The central nexus for this coordination might be a local Carriage Hack Trade Association, but this is fraught with dangers of combinations in restraint of trade. Should there be public intervention?

The provision of Sanford's services, it turns out, requires more than just the horse, the driver, and a carriage. A barn, or terminal, is needed, along with the purchase and storage of necessary inputs—hay, grain, the cleaning and servicing of equipment, a blacksmith, etc. It is quite conceivable that, to some point, increasing the capacity of a terminal is less costly than the duplication of a terminal for each production unit. In addition, there are locational factors involved in the siting of terminals, and these include the geographic distribution of demand, transportation costs for inputs, and the costs of waste disposal. For cost minimization, jointly operated and shared terminals may be required. These raise antitrust problems also.[6]

It is obvious that it is not just Sanford that we are considering. Other industries which may be affected by some or all of these cost factors include commercial aviation, railroads, trucking, ocean shipping, telecommunication services (telephone, radio, television, CATV, satellites and their earth receiving stations, electronic funds transfers, computer networks, etc.), milk distribution, electricity distribution, gas distribution, petroleum distribution, fisheries, and, of course, Sanford's modern counterpart, the taxicab. All have geographical network demand and supply factors, dispatching factors, and terminalling factors involved in their operations. Again metaphorically, Sanford is still there and still regulated, either publicly or privately, for these reasons if for no others.

Other Private Cost and Revenue Characteristics

In the absence of regulations to the contrary, entry into the carriage hack trade is easy. Anyone with a horse and a carriage, together with stable facilities, can ply the streets if and when it seems profitable. Thus, people who keep a horse primarily for private use can, as the occasion warrants, get into and out of the business with very low entry or exit costs.

A bit more concisely, anyone with a horse and carriage has a number of costs which must be borne whether or not they are used for hire. The marginal costs of supplying a seat mile of commercial service is very low once the equipment is purchased. These short-run marginal costs, however, are much below long-run marginal (and average) costs through most ranges of short-run output possibilities. Only when Sanford and his rebuilt Studebaker are used to the point that his food consumption rises drastically, or both he and the carriage depreciate rapidly, do the short-run marginal costs rise, and approach or exceed long-run costs.

There are revenue considerations, also. Revenue per seat mile supplied varies with the load factor, or, in this case, with traffic density. This means that people with equipment not dedicated to public transportation will tend to "skim" the market. Acting as individuals rather than in concert, they will provide service in areas and during hours when passenger demand is high, tending to keep the fare per seat mile at or near the level of short-run marginal costs. Only those with alternative uses for the equipment at other times and places (e.g., personal or private business use), with an alternative value adequate to cover the difference between the short-run marginal costs of taxi service and the long-run average costs, including ownership, will remain in the carriage hack business.

This result looks good from a pure efficiency point of view. But it does not look good to professional operators. Neither does it look good to users who want service in locations or at hours where passenger density is low. The competitive structure and operation of the carriage hack trade would prevent the cross-subsidization of low-density traffic from the revenues of high-density traffic. The price of low-density service, if offered at all, would tend to be high, because the marginal cost of that service (viewed to include forgone revenues from other services) would be high. Service frequency would, of course, be low. Some might wish to regulate in order to avoid this result.

What other industries have similar problems? A good many. They obviously include modern taxi service. Included, too, are the airlines,[7] long-line telecommunications,[8] radio and television,[9] computer services, travel agents,[10] petroleum extraction,[11] and bituminous coal.[12] Sanford is not alone with his regulatory problems.

Externalities

It is possible to argue that the provision of local transportation services to low density geographic areas and time periods has some positively valued externalities. It may tend to spread population more evenly, to reduce congestion, to lower the costs of police and fire services, water, sewage, and trash systems, to reduce the development of concentrated ethnic and racial areas, etc. It is possible to argue this, but curing all of these problems is a large task to put on Sanford's shoulders and on the incomes of selected persons who use his services.

It is easier to argue that, in his present functions in New Market, Sanford provides a positively valued externality to the businesses of the district. He lends charm and ambience to the restoration. Some people like only to look at him or to pat his head and stroke his mane, without taking a ride. The same people are customers of the local bars, restaurants, bookstores, parking lots, and the other modes of transportation used to get to and from New Market. If this is true, a price equal to even the long-run marginal cost of the provision of the rides fails to capture the full social value of Sanford's being in New Market.

There are negatively valued externalities, too. Sanford moves slowly on narrow, heavily trafficked streets. He causes congestion. He occupies a space on a public square with alternative uses. He is not charged for the maintenance of public streets, and he has the additional characteristic of depositing manure which must be removed by someone if unpleasant odors, insects, and disease are to be avoided.

Regulations aimed at dealing with negative externalities abound. They form the basis of the common law of nuisance, which provides for private remedy for noise, smoke, and sunlight violations against property. They also are the basis for common law riparian rights which, not coincidentally, vary among jurisdictions with the amount of water freely available to all. In years gone by, rendering plants (poor Sanford) had to be placed on the leeward side of towns, and steam locomotives were required to stoke their fires and bed them with anthracite before going through urban areas. Zoning, building codes, health codes—even stop signs and traffic lights—are manifestations of regulation which interfere with private decisions that might exhibit negative externalities.

Health and Safety

Related to externality problems are others more directly incident to Sanford's operation. First, there is the question of Sanford's own well-being. The hours of use which might maximize profits could be at variance with those conceived by some as necessary restrictions for his welfare. The same could be true of feeding and veterinary care.

Second, there are questions about the safety of passengers. Is the driver adequately trained for the tasks and responsibilities? Are various emergency situations properly anticipated?

Third, there are questions about the driver. These relate to his working conditions, including hours worked, the adequacy of his training, the availability of sanitary facilities, and, quite possibly, wages. And the public health and safety is involved in ways other than just manure, since Sanford might bite, bolt, or break down in socially costly ways. Someone could get hurt, even though he had no intention of being involved with Sanford at all.

The enumeration of parallel regulatory concerns in other industries is impossible because of its extensiveness. For a few illustrations, consider the Federal Aviation Administration's control of pilot training, pilot physical condition, pilot hours, aircraft design and certification, aircraft maintenance and operating rules, instrumentation, airport construction, and airport operations. Also remember the Bureau of Mines, the Food and Drug Administration, the Product Safety Commission, the Environmental Protection Agency, the Department of Labor, state and local boards of health, and the myriad licensing and certification agencies for nurses, doctors, dentists, veterinarians, podiatrists, chiropractors, barbers, plumbers, electricians, and, of course, teachers. Note that the Interstate Commerce Commission is required, as are many other regulatory agencies, to consider the effects of its regulations on railroad employees.

Without attempting to weigh the merits of such interferences with market processes, it is clear that health and safety issues have been used to extend regulation into many facets of the economy. Sanford is just an isolated case.

REGULATORY ALTERNATIVES

When the scope of regulation is seen in even this abbreviated survey, it is difficult to conclude that the public utility concept is passing, or that social inventiveness has created new, general techniques to deal with regulatory failures. If anything, the scope of regulation has increased. New agencies and commissions have been created, and the responsibilities of existing ones have been enlarged. Public utility regulation—in practice if not in concept—has been extended to activities which were beyond those suggested so eloquently by Justice Brandeis in the New State Ice case.

As a general principle, regulation is appropriate whenever the aggregate gain in social welfare from regulation exceeds the aggregate social cost of regulation, with all side effects considered. Given this initial condition, the form of regulation used, and the amount of regulation, should be that which maximizes the difference between the benefits and the costs. The second condition seems at first to imply the usual marginal conditions for maximization, but the matter proves to be considerably more complex than that.

In the first place, a function describing the social costs of regulation is not independent of a function describing social gains. Different kinds of regulatory machinery entail different costs and produce different results. Thus, there is conceptually a family of different cost functions associated with a family of different benefit functions. By itself, this is not a difficult theoretical problem, but the kinds and degrees of regulation may be virtually infinite in number, and the actual relationships between the regulatory costs and the associated social gains are not known, and cannot be known.

Second, something like a general equilibrium model—or a general equilibrium model truncated to include only significant interrelationships—is needed to account for the effects of regulating one market on other markets in the system. The other markets may be largely unregulated, or they may be regulated in some ways. Changes in natural gas regulations affect the market for gas furnaces, electric heating units, and the regulated distribution of electricity. And these are only first order interactions.[13]

Third, as a practical matter, solutions to many of the regulatory problems raised above require a fairly explicit specification of a social welfare function. It is not enough to use narrow Paretian terms, even when these are modified by Scitovsky-type "bribe" conditions. As we observe social values through social decisions, the welfare function has arguments covering income distribution, ethical propositions of many types, political and institutional preferences, and complex issues involving time and intergenerational transfers. Moreover, there are differences in values among people, and hence, differences with respect to what variables should be included in the social welfare function and the weights attaching to these variables.

Fourth, there are "second-best" problems. The conditions necessary for optimization in a system with a single objective function and a single constraint do not universally apply when an additional, nonredundant constraint is added. With respect to regulation, this means that the rule of equating price to marginal cost does not maximize welfare when any constraint other than that arising from the production function and factor costs is introduced (see Baumol and Bradford 1970; Baumol 1977).

Finally, if these problems in narrow economic theory are not enough, there are the very real considerations of the costs of the regulatory activity and the behavior of regulators. It is obvious that commissioners and their staffs must be paid, and that they incur other expenses. Less obvious are the explicit or implicit regulatory objectives, and the behavior of commissions. Are they "captives" of the regulated, as Gray, Stigler, and others have suggested? Do they behave as "satisficers" rather than optimizers? Does the organization of a commission matter? Are commissioners politically sensitive? Do they really behave in their own best interests, and serve the public welfare only as it coincides with their own? (See Posner 1974; Stigler 1971; Bernstein 1955; Breger and MacAvoy 1974; Friendly 1962; MacAvoy 1965; Noll 1971; Phillips 1977.)

What to Do about Old Sanford

Deciding how to regulate old Sanford optimally — including the alternative of not regulating him at all — now proves to be a difficult if not impossible task. Suppose, for example, that the only problem was that there were the classic form of scale economies. It is not enough to say that all that needs to be done is to set price equal to marginal cost. As we all know, this would yield a negative net return, and Sanford would disappear, even though some people would be willing to pay more than that for his services. Further, forming and operating a regulatory commission itself imposes a social cost. Should Sanford's passengers pay for that?

In theory, lump sum subsidies, neutral with respect to resource allocation, could be used, but the supporting taxes and the subsidies have to be administered even if, as is unlikely, a truly neutral tax-subsidy device could be discovered. The standard solution of a "fair return on fair value" would violate the $P = MC$ rule, and indeed, the rule would have to be violated for the "second-best" result with this additional constraint. This, too, requires administrative costs. Perhaps, but only perhaps, a system of perfect price discrimination would lead not only to the "competitive" output, but would also cover the average costs of production.[14] Yet it is unreasonable to think that any regulator or any operator could enforce anything approaching a perfectly discriminating pricing system, especially if a commodity rather than a service is involved.[15]

The issue raised by waiting times, service availability, and varying demand densities raises vexing regulatory problems. Charging for a service whether or not it is used, or charging a flat fee irrespective of the volume of use, is generally condemned as a violation of the marginal cost pricing rule. It need not be a violation if the demand function has availability as well as actual use in its terms, as may well be the case for Sanford, taxis, telephones, television, banks, airlines, and many other industries. Maintaining service availability has a marginal cost, too, but it would be expressed in terms of the partial derivative of costs with respect to seat miles available, waiting time for a dial tone, an extra TV channel, or something like that, instead of the partial with respect to ordinary output measures. A two-part tariff could then be justified if there were an extension to the usual marginal rules, although it clearly would add to administrative complexity.[16]

The value placed on waiting times and availability varies among customers. Those who place a high value on time are willing to pay more for availability than others with lower time costs. If, in years past, Sanford's carriage was seen with an "Out of Service" or "On Call" sign, with the driver waving off flagging potential riders, it could well have been that he was responding to another fare who was willing to pay more. This is discrimination, of course, but it is not obvious that it violates the extended marginal conditions for optimality or near optimality.

This may be clearer in the case of varying traffic densities, which is really just a variant of the service availability illustration. The cost per seat mile remains much the same across differing densities; the cost per passenger mile varies inversely with density. If, because of the demand for availability, the price elasticity of demand per seat mile varies directly with density—i.e., a low price elasticity accompanies a low density—price discrimination would yield more profit because of both the demand and cost factors.

By previously accepted theory, the fact of higher marginal cost per passenger mile should be allowed for setting price differences, but the less elastic demand should not. This is in accord with the $P = MC$ rule. But, as Baumol and Bradford (1970) have shown (also Baumol 1977; Oi 1971), the existence of a binding rate of return constraint leads to a second-best "inverse elasticity" rule for departures from marginal cost pricing. Price discrimination based on elasticity differences is not so bad after all. It follows that any other additional and binding constraint would also require departures from $P = MC$. The theory, however, is clearer than the means by which regulatory agencies might enforce the proper rules.[17]

In this context, peak load pricing is a response to the demand for availability. It is generally recognized that those who are willing to pay for more capacity—i.e., more availability—should pay capital costs as well as operating costs.

So, too, with those who wish service in low density locations or low density hours.

Alternative regulatory schemes to handle the economies associated with dispatching and terminal facilities are few. The terminals could, it seems, be publicly owned, with space auctioned to competing users (see Demsetz 1968). The dispatching might also be a public service. Relegating them to a government hardly does away with regulatory burdens, however. Moreover, the questions of whether the sum of the bid prices would cover the governmental capital and operating costs, whether discrimination should be allowed, whether certain "standards" need to be established in addition to price, and whether the industry may not dominate the decisions of the agency, remain.[18] The structure of the purchasing firms—monopsonistic, oligopsonistic, or competitive—obviously affects answers to these questions.

Full faith in competition, in a market with sellers possessing complete knowledge and with no transactions or "set up" costs, gives a solution to the problem of operators entering and leaving service on the basis of short-run marginal costs. It is ideal that way. But what if knowledge is imperfect? What if actual and potential operators do not know when it is going to rain during rush hour, or when the winter is going to be unusually cold or the summer unusually hot, or the Arabs are going to impose an embargo? It is not clear at all that the capacity for service which comes from "standbys" will adjust to such uncertainties and exigencies. What if there are transactions costs or other entry costs requiring either or both time and resources? Again, the competitive response may be inadequate, and the "fly-by-night" operators may prevent optimal allocation.

Optimal capacities, as optimal inventories, require provision for buffer stocks to handle random demand and nonrandom, uncertain events. An unpopular way of achieving this in some industries is to bar the entry of the "fly-by-nights," require or permit standby capacity of certified operators, with compensating departures from P = MC for those operators. One wonders whether the costs borne by users to meet contingencies are properly allocated, and whether they should not be borne by society generally. Further, one wonders about permitting nonprice competition to be the incentive for creating the added capacity and the low load factors necessary to handle contingencies. Still, complete deregulation may not be the best alternative in all cases.

The market mechanism, it is alleged by some, will also handle externality difficulties. If Sanford provides positive externalities to business and community, contracts would emerge between his owner and those benefited. These contracts, plus the fees paid by those riding, would capture full social values. If Sanford causes odors and congestion of traffic, his owner would pay those offended, or they would pay him not to operate in manners so offensive. These payments would capture full social costs.

Were there full information on the nature of external costs and benefits, were there no transactions costs, and were there no possibilities of "free riders" because of the quasi-public goods aspects of Sanford's presence, the Coasian solution would be the correct one (Coase 1966). But there is not full information, there are transactions costs, and there are likely to be "free riders" when larger numbers are involved. Consequently, markets fail, as Williamson (1975) has so cogently pointed out in a different context. One might, indeed, want to tax those receiving positive externalities, tax Sanford for the negative externalities, etc., but these policies have administrative burdens and allocative implications. Perhaps direct regulation is sometimes preferable.

Similar considerations affect health and safety, and matters of distributive justice. Markets will fail where health and safety externalities exist. No one has really suggested seriously that markets attend to distributive matters. It is convenient in the theory of regulation to assume—usually implicitly—that equitable distribution, and perhaps health and safety, are handled by other mechanisms, particularly the tax structure. Well, in fact they are not, and there is a great temptation to use the regulatory machinery for these purposes.

It is necessary to repeat that when any of these problems are introduced into the regulatory scheme, the objective function or the constraints imposed on the attaining of objectives become different from those usually contained in regulatory theory. Then the $P = MC$ rule is no longer correct.

CONCLUSIONS

To be perfectly clear, this overview is not intended as an apologia for the continuation of regulation in its present guise. With Commissioner O'Bannon, I suspect Sanford is regulated because, in history, he has been. On balance, it seems that deregulating Sanford would not impose new social costs equal to the cost reduction involved in deregulation. There probably would be net social benefits.

The overview is intended, however, to sound a note of caution. Re-regulation, not total deregulation, may be the prime necessity today. There is another intention. If useful social inventiveness is to occur to fulfill Gray's prophecy, economists will have to contribute more than restrictive equations and graphs. The long worked-over $P = MC$ rule is not very helpful, even if more competition—taken generically—sometimes may be in order. People and institutions are involved, with all the complexities in objectives and constraints that these imply.

Sanford's situation is still with us, and will be for the rest of our lives.

8

CHRIS ARGYRIS

Ineffective Regulating Processes

Organizational learning in private and public entities. Detecting and correcting error. Theories-in-use and intraorganizational problems. Error-hiding, deception, and games as part of normal organizational life. Interorganizational relationships. The regulating and the regulated.

A growing body of research on organizational learning reveals details of the regulatory processes between organizations. This research is based on the underlying assumptions that regulatory agencies and regulated organizations have capacities to learn, and that these capacities exercise a strong influence on how effectively they deal with each other. It suggests that the performance of regulatory agencies will tend to be low for important tasks, and will tend to deteriorate over time. This paper attempts to specify the basis for such a pessimistic prediction.

ORGANIZATIONAL LEARNING

The following case illustrates the problems of detecting and correcting error, problems which are common to both private and public organizations.

The Hundred-Million-Dollar Error

Several years ago, the top management of a multibillion dollar corporation decided that Product X was a failure and should be dropped. The losses involved were in excess of $100 million. Six years before this action was taken, at least five people knew that Product X was in serious trouble. Three of these were plant managers who lived daily with the production problems; the others were marketing officials who perceived that the manufacturing problems could only be solved with expenditures that would drive the product out of the market because of the resulting price increases.

There are several reasons why this information did not get to the top before it did. Those lower down believed at first that with hard work they might turn the errors into success. But the more they struggled, the more they realized the massive size of the original mistake. In considering the problem of communicating the bad news so that it would be heard, they knew that negative facts would not be well received at the upper levels of their company without suggestions for positive action. They therefore lost much time in drafting constructive memos that indicated the realities without too much shock to top managers, since the latter were enthusiastically describing Product X as a new leader in its field.

Middle managers found the memos too open and forthright, in part because they themselves had done the development and marketing studies that led to the decision to produce Product X; the memos thus threw doubt on the validity of their analysis. They wanted time to "really check" the gloomy predictions and, if they were true, to design corrective strategies. If they were going to send the pessimistic information upward, they wanted it accompanied by optimistic action alternatives. Hence further delay.

Once convinced that the predictions were valid, middle managers began to release some of the bad news—but in measured doses. They carefully managed the releases to make sure they were "covered" if management became upset. They drastically cut the initial memo and summarized its findings, defending the cuts on the grounds that long memos always brought complaints from top management. As a result, the top received fragmented information, underplaying the severity of the problem (not the problem itself), and overplaying the control exercised by those below. Top management therefore continued to extol the product, partially to ensure its needed financial backing within the company.

Lower-level managers grew confused and eventually depressed, unable to understand either the continued top-management support or the reasons for new studies to evaluate the production and marketing difficulties they had already identified. They reduced the frequency of their memos and the intensity of their alarm, while simultaneously passing to middle management the responsibility for the problem. And when, in turn, foremen and employees asked local plant managers what was happening, they heard that the company was studying the situation and continuing its support. The foremen were bewildered, but their concern lessened.

How Organizations Learn

In pursuing organizational policies and objectives, organizational learning is a process of detecting and correcting error, one element of which is any feature of knowledge or knowing that inhibits the conditions for learning. When the process enables the organization to maintain present policies or to achieve objectives, the process may be called *single-loop learning*. This is analogous to a thermostat that learns when it is too hot or too cold, thus turning the heat on or off; the thermostat is able to perform this task because it can receive information (the temperature of the room) and take corrective action.

If the thermostat could question itself about whether it should be set at 68 degrees, it would be capable not only of detecting error, but of questioning the underlying policies and goals as well as its own program. That is a second and more comprehensive inquiry; hence, it might be called *double-loop learning*. When the plant managers and marketing people were detecting and attempting to correct error in order to manufacture Product X, that was single-loop learning. When they began to confront the question whether Product X should be manufactured, that was double-loop learning, because they were now questioning underlying organization policies and objectives.

In this organization, as in many others, norms had developed which admonished: "Never openly confront company policies and objectives, especially those which excite top management." Thus, to communicate the truth about the serious problems of Product X would confront a company policy, violate an organizational norm, and defy a second norm which forbids challenging the first. A lot of information about error-hiding therefore would have to be camouflaged, greatly inhibiting double-loop learning.

The Double Bind

To complicate matters, when employees adhere to a norm that says "hide errors," they know they are violating another norm that says "reveal errors." Whichever norm they choose, they risk getting into trouble. If they hide the error, they can be punished by the top if the error is discovered; if they reveal it, they risk exposing a whole network of camouflage and deception. They are thus in a double bind. Whatever they do is necessary, yet counterproductive to the organization; their actions may even be personally abhorrent.

A common way to reduce the tension that results from conflicting aims is to begin to conceive of the error-hiding, deception, and games as part of normal organizational life. The moment individuals reach this state, they may become blind to the errors. This is one reason some employees are genuinely surprised and hurt when accused of disloyal and immoral behavior by those (usually outsiders) who discover the long-standing practices of error-hiding. Note that the camouflaging of technical errors is done by the use of acceptable human games and organizational norms. The existence of human games in turn implies games to hide the games.

It is rare, therefore, that an organization is able to use double-loop learning for its instrumental and policy issues if it cannot do so for the games and norms, because the games and norms act to prevent people from saying what they know about technical or policy issues. The subordinates who knew about the problems of Product X did not speak of them directly, because it would have violated organizational norms and games that were respected and played to ensure survival.

Long-Term Problems

Under these conditions, double-loop learning would occur because of (1) a crisis precipitated by some event in the environment (such as a recession, or a better product marketed by a competitor); (2) a revolution from within (new management) or from without (political interference or takeover); or (3) a crisis created by existing management (often caused by continued losses) in order to shake up the organization.

These choices entail several long-range problems. First, the change usually comes long after its necessity has been realized by alert individuals or groups within the organization. The delay teaches these persons that their alertness and loyalty are not valued. Second, those who are not alert or not as involved are reinforced in their behavior; they learn that if they wait long enough and keep their reputations clean, someone else will one day take action. Third, change under crisis and revolution is exhausting to the organization. Fourth, such changes usually reinforce the factors that inhibit double-loop learning in the first place. Hence, from the standpoint of organizational learning processes, there would be no change.

FACTORS THAT INHIBIT
DOUBLE-LOOP LEARNING

Research suggests that double-loop learning is inhibited by both individual and organizational factors (see Argyris and Schön 1974, 1977). To begin with individual factors:

Model I Theories of Action

Actions are planned and carried out according to individual theories. "If you want to motivate people to perform, pay them well and inspect their production closely" is a proposition contained in many executives' theories for action. Yet we found that few people are aware that they do not use the theories they explicitly espouse; still others are unaware of those they do use. We label the former "espoused theories"; the latter, "theories-in-use." If people are unaware of the propositions they use, then it appears that they design for themselves theories-in-use that are not genuinely self-corrective. Thus, they are prisoners of their own theories.

If this finding sounds questionable, I agree; I, too, doubted our early results. As we developed a model of the theories-in-use, however, which we call Model I (see Exhibit 1), the pieces began to fall into place.

Exhibit 1

Model I

I Governing Variables for Action	II Action Strategies for Actor and toward Environment	III Consequences on Actor and Behavioral World	IV Consequences on Learning	V Effectiveness
1. Achieve the purposes as I perceive them	1. Design and manage environment so that actor is in control over factors relevant to me	1. Actor seen as defensive	1. Self-sealing	1. Decreased effectiveness
2. Maximize winning and minimize losing	2. Own and control task	2. Defensive interpersonal and group relationships	2. Single-loop learning	
3. Minimize eliciting negative feelings	3. Unilaterally protect self	3. Defensive norms	3. Little testing of theories in public	
4. Be rational and minimize emotionality	4. Unilaterally protect others from being hurt	4. Low freedom of choice, internal commitment, and risk-taking		

The validity of the theories that people use to design and carry out their actions is tested by the effective achievement of their objectives. Four basic values have been identified as goals toward which people who operate by model assumptions seem to strive, and that govern their behavior. They are (1) to define in their own terms the purpose of the situation in which they find themselves, (2) to win, (3) to suppress their own and others' feelings, and (4) to emphasize the intellectual aspects of problems, and deemphasize the emotional aspects. To satisfy these purposes, people tend to pursue such strategies as advocating a position while controlling others in order to win that position; controlling the tasks to be done; and secretly deciding how much is to be told and how much is to be distorted, usually to save someone's face.

It can now be seen why Model I theories of action might be difficult to correct. First, the actors do not invite confrontation of the inconsistencies within their theories, or of the incongruities between what they espouse and what they actually use. To do so would risk the possibility that others might seize control or might win, and negative feelings might be aroused—all of which would violate the governing objectives.

Those who observe the actor usually see and react to his or her inconsistencies and incongruities. Since they often hold the same theories of action, however, they say nothing, lest they upset the actor and be seen as insensitive and undiplomatic.

A Practical Example

These governing objectives and strategies are deeply rooted. In leading a seminar with fifteen line officers of a large holding company (mostly presidents of divisions), eight financial officers of these divisions, the headquarters financial officer, and the head of the entire company, I began to realize that the line officers were seriously concerned that the financial types—with their financial information systems—seemed to be increasing their power with the chief executive officers. The finance people, who sensed this concern and interpreted it as natural defensiveness, wished they could do something about it.

Because both groups wanted to correct the problem, I asked each of the line and financial officers to write a short case. On the right side of the page, they were to write a scenario on their approach to discussion of the issue with their financial or line counterparts. On the left side, they were to write anything that they thought or felt, but probably would not communicate. I then summarized the findings, and presented them to both groups.

Some interesting patterns emerged. In all twenty-three cases, the scenarios dealt primarily with surface aspects of the problem. For example, the line officers emphasized the frustrations connected with filling out so many forms, the inability to get financial results quickly enough, while being loaded—indeed, overloaded—with information they did not need. The financial officers, on the other hand, said the forms were complex because the banks demanded the information; if the financial reports were not coming out fast enough, they would try to speed them up.

The information on thoughts and feelings *not* discussed was central in both groups. For example, ''Here comes the runaround again,'' ''Why don't they say that they want to control this place?'' or ''He [the financial man] demands reports to impress his boss.''

Moreover, members of each group knew they were withholding information and covering up feelings, and they guessed that the others were doing the same. Information that each side considered incomplete or distorted, however, was not up for discussion. Such issues, if not discussed, still had to be solved, so the views of others were inferred. The participants could test such inferences only indirectly, and were unable to discuss their testing methods.

ORGANIZATIONAL LEARNING SYSTEMS

People who are programmed with Model I theories-in-use will tend to create particular kinds of learning systems within their organization. We identify this system as Model 0–I.

The first components of Model 0–I learning systems are the *primary inhibiting loops* (see Exhibit 2). These arise when attempts are made to solve double-loop problems by using Model I theories-in-use. As we saw in the example above, there was a tendency for all parties to withhold information that was potentially threatening, and the act of cover-up itself was closed to discussion.

It was thus highly probable that people in each group would view much of the information they received from others as being inconsistent, vague, and ambiguous. Under these conditions, the detection and correction of error is highly unlikely. To compound the problem, the very qualities of inconsistency, vagueness, and ambiguity are not discussable. These two conditions combine to make it highly likely that primary inhibiting loops will increase the ambiguity and inconsistency of any information involved in a double-loop problem.

Secondary inhibiting loops arise in part from the fact that people are unaware of theories that they use to design and manage their actions. Since they are unaware of these theories-in-use, they tend to be blind to the impact they have on others. The blindness compounds the problem, and so we have loops nested within loops that inhibit learning. Model I blinds people to their weaknesses. In a recent study, for instance, six corporation presidents were unable to realize that they were incapable of questioning their assumptions and breaking through to fresh understanding (Argyris 1976). They had the illusion that they could double-loop learn, when in reality they just kept running around the same track.

President *A* told the group that Vice President *Z*, whom he had viewed as a prime candidate to be the next president, was

Exhibit 2

Model II

I Governing Variables for Action	II Action Strategies for Actor and toward Environment	III Consequences on Actor and Behavioral World	IV Consequences on Learning	V Effectiveness
1. Valid information	1. Design situations or encounters where participants can be origins and experience high personal causation	1. Actor experienced as minimally defensive	1. Disconfirmable processes	1. Increased effectiveness
2. Free and informed choice	2. Task is controlled jointly	2. Minimally defensive interpersonal relations and group dynamics	2. Double-loop learning	
3. Internal commitment to the choice and constant monitoring of the implementation	3. Protection of self is a joint enterprise and oriented toward growth	3. Learning-oriented norms	3. Frequent public testing of theories	
	4. Bilateral protection of others	4. High freedom of choice, internal commitment, and risk-taking		

Exhibit 2

Model O-1
Learning Systems that Inhibit Error Detection and Correction

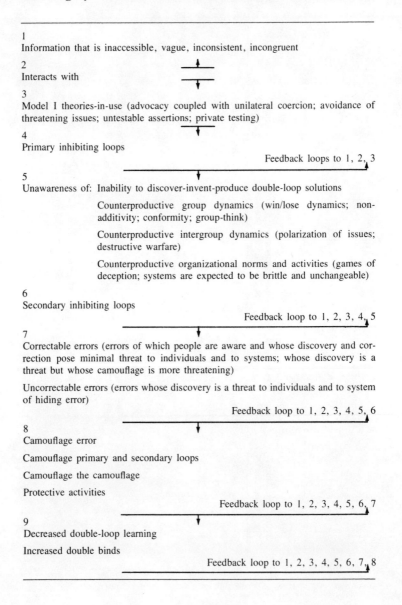

1
Information that is inaccessible, vague, inconsistent, incongruent

2
Interacts with

3
Model I theories-in-use (advocacy coupled with unilateral coercion; avoidance of threatening issues; untestable assertions; private testing)

4
Primary inhibiting loops

Feedback loops to 1, 2, 3

5
Unawareness of: Inability to discover-invent-produce double-loop solutions

Counterproductive group dynamics (win/lose dynamics; non-additivity; conformity; group-think)

Counterproductive intergroup dynamics (polarization of issues; destructive warfare)

Counterproductive organizational norms and activities (games of deception; systems are expected to be brittle and unchangeable)

6
Secondary inhibiting loops

Feedback loop to 1, 2, 3, 4, 5

7
Correctable errors (errors of which people are aware and whose discovery and correction pose minimal threat to individuals and to systems; whose discovery is a threat but whose camouflage is more threatening)

Uncorrectable errors (errors whose discovery is a threat to individuals and to system of hiding error)

Feedback loop to 1, 2, 3, 4, 5, 6

8
Camouflage error

Camouflage primary and secondary loops

Camouflage the camouflage

Protective activities

Feedback loop to 1, 2, 3, 4, 5, 6, 7

9
Decreased double-loop learning

Increased double binds

Feedback loop to 1, 2, 3, 4, 5, 6, 7, 8

too submissive and did not show enough initiative. The presidents questioned *A* carefully, and they soon produced evidence that *A* might be the cause of *Z*'s behavior. *A* was surprised and irked about his own lack of awareness, but he was pleased with the help he got, and invented a solution based on the new diagnosis—"to lay off the vice president and give him more breathing space." To his colleagues, this solution was simplistic, and they told him so. As one said, "If I were *Z* and you suddenly changed by letting me alone, I would wonder if you had given up on me." *A*, again surprised and irked, nevertheless tried out the solution that he and the others finally designed, with his peers acting as *Z*. What he produced, however, was not what he and his colleagues had designed.

The point is that *A* honestly thought that he was doing the right things. What he learned was that he did not have the skills to discover, to invent, to produce double-loop solutions, *and* that he was unaware of this fact.

People provide incomplete and distorted feedback to each other; each knows that the other knows, and each knows that this game is not usually discussable. The second set of factors helping to create secondary inhibitions, therefore, is composed of the games people play in order not to upset each other. These games can become complex, and can spread quickly throughout an organization. A third set of factors causing secondary inhibiting loops is in the competitive win/lose dynamics; the low trust and risk-taking in groups that results from using Model I theories-in-use. The fourth set of factors involves the interdepartmental competitive dynamics, such as "throwing the dead cat in someone else's yard" during a budget meeting, or "creating fires to motivate other departments to cooperate."

All these games are not formally sanctioned by the organization. Hence the double bind that was mentioned at the outset will affect the more loyal employees. They will feel the dilemma deeply. If they ignore the Model 0–I learning system, the organization's problem-solving will not be effective;

if they surface it, they run the risk of incurring the wrath of the people above, below, and around them who believe it makes no sense to open Pandora's box.

INTERORGANIZATIONAL RELATIONSHIPS BETWEEN REGULATORS AND REGULATEES

The theoretical framework just presented purports to deal with any pyramidal organization, public or private. It should apply in varying degrees to all regulating and regulated agencies, and to the relationships between them. Regulating agencies and the regulated organizations should not be good at detecting and correcting errors (especially of the double-loop variety), *and* both should have vested interests in hiding these limitations lest another interest (such as Congress or its members) decides to open up the can of worms. This fear, by the way, may not be realistic; Congress probably has its own Model 0–I learning systems. Hence it, too, would be unable to generate valid solutions, and would be careful to hide the fact. More specifically, we would predict:

1. Regulating and regulated organizations will tend to create interorganizational relationships that are consistent with their respective Model 0–I learning systems.

For example, relationships between private and public organizations, or those between public organizations, should be characterized by games such as win/lose dynamics and deception. These games should be camouflaged, and the games and the camouflage should not be directly discussable by the participants when they act as agents for their organizations.

Bardach (1977) has described in detail many of the relationships between national, state, and local governmental agencies as well as between governmental agencies that deal with private enterprises. He found that the major characteristic of their relationships was a complex set of games that

were played in appropriate camouflage to assure their survival. For example, there exists "implementation politics"; at
their core, these involve a complex set of interrelated games
with specified players, roles, stakes, tactics, and rules. These
games form a system of activities which lies at the heart of
the implementation process.

To begin with, three sets of games relate to the following
three objectives: the diversion of funds, influence over goals,
and influence over administrative actions. Examples of political games to divert resources include Easy Money (making
off with funds in exchange for program elements of significantly less value); Budget Games (moving money; making
certain that all moneys are spent, even at the risk of failure of
a quickly funded project; and intergovernmental "revenue
sharing"); Easy Life (compensating for low salaries by de-
signing the work environment to suit personal tastes); and
Pork Barrel.

The second set of games is used to deflect policy goals. As
examples: Piling On (adding a large number of additional objectives to a successful program); Up for Grabs (defining programs with minimal bureaucracy and modest budget, thus encouraging bureaucrats or others to stay away from the programs); Peace (defining programs to keep peace between ex-
tremists or zealots and those conservatives who scrutinize the
former, and who could terrorize agencies charged with program administration).

The third set of games arises from the dilemma of adminis-
tering programs. Tokenism attempts to appear to contribute to
a program, while privately conceding only a small contribu-
tion. This leads the agency to develop monopoly power
which, in turn, produces a new set of games on the part of
other agencies or on that of the clients which the legislation
was designed to assist. Included are Do Without, Create a
New Monopoly, Foster Competition, Buy Agency Off,
Co-opt Agency, and Build Institutions with Countervailing
Power.

Massive Resistance is another major game played by agencies. The actions that may be developed to counteract it include Prescriptions (orders), Enabling (give added resources), Incentives (encourage cooperation), and Regulations (to make deterrence unlikely).

All of these multilevel games exist in social entropy—a state of slow social deterioration—and help to reinforce it. Social entropy is not only encouraged by the games, which reinforce it, but it is doubly reinforced by the incompetency of the civil service (especially at the higher levels), by variability in the objects legally subject to bureaucratic control, and by the quality of coordination among various agencies (which, as might be surmised, tends to be low).

The games produce a good deal of defensive reaction. Individuals, groups, and organizations consume time and energy in avoiding responsibility, in defending themselves against maneuvers by other game-players, and in setting up situations advantageous to their own game-playing strategies. These defensive reactions, in turn, produce a new set of games which reinforce the original games, the defensive reactions, and themselves. They include Tenacity (stymie progress), Territory (staking out one's action space), Not Our Problem, Old Man Out, and generating a Particular Reputation.

The games form a system of rules and norms for effective behavior. Actors must play within these constraints if they are to succeed. They must also act as if the games do not officially exist. All sides are playing; all sides know that the others are playing; and all sides know that the games are not publicly discussable. This makes it highly unlikely that double-loop errors are going to be detected and corrected.

2. Effective regulation requires the ability to influence internal problem-solving activities and the learning capacities of organizations.

The newspaper industry has attempted to regulate the behavior of its members through the use of a Newspaper Council, a regulatory agency to which persons with grievances related to published news items may appeal. The Newspaper Council has the right to investigate all complaints, as long as the paper in question is one of its members. The fundamental assumption is that the council can acquire and assess evidence regarding the validity of a particular news article. The difficulty is not that such data is unobtainable, but that the causes of such errors may be beyond the scope of the council's authority and competence to investigate.

A recent study (Argyris 1974) suggests that many of the reporters are not aware that they are distorting the news, nor are they aware that the predisposition to distort the news may be related to the quality of the Model 0–I learning systems within the newspaper. The learning system contained components, for example, that created many complex frustrations for the newspaper people which appeared to be uncorrectable. These same components (e.g., deception, win/lose, conformity to higher authority, etc.) were key qualities of the Nixon White House, condemned by these reporters through their published articles. The distortion of the reporting—by exaggerating its existence and magnifying its impact within the White House—could be related to the pent-up frustration felt by the reporters and editors toward their own organization. Thus, the council could judge a particular article as distorted, it could warn or punish the newspaper, the paper could print an apology—and none of these actions would correct the cause of the errors.

A recent study by the Rand Corporation (Elmore 1977) of three hundred federally funded educational programs concluded that:

nothing the federal government did in its management of the programs seemed to have much influence on the success or failure of the implementation. In a follow-up in-depth study of the successful programs, the causes were found to be factors at the local level such as the motivation of participants, the commitment of the local people, and the internal milieu of the local organization. All of the

characteristics of successful projects that the Rand analysts identified were factors over which federal administrators typically have
very little control.

In my experience with the Office of Education, most of its
top administrators were aware of this state of affairs, and
could predict the results even before the study was made.
They continued to give out the money, however, because of
their goals: to develop strong constituencies, and not to return
funds to Congress. Their desire to develop strong constituencies was not so much to guarantee better education for children, but to guarantee a longer life for the Office of Education itself.

3. Although regulators and regulatees may differ with each other
   on substantive issues, they will tend to use similar strategies to
   protect themselves if under attack.

For example, both will strive to hide the problem-diagnosing
and problem-solving deficiencies of their learning systems.
They will also attempt to place the blame onto the other organization. But in pressing its claim that the other is at fault,
the accusing organization will do its best to avoid methods
that cause to surface any underlying double-loop problems. If
this should occur, the accusing organization runs the risk of
having its own Model 0–I learning system exposed.

4. The long-run strategy of regulators is to strive to translate or
   reduce double-loop problems into single-loop problems.

One way to do this is to decompose problems into smaller
problems, and then to focus on detailed specifications. If regulatees are seen by the regulators as always trying to find
loopholes, then the duty of the regulator is to plug up such
loopholes ahead of time. This will lead to myriad specifications, since regulatees are innovative in finding loopholes.

As the pile of specifications becomes high, the regulatees
can mount their attack: namely, that they are swamped with
regulations and specifications. In turn, the regulators will insist that they have no alternative. Instead of dealing with the
underlying problem (e.g., neither side trusts the other), the

usual solution is the creation of manuals on ways to comply with specifications. Ironically, this tends to drive out the honest regulatees who see no sense in being hampered by specifications designed for dishonest regulatees. HUD provides an excellent illustration of this problem. In order to deal with dishonest builders, HUD developed rigid specification and inspection procedures which drove out many of the honest builders, leaving HUD with those builders who made the procedures necessary in the first place. Hence, a self-sealing process that rewards the incompetent.

Lipsky (1976) has shown that translating double-loop issues into single-loop issues is permeating the street-level bureaucracies such as the police, welfare, school, and court systems. Police and judges, for example, create "shortcuts" in arrest and trial procedures because they have inadequate resources for law enforcement. Another coping mechanism tries to create an image of "bad guys" and "good guys"; needless to say, "we are the good guys." Hence, stereotyping occurs—"most businessmen cannot be trusted," "bureaucrats enjoy red tape."

5. The causes of ineffectiveness within the regulating agencies, and in their capacity to regulate effectively, will not be corrected without changes in the theories-in-use, at least in those of the top and middle administrators, and in their Model 0–I learning system.

The proliferation of rules and regulations about how to regulate, or the development of heavier penalties for ineffective performance, will not tend to correct the underlying causes. For example, Motta (1976) reports that national planners in one of the largest countries in South America concluded that many of the governmental bureaucracies were unable to detect and correct their own errors—not to mention the errors of those organizations that they were supposed to monitor. They poured in financial and human resources to change the bureaucracies, and failed. In desperation, they eventually created totally new organizations specifically designed not to generate the deception and rigidities of Model 0–I learning systems. Yet the organizations began in a few years to develop the very characteristics that they were designed to avoid.

CONCLUSION

People are programmed with Model I theories-in-use which, in turn, necessarily create Model 0–I learning systems. These factors combine to make it unlikely that any organization, including those that regulate, will be effective in double-loop learning. To the extent that effective regulation requires the solving of double-loop problems, the regulating agencies will tend to fail.

Attempts to tighten regulations, to close loopholes, to create new controls, will be effective, at best, on single-loop issues. Because organizations and their agents do not know how to control the quality of double-loop learning, and because they are unaware that this is the case, such attempts will fail on double-loop issues.

The consequence of "tightening" activities is to increase the threat of being caught; hence, the double bind of the participants mentioned at the outset. They may react by hiding behind the myriad rules and regulations required by new controls, and may seek new games and new camouflage. Nor will the typical educational programs on decision-making or strategic planning be effective, since they focus on the espoused theories of action of individuals and organizations.

Corrective measures must focus on the theories-in-use.* The first step to effective regulation, therefore, must be to look within the regulating and regulated organizations.

---

*Examples of attempts to alter individual and organizational theories-in-use may be found, respectively, in Argyris (1976) and Argyris and Schön (1977).

9

PAUL H. WEAVER

Regulation, Social Policy, and Class Conflict

Social-science theories of government regulation. The "iron triangle." Reform of older programs. Deregulation movement. The adversary posture of new regulation. The public interest and special interest: the Old and New Regulations. The objectives: control of the marketplace and class politics. The new class and its ambitions.

Some time ago I received a letter from a friend of mine, a political scientist who is an author of one of the best-selling introductory textbooks on American government. He and his coauthors were preparing a revised edition, and they wondered if I would be willing to review the chapters on government regulation of business in light of the reporting and writ-

ing I had done on the subject for *Fortune* magazine. After a
certain amount of haggling over the fee—in practice, the authors' liberality with other people's money (in this case, the
publisher's) was not what one would have guessed from their
political views—I accepted. Shortly thereafter the book ar-
rived, and, curious as to what it would have to say, I immediately opened it and started to read.

The theme of the chapters in question was straightforward
enough: government regulation of business, they insisted, is a
disappointment at best, and more often than not an utter failure and scandal. Its purpose is to make private economic activity safe for liberal democracy by remedying imperfections
in the marketplace that prevent business activity from being
self-regulating in the manner posited by Adam Smith. Yet in
the overwhelming majority of cases, according to the
textbook, this purpose does not even come close to being
achieved. The regulatory agencies do not control business
power; they are controlled by it. They do not serve the public interest, but promote special interests at the expense of the
public.

These conditions prevail, the chapters suggested, because
the politics of the regulatory agencies are dominated by what
some political scientists have described as an "iron
triangle"—a coalition made up of the regulated industry, the
regulatory agency, and the congressional subcommittees with
jurisdiction over it. Exploiting the generality of the agency's
legal mandate and the breadth of its official powers, the
members of this unholy trio so arrange things that regulatory
policy works to their own narrow advantage rather than ben-
efiting the people as a whole. And they can do this with
impunity, year in and year out, because their interest in regulation is intense and direct, whereas that of the public is weak
and diffuse and so goes unrepresented. In short, the textbook
argued, the politics of regulation is an exercise in subversion
and injustice, and the lesson it teaches is that the institutions
of liberal democracy are impotent in the face of special interests, especially business interests.

None of the text's account of government regulation was unfamiliar to me, nor will it be to any other student of the subject; it represents a reasonably accurate thumbnail sketch of the social-science and journalistic literature on the regulatory agencies. Nevertheless, within minutes I found myself dismayed, and by the end of the first chapter I was aghast.

Now I will admit I was put off, perhaps to an unreasonable extent, by the resolute vagueness of the exposition (intended, apparently, to connote objectivity), by the relentless, if covert, editorializing, and by the absence of persuasive detail. I also was irritated by the authors' failure to convey a sense of the diversity of social-science interpretations. The differences between "capture" theories of regulatory failure like that of Samuel P. Huntington (1952), "life-cycle" theories such as the one advanced by Marver Bernstein (1955), and "original intent" theories of the sort proposed by Gabriel Kolko (1963) and others, were scarcely broached.[1] Little was made of the competing argument, developed by such scholars as Louis Jaffe and James Q. Wilson, that the real bias of the regulatory agencies is not that they favor the regulated, but that they have an enormous stake in regulating per se, and that the "special interests" the agencies really serve are those involved in the regulatory process itself—lawyers, judges, environmental consultants, business lobbyists and so forth. Moreover, the text almost completely ignored the fascinating body of empirical research, mostly by economists, on the often perverse practical consequences of regulatory programs. The author most frequently cited in the footnotes was not Merton Peck or Sam Peltzman or Roger Noll or Paul MacAvoy, but—Ralph Nader and his various *doppelgangers*.

Yet my quarrel was not really with the textbook, which is not bad as such things go. What mainly horrified me was that the social-science theories the textbook was describing bore no relationship worth speaking of to what I had observed and pondered during some three years of writing about government regulation of business.

THE OLD REGULATION

Consider, to begin with, the political processes that surround
the older regulatory agencies—those founded between 1887,
when the Interstate Commerce Commission was established,
and the outbreak of World War II. With exceptions, most of
these agencies are cartel-like in structure and effect; they are
organized on an industry-by-industry basis, and are more or
less mandated to protect as well as regulate. Characteristic
examples are the ICC itself (which regulates railroads, trucking, and barges), the Civil Aeronautics Board (airlines), and
the Federal Communications Commission (television, radio,
and telecommunications). These are the agencies to which the
regulatory literature has empirical reference, so it is not surprising that there should be some points of correspondence
between their actual behavior and the social-science account
of it. Yet even in the case of these older agencies, there has
arisen in recent years a large discrepancy between social science and reality.

Since the fall of 1974, for example, there has been under-
way in Washington a concerted, broad-based, and so far
fairly successful movement to reform, and in some instances
to abolish, the older regulatory programs. This movement is
the undertaking of a peculiar coalition of *laissez-faire*
economists, conservative Republicans, "consumerists," and
liberal politicians. The two former groups are motivated particularly by their beliefs about limited government; the two
latter seek to save consumers money and to deprive business
of what they regard as illegitimate political advantage.

According to the political science of regulation, this
movement for deregulation simply shouldn't exist; the public
interest in regulation is supposed to be inherently too diffuse
to sustain any significant, ongoing challenge to the hegemony
of the "iron triangle," whose members are supposed to be
able to turn regulatory programs to their own selfish purposes
with comparative ease. Yet in the real world, just the oppo-

site is the case these days. A deregulatory movement does exist, and has made considerable headway. It has been pushed enthusiastically by the Council of Economic Advisers, the Antitrust Division of the Justice Department, elements of the Office of Management and Budget, and other agencies in the Executive Branch. It has enlisted the support of two presidents. It has strong backing from liberal Democrats as well as from conservative Republicans on the Hill, and is being carried forward by a number of congressional subcommittees, including several whose members ought to be in the front ranks of those defending the "iron triangle." Already the deregulators have had some successes. They have lessened somewhat the ICC's powers to set railroad rates, and they have pushed through legislation prohibiting state fair-trade laws. This past year, with strong support from Senators Cannon and Kennedy and the endorsement of President Carter, a bill to cut back airline regulation substantially has progressed to the point of enactment in the Senate. Passage in the House, though not a certainty, is entirely possible. And significant reforms in other agencies could well be in the offing, too.

The case of airline deregulation illustrates with particular force just how misleading and fallacious the standard political-science account of regulatory politics has become. The theory of the "iron triangle" holds that regulatory agencies are always and everywhere the unyielding defenders of their programs and prerogatives. The reality in this case is that the CAB itself has been one of the most active advocates of airline deregulation. Under two chairmen—first John Robson, now Alfred E. Kahn—the five members of the CAB have unanimously asked Congress to curtail their agency's power to determine airline rates and routes. Even more astonishingly, the CAB's professional staff has come out in support of the same idea—and it did so before the commissioners did. Two years ago, a committee of senior civil servants at the board issued a long report, the key conclusion of which was that the CAB should be relieved of a large portion of its powers.

The theory of the "iron triangle" also says that the typical regulatory program is defended to the death by the regulated industry. In the case of airline deregulation, the reality is that the Air Transport Association (the trade association of the scheduled airlines) does not have a position on regulatory reform. Several carriers, including the nation's biggest airline, United, favor a measure of deregulation, and barely half the members of the industry are actively opposed to major reform legislation.

The literature further holds that congressional subcommittees are a mainstay of the "iron triangle," and can be counted on to turn back any congressional pressures for change. In the case of airline deregulation, the reality is that Senator Howard Cannon of Nevada, who is chairman of the Senate Commerce Committee's subcommittee on aviation, has been publicly committed to airline deregulation for almost two years now; that his subcommittee has reported a deregulatory bill to the full committee; and that the full committee has reported a bill to the whole Senate for a vote. The House subcommittee, though not yet as active as its opposite number, could well become so. Its chairman is also on record as favoring airline deregulation.

In other words, the "iron triangle" that should be effortlessly smashing the deregulators' assault on the CAB is doing nothing of the sort. It has scarcely a single member who reliably defends regulation, and most of the actors who should be supporting CAB policies these days are busily attacking them! The airline case, though extreme, is not an isolated instance. Similar weakness is visible in other " iron triangles" today—in the House subcommittee on communications, which has been conducting a root-and-branch review of FCC regulatory programs; in the Antitrust Division, which has urged repeal of the Robinson-Patman Act; and in many institutions concerned with banking regulation, which had begun an agonizing reappraisal of that policy area long before Bert Lance began—or ended—his ill-fated stay in Washington.

The fact is that in a great many regulatory arenas the "iron triangle" no longer exists, or has been severely weakened. (One regulatory reformer now speaks of a "rubber triangle.") The standard political science of government regulation is simply in error when it asserts that regulatory policy is always and everywhere controlled by the regulated, that it is essentially immune to outside criticism and reform, and that the existence of the "iron triangle" thus demonstrates a deep contradiction at the heart of American democracy. The truth is that the "iron triangle," where it exists, was and is a political coalition like any other—sometimes successful, at other times not, and always dependent over the long run on the good opinion of the people.

THE NEW REGULATION

In fairness, it must be said that the theory of the "iron triangle" was an honest mistake. The scholars who propounded it did so, for the most part, on the basis of careful research, and if they overgeneralized their findings, their work remains useful as an account of episodes or eras at the agencies in question. And yet, even as description, the literature on regulation is getting to be very misleading.

Over the past decade, the federal regulatory establishment has been greatly expanded by a long series of new laws in the areas of health, safety, and environment. For a variety of reasons—not the least of which is that legislators or their aides are aware of the social-science literature—the new regulatory agencies are utterly unlike the old ones. And since the new agencies as a group now far overshadow the old ones by any measure one might invoke—social impact, number of people employed, amount of federal money spent, etc.—the literature, merely by remaining on the library shelves, has come to convey a seriously inaccurate impression of what regulatory agencies in general are like and how they work. (Scholars are only now beginning to do serious research on the behavior of the newer agencies.)

For example, the literature says that government regulation of business typically is based on terse statutes that confer extremely broad powers on the agencies and provide little specific policy guidance save to enjoin the regulators to act in the public interest. As a result, according to the literature, regulatory agencies have legislative as well as administrative functions, and therefore are particularly vulnerable to pressure from special interests.

This is indeed a reasonable statement to make concerning the ICC, FCC, CAB, and most of the other older regulatory agencies. But it isn't at all true of most of the newer ones. Typically, the laws establishing these newer agencies are extraordinarily lengthy and specific. The Employee Retirement Income Security Act, under which the IRS and Labor Department jointly regulate private pension plans, runs to more than two hundred pages, and spells out in excrutiating detail what kinds of information are to be gathered by which bureaucrats, when the information is to be collected, and even how often they are to repeat the process. The Environmental Protection Agency administers statutes that fill hundreds of pages in the Federal Code. The Clean Air Act is so specific that it spells out precise pollution-reduction targets and timetables, and leaves the EPA virtually no discretion whatsoever. And these detailed specifications have teeth in them. For the laws establishing the New Regulation typically give nearly everyone an all but unlimited standing to sue the agency in question for any seeming failure to do precisely what the law tells it to do. Citizen groups and other organizations have made liberal use of this opportunity, and the courts have not been notably latitudinarian in their reading of the statutes.

The literature on regulation also says that regulatory agencies are prone to cooptation by the regulated interests, because they are organized by industry. That may be true of the Old Regulation, but it isn't the case with the New. The new regulatory agencies were deliberately organized along functional lines, and their jurisdictions therefore cut across industry boundaries. The EPA, for example, deals with pollution problems created by all industries, and OSHA regulates safety and health conditions for workers in all industries. The Consumer Product Safety Commission controls the safety of virtually every consumer product on the market, and so involves itself in the design and marketing of everything from rag dolls to lawn mowers. The new regulatory agencies are accordingly resistant to cooptation by any single industry. If they are vulnerable to cooptation at all (and they are), it is to cooptation by safety- or environment-oriented groups, not by business organizations.

The social-science literature also paints a picture of a comfortable, cooperative relationship between regulator and regulated. That typically is the case with the old regulatory agencies, whose employees usually do feel responsible for the economic well-being of the industry they have jurisdiction over—often, as with the CAB, because the law explicitly instructs them to. But this is not at all true of most of the newer regulatory programs. They were established to operate as the adversaries of the interests they regulate, and typically it is as adversaries that they administer the law. Not, to be sure, that they have much choice in the matter. The New Regulators for the most part are mandated to pursue their appointed goals more or less singlemindedly, with little or no concern for the cost and consequences of the pursuit. The EPA, for instance, is explicitly forbidden by law to pay attention to cost in setting and enforcing the nation's primary ambient air-quality standards. Similarly, OSHA may not take account of the cost of health regulations, except in the extreme case that they might push a company into bankruptcy.

By and large, the new regulatory agencies are true to the spirit of these laws, and where they are not, suits by environmentalist, labor, or other such groups put them back on the straight and narrow.

The New Iron Triangle

Thus, in the new regulatory agencies, there is no traditional "iron triangle" at work behind the scenes. To the contrary, the New Regulation is controlled by what can only be described as a *new* iron triangle made up of "public interest" groups, the press, and the federal government as a whole (especially the courts and Congress). Whereas the members of the old "iron triangle," at least while it lasted, were responsive mainly to the concerns of business, the members of the new iron triangle are motivated by a concern for health, safety, and the environment—and by a passionate sense of opposition to the members of the old "iron triangle." The new iron triangle is not omnipotent, but today it is in the driver's seat as far as the New Regulation is concerned. It is significant, for example, that the movement for deregulation, which is strongly supported by the members of the new iron triangle, addresses itself only to the Old Regulation; the New Regulation has so far been exempt from its animus, and is likely to remain so.

REGULATION AND THE PUBLIC INTEREST

The social-science literature's lurid overstatement of the power and permanence of the old "iron triangle," and its failure for some ten years now to acknowledge the political and institutional realities of the New Regulation, are not random errors. They are part and parcel of a larger undertaking—that of declaring regulatory programs to be failed acts of public policy. According to the literature, the agencies are so encumbered by special interests that their activities serve no identifiable public interest. Regulators may try to give people the impression they are rendering a public service, but these efforts are a fraud—mere "symbolic politics," in the phrase of one widely footnoted political scientist. The reality, the literature maintains, is that regulation is a rip-off without redeeming social value.

The notion that regulation is the antithesis of proper public policy and that it is impotent to do anything but harm to the common weal is, to me, truly bewildering. It bears no relationship to anything I have observed, and—what is at least as important—it bears no relationship to any intelligible conception of the public interest in relation to private interests.

To be sure, government regulation serves all kinds of private interests. It protects the airlines and truckers from most relevant kinds of competition. It enables well-connected Washington lawyers to make $500,000 a year. It gives small businessmen a degree of protection against the effects of price discrimination. It has created an enormous and growing market for air-pollution-control equipment and the services of workplace-safety consultants, who are doing very nicely these days. It has raised prices in the paper industry by driving out of production the old, marginal paper mills that were the first to cut prices when demand was soft, but were ferocious polluters of the waterways and thus had to be closed down when EPA's standards went into effect.

Regulation has done all these things and many more—but this in itself is not evidence that it does not serve public ends. Yet this is what the political science of regulation suggests— that the public interest and private interests are at war with each other, and that in the nature of things a program serving the one cannot serve the other. On this assumption, the fact that private interests intervene in regulatory affairs or benefit from regulatory policy is taken to signify that public ends are being subverted.

Not only is this notion wrong in general, it is also profoundly misleading as a guide to understanding the reality of any particular program or agency. For it is impossible to contemplate regulation with even a half-open mind and conclude that it is powerless to promote public goals or to advance a conception of the public interest. The point is particularly evident in the case of the New Regulation. That it actually does pursue the goals of health, safety, and a clean environment, even when they collide with private interests, is obvious to even the most casual observer. Already the EPA has required private parties, including some of the nation's biggest and most influential industries, to spend tens of billions of dollars on pollution control. By the mid-1980s it will have required the direct investment of well over a hundred billion dollars, and God only knows how much more in operating expenses, inflation, and other social costs.

This enormous reallocation of national resources required by the New Regulation has already begun to produce many of the desired results. (Whether these are worth what they cost is another question, of course.) Water quality has improved substantially in many areas. Ambient air quality has risen in a number of important respects since the EPA went to work five years ago. The number of deaths attributable to accidental ingestion of aspirin by infants has fallen dramatically since child-proof caps on bottles of aspirin were introduced, first at the suggestion of the FDA and later under the order of the Consumer Product Safety Commission. Auto emissions are now some 90 percent lower than they were before auto pollution became a concern of public policy. To be sure, not all regulatory programs have achieved very much in terms of their ultimate goals. Despite the billions that have been spent on occupational safety and health measures, it appears that the sickness and injury rates of the domestic labor force have not been changed significantly. Yet this seems less a reflection on OSHA's political integrity, which is nothing if not formidable vis-à-vis business organizations, than a consequence of the inherent difficulty of lowering injury rates.

The older regulatory agencies also serve public ends, although these admittedly are harder to discern. Partly this is because their enabling statutes do not lay down any concrete public purposes for the regulators to pursue. And partly it reflects the fact that the most obvious and immediate effect of their programs is simply to transfer wealth from one part of the population to another—from the risk-accepting to the risk-averse in the case of banking regulation, or from certain kinds of shippers to certain categories of truckers in the case of the ICC's regulation of trucking. Yet there is no necessary contradiction between serving public interests and private interests at the same time, and if one is willing to entertain the notion that the Old Regulation might be serving intelligible public ends (as the social scientists of regulation in general are not), it is possible to discover a number of these.

One public purpose clearly advanced by the Old Regulation is that of saving "free enterprise" from big business—i.e., of preserving competition (or at any rate, competitors) to a greater extent than the "natural" dynamics of a free market would allow. The Antitrust Division and Federal Trade Commission do this by restraining monopolies, trusts, and big companies generally. The Robinson-Patman Act does it by trying to curtail the natural advantages of big corporations in purchasing supplies. And the ICC and CAB, among others, do this by "rigging" the trucking and airline industries to permit more companies, and more small companies, to exist than would otherwise be the case.

Another public purpose that has been advanced by the Old Regulation is that of helping to integrate a diverse, localistic, continental population into a single, interdependent, national society. The older agencies have done this in many ways:

1. With the blessing of the FCC and state utility commissions, the Bell system has created an elaborate network of cross-subsidies, one effect of which, it appears, is to lower the price of telephone service to residential customers below its true cost. This encourages private users of

telephones, for example, to speak with, and so to maintain ties with, friends and family, even over long distances.

2. The FCC's informal requirement that a certain minimum of a television broadcaster's air time be devoted to public-affairs programming causes more public-affairs broadcasts, especially documentaries, to be shown than would otherwise be the case. This, in turn, has encouraged citizens to concern themselves with political affairs, and has helped to create a genuinely national politics based on national issues and a national agenda.

3. The CAB's regulation of the airline industry has given airlines an incentive to operate excess capacity on their routes, which, in turn, has caused service levels to be higher than they would be in an unregulated air transportation market. That is, more routes are flown more frequently, and with better equipment, than would otherwise be the case. As a result, air travel is more convenient and attractive, especially for business travelers, if also more expensive. This has helped to increase mobility and to promote national social and economic integration without diminishing the decentralized, localistic structure of American society.

4. More generally, by establishing uniform national standards of safety, security, and the like in such industries as banking, securities exchange, food, and drugs, the Old Regulation has reduced the risks and costs of engaging in anonymous commercial transactions over long distances, and has thereby helped to provide the benefits associated with larger, less fragmented, national markets.

The Old Regulation has also helped to domesticate and legitimate large corporate business. Americans have long been suspicious of big business, whose resources they perceive, not unreasonably, to be vastly disproportionate to those of an individual customer. The regulation of airlines, banks, and local utilities has arguably curbed tendencies toward corporate rapacity, and certainly it has eased consumers' mistrust. That is why public opinion polls show that, in general, the most highly regarded industries in the United States are regulated industries—banks, electric utilities, and airlines, for example. Indeed, these three are among the most highly esteemed of all American institutions of all sorts, whether economic, religious, political, or social.

The Old Regulation has also helped to make America a nation of homeowners. By establishing the savings and loan association as something distinct from a commercial bank, for example, and by giving it special obligations to provide mortgage loans, banking regulation (together, to be sure, with the federal tax code) has lowered the cost of homeownership relative to the alternatives, thus encouraging Americans to be homeowners and suburbanites. One may debate whether this is good or bad, but what cannot be questioned is that banking regulation has advanced a conception of the public interest.

REGULATION AS SOCIAL POLICY

If government regulation of business isn't an interest-group rip-off, what is it? What role does it play and what meaning does it have in the American scheme of things? Obviously, this question goes beyond the scope of any essay (not to mention the state of our knowledge), yet some parts of the answer seem clear enough.

The first point that must be grasped is that, despite all appearances and representations to the contrary, government regulation of business is not primarily an instrument of economic policy. To be sure, it is conventionally spoken of as if it were. Defenders insist that regulation is intended to remedy "market imperfections" and to "internalize externalities," and their opponents counter with stories and studies illustrating the economic absurdities so often committed by regulatory programs. All such arguments, however, are beside the point. If regulation were really founded on a belief in markets, its scope, at least potentially, would be practically unlimited: *all* markets, after all, are significantly flawed. At the same time, government would not be so quick to replace market processes with administrative ones, since no market is by nature completely inoperative or beyond hope of reviving—not even those that we refer to, usually inaccurately, as "natural monopolies."

The real purpose of government regulation is not to correct the deficiencies of markets, but to transcend markets altogether—which is to say, government regulation is not economic policy, but social policy. It is an effort to advance a conception of the public interest apart from, and often opposed to, the outcomes of the marketplace and, indeed, the entire idea of a market economy. (That is why economists of all political views end up being so critical of government regulation, at least as it works out in practice. They think regulatory policy should make sense economically—which, of course, it never quite does.)

The second thing that must be understood about government regulation is that, being social policy, it is a manifestation not of interest-group politics but of class politics. To be sure, interest groups are active in every regulatory arena. But government regulation is more than a narrow matter of "who gets what." It also asserts a set of values, a world view, and policy of this larger sort is never created by mere interest groups, but by classes—groups that possess a distinctive "culture" and relationship to the means of production, and that intend to dominate and define the society, i.e., to rule. The class basis of regulation, incidentally, is one reason why so much regulatory policy is an intellectual scandal, as when it mandates zero pollution of the waterways by 1985 (which is lunacy even as an ideal) or allows the Bell system monopolies (e.g., over the manufacture of telephone receivers) that are not necessary to maintain a network of telephone service. When policy is not just a means to an end, but a symbolic assertion of a class sense of destiny as well, government easily becomes an exercise in gratuitous excess.

THE OLD PROGRESSIVES AND THE NEW CLASS

With these two points understood, it is possible to grasp the central and controlling truth about this entire phenomenon — namely, that the two kinds of government regulation in the United States today represent the social policy of two different classes and embody radically different political philosophies. The Old Regulation, for the most part, is the social policy of that curious class of reformers, professionals, politicians, and businessmen around the turn of the century who blended the "populist" and "Progressive" impulses into a body of political views that eventually transformed a traditional, bourgeois political economy into the mixed corporate order we know today. The New Regulation, by contrast, is the social policy of what is often described these days as the "new class" — also largely professional and managerial, like its turn-of-the-century counterpart, but committed to "humanistic" work in the not-for-profit and public sectors, and generally hostile to the economic accomplishments and political vision of the Progressive era.

The Old Regulation is an expression of a much larger movement in American social history — the effort, which began in earnest around the turn of the century, to create a modern economy that would deliver the enormous economic growth and other social benefits made possible by large-scale, technologically progressive, corporate capitalism without sacrificing the benefits of traditional, bourgeois "small business" — its economic efficiency, its natural legitimacy, and above all its capacity to make the idea of individualism an economic reality. This broader effort was supported by an odd coalition of small businessmen and farmers, liberal economists, reformist politicians, and a new breed of corporate managers, and it gave rise to the corporation, modern transportation and communications, and other institutions as well as the Old Regulation itself.

The policies advocated by this energetic class of social innovators and political reformers pointed in divergent directions. On the one hand, through such statutes as the Sherman and Clayton Acts, they sought to break up excessive concentrations of economic power, and thereby to restore, insofar as possible, market conditions of the sort envisioned in classical economic theory. On the other hand, they also established a long series of cartel-like regulatory commissions explicitly intended to replace market processes with political and administrative ones. In part, the purpose of these commissions was to cushion "small business' against the rigors of the marketplace and the innate strengths of big business. And, as in the cases of the airline and telephone industries, their purpose was also partly to enable big corporate business to provide the social benefits of modern technology faster, or in greater abundance, than the market by itself would allow.

Yet though this class was both for the market and against it, for big corporate business and against it, for small business and also anxious to transcend its limitations, its position did have an underlying coherence: a clear and persistent dedication to basic values of the liberal tradition—science, economic growth, widespread prosperity, the rule of law, the idea of progress, and above all, the primacy of the individual. It was the fate of the members of this class, however, to live at a time when traditional liberal forms were no longer compatible with the fullest possible realization of liberal social ends. The marketplace, for example, still performed many useful functions. Yet with the rise of the big corporation, it seemed less and less effective in providing the social and political benefits inherent in the institution of small business. At the same time, the logic of the market prevented big corporations from realizing to the maximum practical extent the full benefits of modern technology—for instance, universal enjoyment of inexpensive, reliable, and high-quality telephone service. Thus the Old Regulation represented an effort to transcend traditional liberal forms like the free marketplace for the purpose of promoting liberal values.

THE NEW REGULATION AND THE NEW CLASS

The New Regulation could hardly be more different. It is the social policy of the new class—that rapidly growing and increasingly influential part of the upper-middle class that feels itself to be in a more or less adversary posture vis-à-American society, and that tends to make its vocation in the public and not-for-profit sectors. Over the past decade it has come to be represented by a broad constellation of institutions—the "public interest" movement, the national press, various professions (law, epidemiology), government bureaucracies, research institutes on and off campus, the "liberal" wing of the Democratic party, and the like. By means of its regulatory policy, the new class is, among other things, bringing about what Murray Weidenbaum has described as the "second managerial revolution." The first managerial revolution, of course, involved the displacement of the old bourgeois class by the corporate managerial class, and a corresponding shift from purely private economic institutions to quasi-public institutions like the corporation. The second managerial revolution is transferring power from the managerial class to the new class, and from quasi-public institutions to fully public ones—i.e., to the government.

The announced objective of the New Regulation is to promote health, safety, a cleaner environment, and a more open political process. But that is not all the New Regulation is about. For the members of the new class seem less interested in maximizing the overall health and safety of American society than in reducing the health, safety, environmental, and political costs of the modern capitalist order—which is a very different thing indeed, since liberal capitalism has itself brought about, and continues to sustain, large improvements in the health, safety, environment, and political life of the country. These benefits, to be sure, have price tags on them, but working to lower those social costs is not the same as seeking to increase the overall welfare of the society, as the record of the New Regulation itself shows. The now-

infamous Thalidomide Amendments, enacted in 1962 to prevent the introduction of dangerous new drugs, appear to have
delayed the introduction of all kinds of new drugs, safe and
dangerous, to the point where more deaths have been permitted than prevented. Similarly, the efforts of Common Cause
and other "reform" groups have considerably reduced the
influence of traditional interest groups, e.g., labor, trade associations, and the like. But they have not thereby appre-
ciably "opened up" the political process. They have merely
transferred power from those who produce material goods to
those who produce ideological ones—to the intellectuals, policy professionals, journalists, and "reformers," who are arguably much less representative of the American people as a
whole than those whose influence has been curtailed.

Outcomes like these are not accidental. They faithfully reflect the underlying interests and ethos of the new class itself.
With each passing year it becomes clearer that the real
animus of the new class is not so much against business or
technology as against the liberal values served by corporate
capitalism and the benefits these institutions provide to the
broad mass of the American people: economic growth,
widespread prosperity, material satisfactions, a sense of
nationhood, a belief in an open and self-determined future,
and the many options and freedoms these make possible for
ordinary citizens.[2] The real ire of the new class, and the fire-
power of its social policy, are directed, not merely at those in
business who (in Lewis Lapham's marvelous phrase) "go
around making things without permission," but also, and
perhaps especially, at the mass of Americans who go around
doing and enjoying things without permission.

For instance, a cardinal principle of the New Regulation is
that of "internalizing the externalities"—making manufacturers and consumers pay the social costs of modern goods
and services. The idea, as an idea, does have a certain attractive neatness about it, and put into practice it does indeed
cause the environment to get cleaner and products to get

safer. But in practice it also raises the price of the goods and services in question, or decreases their utility. Either way, "internalizing the externalities" is a form of taxation, and taxes always discourage the production and use of the thing taxed. In this sense, the new class, though it marches under the banner of "consumerism," is in fact working against the widespread enjoyment of consumer goods and services that liberal capitalism makes possible.

The hostility of the new class to acts of consumption by consenting adults is paralleled by a vigorous opposition to all institutions that promote consumption—advertising, the corporation, and above all, the Old Regulation. It sees the Old Regulation in much the same light as social scientists do, as representing a kind of theft of the symbols and power of the state by interest groups for selfish purposes. Accordingly, the new class is at the forefront of the movement to deregulate such older regulated industries as trucking, the airlines, banking, and so on, even as it seeks to extend the New Regulation.

CONCLUSION

So it is obvious that government regulation of business raises some crucial issues for American politics and American social science. They are not, however, the issues that predominate in current discussion of this much-discussed subject. To critics associated with the Left and (what is by no means the same thing) the new class, the central issue posed by regulation is one of the integrity of democracy itself in the face of "corporate power" and "interest-group politics." But this, as we have seen, is a wildly misleading definition of the problem. While interest groups do happily graze in these pastures, the overriding truth is that the authority of American government is nowhere more dramatically demonstrated than in the regulatory agencies, which are a veritable cornucopia of public philosophies and social-policy enterprise. Indeed, if regulation raises an issue in this respect, it is the question of the fate of the traditional private sector, which has manifested a worrisome political and moral weakness in defending itself against both managerial and new-class notions about the primacy of bureaucratic, quasi-public, and public institutions.

Nor are the important issues of regulation the ones which figure so prominently in the arguments of economists, conservatives, and deregulators—for example, the question of whether a measure of "economic rationality" can be restored to this sector of public policy through the establishment of market-type mechanisms (effluent charges, for instance) or the infusion of cost-benefit consciousness into regulatory organizations. These, to be sure, are not utterly irrelevant concerns: prodigality with other people's resources is the rule rather than the exception in the regulatory process, and with the explosion of new agencies in recent years, this habit of mind has been exacting a heavy toll on the nation's wealth and growth. Yet outside a narrow range, these concerns seem to beg the question. Efficiency is desirable—but efficiency at what and for whom?

The current debate over regulation is unsatisfactory, it seems to me, for a simple reason. Contrary to what nearly everyone has assumed for decades now, government regulation of business is not a political backwater or public-policy sideshow, an affair of mere interest groups and narrowly economic concerns. To the contrary, it is a direct and consequential expression of the central social and political currents of twentieth-century American life. As such it raises squarely, and in a peculiarly puzzling way, the ultimate issue of American politics: that of the meaning and fate of the idea of liberal democracy. Both the Progressive-managerialist class and the new class have an obvious connection with the liberal tradition, but both also are carriers of ideals and structures that, at the very least, do not sit comfortably with the liberal orthodoxy. The ethos of the Progressive class is mostly a familiar one whose lineage traces directly back to Lockean notions of reason, science, growth, and social harmony. On the other hand, its notions of transcending the rough and tumble of both the marketplace and (to some extent) democratic politics, and its unrelieved materialism, seem more than faintly heretical. The relationship of the new class to liberal values, it seems to me, is a good deal more problematic. In comparison to that of its Progressive-managerialist predecessor, the ethos of the new class, as if by a generational mutation, is by now so systematically statist, so indifferent to the liberal promise of individual autonomy and social abundance, so hostile to the achievements and aspirations of so many liberal institutions, that it strikes me as being more heresy than not.

But whatever one concludes about these questions, liberal values are the issue. And they, of course, are the things that our enormous literature on government regulation ignores above all. In part this is because so much of that literature is so tendentiously allied with the new class cause (writers are not without their own class interests), so anxious to discredit the Old Regulation, and so avid to justify the exercise of more and more state power over private persons and organizations that it literally refuses to acknowledge the realities that impress themselves so forcefully on even a casual observer of the regulatory agencies. And beyond that, there is the fact that modern social science scarcely has the words to describe the ultimate dimensions of government regulation for what they are. To economists, regulation is chiefly a matter of mere pecuniary quantities and the narrow "efficiencies" envisioned by the idea of a market. To political scientists and newsmen, the agencies are for the most part simply a battleground for an ongoing Armageddon between the "interests" and the people. All of which is to say that social science is as much afflicted as every other liberal institution by the one great weakness of modern liberalism: being ''pragmatic'' and distracted by the promise of a progressive future, it has a hard time recognizing its organizing principles for what they are, and an even harder time remaining true to them. That, of course, is the problem of government regulation as well.

IV

Postscript

10

A. LAWRENCE CHICKERING

Regulation: Hopes and Realities

The intellectual case for and against regulation. The older economic regulations and the new social regulations. Efficiency and transition: banking, transportation, energy, health, marketing. Business opposition to deregulation. The importance of gradualism. The public attitude toward business and toward regulation: some unanswered questions.

In the past several years, government regulation of business has come under serious intellectual attack for the first time in this century. Until recently, except for a few recalcitrant economists, the intellectual case for regulation seemed secure. But since the early 1970s the tradition of economic regulation, which began with the Interstate Commerce Act in

1887, has come under increasing intellectual fire from the Left—whose members have joined more traditional economists in concluding that the regulators have been "captured" by the businesses they are supposed to regulate. With this intellectual reinforcement, the idea of deregulation has attained a respectability and public standing it has never had, under presidents representing both political parties.

Despite rising intellectual concern, regulation continues to grow, so that government now influences or controls most major economic decisions in the United States. MacAvoy concludes that the control sector of the American economy has grown from about 7 percent to nearly 30 percent in the past decade, with much of the rest of the economy being influenced in a variety of ways by general regulations on prices, quality, and the environment. The effect of all this on the productivity of our economy is considerable—MacAvoy estimates on the order of one-half percent in lost productivity growth per year.

Some reforms have been enacted, such as elimination of fair-trade laws in a number of states, and hope for deregulation persists in the airline industry, as discussed by Kahn. But significant decontrol has not occurred and is not in prospect.

This book concentrates on the older tradition of economic regulations, managed by the older regulatory agencies (ICC, CAB, and state public utility commissions, among others), which should be distinguished from the newer class of "social regulations" governing health, safety, and the environment. In fact, the latter have emerged in the past half-dozen years under sponsorship of consumer and environmental movements, precisely as the former were falling from intellectual favor.

The book considers issues at several levels. At the first are questions about efficiency: Are particular regulations efficient? Do the benefits exceed the costs? If not, as is often true, what special economic (efficiency) problems arise during a period of transition, as regulation is reduced and competition increased? What political and social factors obstruct reform? And what, if anything, may be done to mitigate them? And finally—apart from issues of efficiency—what does the current state of regulation suggest about the underlying philosophical and social currents which may ultimately determine any given level of regulation in society? This last question is particularly important, both because it is little studied, and because it may hold the ultimate answer about why regulation persists as it does in the face of widespread concern and dissatisfaction.

THE FIVE AREA STUDIES

Since all markets are imperfect, the essential efficiency question about regulation is whether the benefits of correcting particular imperfections by regulation exceed the costs. When is regulation "worth it"? This question runs through the five area studies in the book—on banking, transportation, energy, health, and marketing. The question is supplemented by the transitional problem of how to fashion policies which will increase efficiency without disrupting the financial health of an industry.

Where regulations induce inefficiencies, competition and the market will tend to break them down, as business moves away from the regulated to the unregulated sector. Jacobs discusses this problem in his analysis of deposit-type financial institutions—primarily banks and savings and loan associations, which are losing depositors who are looking for higher interest rates. Smith sees the same phenomenon in recalling how the price control and entitlements program on old oil, following the 1973 oil embargo, had the effect of subsidizing imports from OPEC, thereby increasing our dependence on foreign energy sources. The growth of unregulated airline charter business is a major factor indermining regulation of the airlines, discussed by Kahn; and Zeckhauser and Feldman observe similar responses in health care regulation.

Smith analyzes the recent history of energy regulation, and concludes that in trying to correct past regulatory mistakes, the president's National Energy Plan will create serious inefficiencies in the allocation of energy resources by setting arbitrary energy consumption targets.

In health care, regulations are undermined, as attempts to limit the system in one way (such as length of stay in hospitals) tend to produce compensating responses elsewhere (such as increased admissions). Zeckhauser and Feldman conclude that health care regulation has thus accomplished few of its goals, but has not been as harmful as critics fear. Unfortunately, the authors conclude that neither reforms nor deregulation can solve major problems in this industry, in which most of the traditional conditions for a market are not met.

Holton considers marketing regulations in the same terms: what role should regulation play in producing a socially efficient amount of product information? His analysis stands in marked and interesting contrast to the comments given by discussant Jones, whose preoccupation with maximizing consumer access to information with little regard for cost is characteristic of important elements in the consumer movement. Button, representing Sears Roebuck, points out that providing good product information is good business, but that giving too much information is costly, and lowers its value to consumers. Holton concludes, ironically, that abundance itself is responsible for our greatest information problem: people do not have time to acquire the information to become expert buyers of everything, and rising affluence can only aggravate this problem.

Phillips, in his overview of the problem, reveals the difficulties in seeking optimal regulation and efficiency, and Argyris exposes the practical question of why the costs of regulation so often exceed expectations. His consideration of obstacles to organizational learning applies to both public and private organizations, but the problems are particularly great without the benefit of profit and loss statements to provide ultimate discipline. Zausner's recollections of experiences at the Federal Energy Administration are also of value in comparing regulation's hopes and realities.

POLITICS AND THE ROLE OF BUSINESS

If regulation has produced few successes and many failures, the question arises why reform has been so difficult. It is clear from a number of these chapters that a major reason is the political role of business itself in the regulatory process. *In general*, most businessmen are fiercely opposed to regulation and to all government interference in the economy; but *in particular*, when faced with specific proposals for deregulation, individual businessmen and business organizations often oppose deregulation and reform.

MacAvoy states the basic problem:

The industry representatives respond that the proposals [for deregulation] represent the worst rantings of economists who have not worked in industry and have little evidence or knowledge as to how the system really operates. . . . Regulation is much more complex than it appears, and despite indications of ill-effects, deregulation would be worse.

O'Brien, representing the trucking industry, follows this scenario exactly, even to his criticism of academics, "who deal mainly in theories."

The "capture theory" is a major theme in regulatory literature. As already noted, the idea that industry has taken over the agencies that are supposed to regulate it is probably the single greatest reason why the political Left have turned away from the older regulations. Unfortunately, the ambivalent role of business itself in regulation is still largely undiscussed and undiscussable in organized business circles. The comments by Gilbert and Brinegar, representing banking and energy, throw light on this problem.

In his comment on transportation, Hillman notes that fairness is a significant element of the problem. Despite its inefficiencies, regulation has nevertheless induced significant business investments in reliance on it, and that reliance deserves consideration. This problem suggests the possibility of at least partial compensation as part of transitional strategies for deregulation; the issue is important, both morally and politically.

The problem of opposition by regulated interests to regulatory reform is curious when set next to the conclusion, mentioned earlier, that over time regulation will tend to drive business away from the regulated to the unregulated sectors. If regulated industries do lose out in the long run under regulation, why do they oppose reforms which would increase their ability to compete? The paradox is particularly clear in Jacobs's discussion of banking; he concludes that if present trends continue, banks will be *forced* to support reform.

Gilbert identifies what may be the major problem: uncertainty. People will almost always prefer the known to the unknown, even under adverse circumstances; uncertainty is intolerable, and for industries long accustomed to regulation, the prospect of an unregulated environment offers more uncertainty than most people can tolerate. This problem reemphasizes the importance of the *transition,* and of gradualism—not only on substantive efficiency grounds, but also to encourage industry acquiescence and support for reform. In this light, the extensive discussions of gradual, transitional strategies by Jacobs and Kahn, in considering deregulation of banking and transportation, are particularly important.

The constructive participation of business representatives in this book indicates the extent of opportunities to encourage business cooperation in reasonable plans for deregulation and reform. As Weaver points out, individual industries are not monolithic in their views on regulation, and the "iron triangles" are proving much softer than was previously supposed. But the best approach for enlisting industry cooperation may be education concerning the stake that regulated industries have in reform to maintain their competitive positions.

On the other hand, even if extensive deregulation continues to be impossible, the relentless movement of business away from regulation inevitably weakens the hold of the regulatory apparatus. For this reason, MacAvoy concludes his chapter by encouraging businesses not to hope too much for regulatory reform, but rather to invest their resources and ingenuity in working through regulations—and around them. As an instrument of social control, regulation—at least, of the command type—is manual and therefore crude; the automatic feature of markets explains why regulation so often fails to control them.

REGULATION AS SOCIAL POLICY: SOME UNANSWERED QUESTIONS

The primary focus for most studies of regulation is efficiency, reflecting the dominant interest of economists, who do most of the studies. But efficiency is not the only social value supporting regulation; and the continued growth of regulation in the face of mounting evidence of its inefficiency raises unanswered questions about other, competing values which may be supporting regulation.

Weaver raises this problem in considering regulation as social policy, and his discussion is particularly helpful in distinguishing the social policy underlying the old regulation from that underlying the new. The old regulation, like the old liberalism which promoted it, was committed to material progress and economic growth (i.e., to efficiency), but it was also committed to the competing goal of smallness—to the benefits, as Weaver puts it, "of traditional 'small business'—its . . . natural legitimacy, and above all, its capacity to make the ideal of individualism an economic reality."

The new regulation of health and safety, on the other hand, grew out of the animus against material progress and economic growth which began with the New Left in the later 1960s and became explicit in the environmental and no-growth movements of the 1970s. Thus, unlike the older liberals, the new liberals have become suspicious of efficiency, if not downright hostile to it. This attitude is also expressed in opposition to everything big, both public and private—which are seen as bureaucratic—and support for everything small.

Although their general commitments are very different, the commitment to smallness that binds the old regulation and the new may highlight the competing social value which regulation often serves in preference to efficiency. The issue of smallness recalls the problems of lost community, and of declining social trust that depends on close personal relationships and contact.

These issues are particularly interesting in light of survey data which consistently show great differences in public attitudes toward regulation in general and regulation in particular. In general, the American people are overwhelmingly pro-capitalist and anti-regulation; but their attitudes toward small business are consistently higher than those toward big business, and their attitudes toward regulation of particular industries seem to be closely related to the degree of social contact between the business and individual consumers. Thus, the industries showing lowest consumer satisfaction and highest support for increased regulation are oil, electric power, and automobile manufacturing; while those with best customer satisfaction and lowest support for regulation are those which maximize contact—banks, supermarkets, and retail department stores.

These results suggest that when social contact (smallness) and efficiency conflict, people will tend to give up some (and, perhaps, much) efficiency for contact, even though it makes them poorer. The implications of this are very great, especially for those in business and elsewhere who are concerned that the growth of regulation may lead to bureaucratic totalitarianism. In this light, those concerned about regulation would do well to go beyond consideration of abstract property rights and consider *what forms of private property* stir greatest passions in their defense, as well as what means of communication and social interaction will maximize social contact.

The problem is within the power of individual businesses to control. How they respond may determine the future growth of regulation.

NOTES

3. Alfred E. Kahn: "Deregulation of Air Transportation—Getting from Here to There"

1. I refer to the fact that the continued *availability* of this service is itself economically valuable, entirely apart from the extent to which it is actually used. The availability of the scheduled service option is in the nature of a public good, which may not be supplied in economically optimal quantities in a freely competitive market. Some eleven years ago, in an article called "The Tyranny of Small Decisions," I observed that major social decisions about which goods and services will continue to be provided are based on the results of a whole series of individual purchases. When I decide whether to fly on a charter or a scheduled flight—or when, years ago, I decided to take an airplane out of Ithaca rather than the night train—I make that decision by comparing the respective costs and benefits of the one versus the other at that particular time, but without considering the possibility that a series of individual decisions by me and most other people to choose the first can result in a loss of the opportunity to choose the second. It was just such a series of decisions to take the airplane, car, and bus out of Ithaca that resulted in the disappearance of the night train. Had I been asked, however, I would have responded that the continued *availability* of that night train was something of value to me; yet the value of preserving that option was never expressed in the marketplace.

The same may be true about scheduled airline service: if there is enough leakage of traffic—whether to charters, to Super-Saver, or to Budget fare—on a purely price basis, is there a danger that we may have to suffer a decline in the availability of the scheduled option, to our regret?

My tentative resolution of this concern is that we should be receptive to proposals by the scheduled airlines to compete with supplementals by offering special combinations of services and fares designed to enhance the competitive viability of the scheduled service itself, notably by filling empty seats on scheduled flights.

This general prescription raises extremely interesting and difficult questions about the proper conditions for effective competition between scheduled carriers on the one hand and charters—specifically, tour operators and supplementals—on the other, questions about what kinds of cost criteria, if any, to apply to these special fares; about the proper definition and measurement of short-run and long-run marginal cost; about the proper limits of price discrimination; about defining and enforcing prescriptions against predation; and, more generally, about how to preserve effective competition in the marketplace as carriers are permitted increasing freedom to price. These constitute the most interesting problems now facing us.

2. The actual marginal cost depends upon whether the number of empty seats available for standbys exceeds the demand at a zero price, in which case the marginal cost is zero, apart from customer costs; if the number is less than the quantity demanded, the true marginal cost is the value of the flight to the customer who would have submitted the highest unsuccessful bid had the seats been auctioned off.

3. The same observation applies to the short-run marginal oportunity cost of discount traffic, defined as the value of the seats to the marginal regular fare-paying customers displaced. The lower the discount fare, the lower the point on the rising short-run marginal opportunity cost function (rising, because the more seats sold at low fares the greater the probability of sacrificed sales at regular fares) at which the carrier will reach an equilibrium between the value of taking on an additional discount customer and the opportunity cost—i.e., the mean expected value of the seat to the would-be regular fare-paying customer displaced. If the discount fare were $50 rather than $100 (above customer costs), obviously the carrier would have an incentive to offer additional seats at that price only up to the point at which the probability of its having to deny a seat to a $200 regular fare-paying customer was 0.25, rather than the 0.5 in our previous example; a discount fare of $50 thus ensures a marginal social opportunity cost of $50.

4. V. Kerry Smith: "Regulating Energy: Indicative Planning or Creeping Nationalization?"

1. There appears to be a somewhat similar conviction in some of the earlier regulatory legislation. The next two sections discuss the motives for regulation, and how they relate to special features of an exhaustible resource's allocation through private markets.

2. Erickson and Spann (1974) have described our energy problems as a "policy-induced" crisis.

3. This comment refers to some confusion introduced in Schultze's (1977) comparison of incentive versus command-and-control approaches to government intervention. At various points in this discussion he seems to imply that the use of a price as an instrument to effect some policy goal assures the same efficiency results as the existence of a market. This view is simply not correct. The existence of a price does not imply that the optimal resource allocation conditions which are present with perfect markets will be maintained. Russell (1977) has recently made a related point in his discussion of effluent-charged systems.

4. The Organization of Arab Petroleum Exporting Countries (OAPEC) is a subset of the Organization of Petroleum Exporting Countries (OPEC). The specific definitions are given as follows:

OPEC member nations—Venezuela, Iran, Iraq, Kuwait, Qatar, Saudi Arabia, Algeria, Libya, Nigeria, Indonesia, Ecuador, Gabon, United Arab Emirates.

OAPEC member nations—Egypt, Iraq, Kuwait, Qatar, Saudi Arabia, Algeria, Libya, United Arab Emirates.

5. The domestic demand for crude oil increased by 75 percent over the period 1963 to 1976 and is expected to increase, without constraints on demand, at an annual rate of about 4 percent, reaching a 25-million barrel per day consumption rate in 1985.

6. Russell (1977:319) reports producer prices in constant 1976 dollars for energy resources as follows:

Year	Natural Gas[a]	Domestic Crude Oil[b]
1950	14.5	5.62
1955	21.7	5.77
1960	27.0	5.55
1965	29.5	5.42
1970	28.3	5.26
1975	46.5	8.02
1976	58.0	8.18

[a]Cents per thousand cubic feet at wellhead.
[b]Dollars per barrel at wellhead.

7. Schultze (1977:90) has argued that:

> the economic and social forces that flow from growth and affluence will continue to throw up problems and attitudes that call for intervention of a very complex order. . . . We cannot afford to go on imposing command-and-control solutions over an ever-widening sphere of social and economic activity.

It is clear that we have expanded the range of issues which require intervention. Macro efficiency as an objective of regulatory programs is simply one example.

In addition, the avenues for intervention have expanded, in part as a result of the issues raised by Schultze, but also due to a growing recognition of the side effects of our private production and consumption decisions. Externalities have gone from bucolic examples to central concerns of many regulatory programs.

8. This description is necessarily brief. Further elaboration can be found in Phillips (1975*a, b*), Schultze (1977).

9. See Schultze (1977:68-72) and Baumol (1977) for further discussion.

10. Consideration of the three Ps of regulation also helps to classify the existing models of regulatory behavior. Most focus on *practice*. Stigler's (1975) work, which implicitly calls for viewing regulation within a demand and supply framework, as well as Peltzman's (1976) extensions to it, can be considered examples of this focus on practice.

11. Schultze (1977:83) observed that:

> two sets of factors seem to be responsible for the output-oriented nature of most social intervention. First, our political traditions place a high premium on preventing the government itself from imposing direct harm on individuals. We have typically accomplished this objective by carefully specifying the rights and duties of both government and individuals, and providing liberal opportunities for individual adjudicatory procedures. . . . Second, the roundabout and indirect process by which the price system determines outcomes is not well understood, and on the surface seems much less certain of achieving results than does the direct specification of outputs.

12. Freeman (1977:16) has discussed regulation in relationship to environmental quality programs and notes:

> The regulatory process consists of two specific tasks. The first is the legislative or rule making task which involves the translation of general criteria and objec-

tives into specific rules, standards and directives. The second task is the implementation and enforcement of these rules and standards. The ways in which both of these tasks are performed affect the economic welfare of the parties whose actions are being regulated; they help to determine the magnitude and distribution of the costs and benefits of regulation.

13. Smith and Krutilla (1978) have offered an additional reason for questioning the outcomes of a private market in allocating an exhaustible resource. It may be that the production and consumption processes involving such resources utilize the services of common property resources, and there is no reflection of these effects in the market transactions for the exhaustible resource. This view would imply that externalities were present, and would therefore provide a rationale for intervention.

14. The extraction patterns of a competitive and a monopolistic firm will be identical if the market demand function is isoelastic. See Stiglitz (1976) and Kamien and Schwartz (1977) for discussion of this case.

15. For discussion of alternative views, see Rice (1976:chapter 2), Davidson (1963), and Davidson, Falk, and Lee (1974).

16. Davidson, Falk, and Lee (1974:414-15) have observed the following qualifications on the efficiency of market allocations of exhaustible resources:

The market price system can provide guidance on an optimal resource allocation over time only under the following conditions:

1. Well-organized forward markets exist *for each date* in the future.
2. Consumers know *with actuarial certainty* all their needs of energy resources *at each date*.
3. Consumers are able and willing to exercise all these future demands by currently entering into forward contracts *for each date*.
4. Entrepreneurs know *with actuarial certainty* the costs of production associated with production flows *for each date*.
5. Sellers can choose between an immediate contract at today's market price and a forward contract at the market price associated with any future delivery date. . . .
6. Entrepreneurs know *with actuarial certainty* the course of future interest rates.
7. The social rate of discount equals the rate at which entrepreneurs discount future earnings and costs.
8. *No false trading* occurs—that is, no production or exchange ever takes place at nonequilibrium prices.

17. For further discussion, see Heal (1975), Stiglitz (1978), and Nordhaus (1973).

18. His definition of indicative planning contrasts with that of Stiglitz, and is closer to what is described in Meade (1972).

19. Davidson (1963) has defined these effects as the negative marginal user costs associated with the rule of capture.

20. Page (1977:9) is a notable exception. He argues that:

Markets can be expected to allocate resources more or less efficiently relative to a given distribution of wealth or market power (a hypothetical ideal market would actually achieve efficiency). But markets cannot be expected to solve the problem of what is a fair or equitable distribution of wealth, either among different people at a point in time (intratemporally) or among different generations (intertemporally).

21. For further discussion, see Smith and Krutilla (1978).

22. Intratemporal equity does seem an objective of much of the post-1973 policy. See Montgomery (1977) for further discussion.

23. These factors may not be as crucial for the efficiency of private market allocations of other resources.

24. Nordhaus (1973) did *not* proceed beyond the level of the principles of social intervention. He did not consider how indicative planning might work.

25. See Davidson (1963:96–97) for further discussion of its effects.

26. This conclusion assumes that nonmarket allocation schemes will not limit the availability of the energy resources.

27. These estimates compare with $33.7 million and $41.0 million in 1975 and 1976 respectively. See Zarb and MacAvoy (1976:143).

28. This summary is based on the House version of the legislation underlying the NEP.

29. The rebate programs for insulation, gas guzzler automobiles, and the gasoline tax are designed to impact the private household component of the demand.

30. The process of giving exceptions under existing regulatory actions of FEA has been one of the most suspect aspects of its policies. The Presidential Task Force on Reform of FEA Reglations noted that (Zarb and MacAvoy 1976:239): "the general evaluation of the exceptions process from one which grants truly 'exceptional' relief toward one rule of general application to large numbers of individuals has given rise to serious problems." Among them are the difficulties associated with using the exception process to make general rules. This can lead to vested interests in the regulatory process, and change policy by incremental decisions without conscious agency-level decisions.

Despite these conclusions concerning the current regulatory framework, the NEP provides a similar mechanism for exemption from taxes to industrial users of oil and gas.

The first Senate bill to be passed from the NEP package changes the use of exemptions in the mandatory conversion to coal program. It requires that electric power plants using gas convert by 1990, but does not require conversion of oil-burning plants. Moreover, the size threshold of the boilers of industrial customers mandated for conversion has been increased. Industrial conversion is specified to be mandated only on a case-by-case basis (*Washington Post,* 9 September 1977).

While these provisions serve to reduce the role of the exemption process, they simply replace it with nearly as complex command-and-control forms of regulation.

31. See Congressional Budget Office (1977) and Russell (1977*a, b, c*).

32. If the objectives of specified consumption levels, minimal macro disruption, and equity in access to energy are accepted uncritically, then it is not clear that a value-rationing scheme would not be better than these systems. This system would allocate equal ration points for a scarce factor-imported oil to producers, and equal ration points to consumers of petroleum products. Each group would be permitted to trade separately in its own type of coupons, but producer and consumer coupon exchanges would not be permitted. Money prices could be freely set in markets. This would assure equality of the rates of exchange of resources among producers and among consumers, separately. While there would be a divergence between the marginal rate of substitution in consumption from the rate of transformation, the inefficiency may well be small. See Tobin (1952:545–48) for more details.

Moreover, when existing regulatory programs are evaluated in a framework that reflects their "disequilibrium" character (see Malinvaud [1976]), it is not clear that the transition would *not* be a Pareto improvement.

5. Penny Hollander Feldman and Richard J. Zeckhauser: "Sober Thoughts on Health-Care Regulation"

1. We do not argue that any absolute measure of inefficiency motivated regulatory interventions. It is almost impossible to determine what $1,000 of health resources should buy. What we can determine is that they are not buying nearly as much as they were five years ago or in some other location. Thus, one of the most powerful arguments for limiting health expenditures is the observation that health outcomes do not vary perceptibly across geographic areas that are equivalent, except that one consumes dramatically more medical resources than the other. Dramatic variations in health-care resources use, apparently unrelated to differential health needs, have been documented by Wennberg and Gittelsohn (1973:1102–8).

2. This would not explain, however, insurance against relatively low levels of expenditures, say, for normal quantities of doctors' visits. Part of the explanation lies in the government's subsidy of health insurance premiums. (Expenditures are only deductible over 3 percent of income.) Part undoubtedly relates to consumer misunderstanding and error. Many motorists, it is alleged, have collision policies with deductibles that are far too modest.

3. Society's prohibition of narcotics, certain dangerous products despite ample warning, and suicide, represent other ways that consumer sovereignty is overridden in a manner consistent with the attitude that an individual's health (as opposed, say, to his recreation) is a concern for society as a whole.

4. Much of the discussion in this section reflects the analysis of Feldman and Roberts (1978).

5. See, for example, the debate on coronary artery by-pass surgery in Braunwald (1977) and "Special Correspondence" (1977).

6. Richard H. Holton: "Advancing the Backward Art of Spending Money"

1. The most recent large-scale survey which sheds some light on this question appears to be the one conducted by Louis Harris and Associates and the Marketing Science Institute, commissioned by Sentry Insurance, undated but published in 1977, and based on interviews conducted during the period November 1976 through February 1977 (see Sentry Insurance [1977]). The Harris poll shows the responses for the total public and also for groups of leaders, two of which are "consumer activist" and "senior business manager."

2. A recent survey of over 3,400 business executives reveals that businessmen consider the second most important reason for the growth of consumerism to be "consumers feeling a growing gap between product performance and marketing claims" (Greyser and Diamond 1976:5). Interestingly, 48 percent of the respondents agreed (either "strongly" or "somewhat") with the statement that "In general, advertisements do not present a true picture of the product advertised."

3. This assumes that the retailer has access to all brands, i.e., that none are foreclosed to him because other retailers in the area have an exclusive geographic franchise for the brand.

4. Porter (1976), in his excellent study, emphasizes that the role of the retailer in the information process differs significantly as one moves across the spectrum from convenience goods to nonconvenience or shopping goods. So we would expect these different information sources to be used to differing degrees among the many goods the consumer buys.

5. For a discussion of the problems of setting safe design standards for what might seem to the uninitiated to be a simple product, namely, ladders, see "Setting Safety Rules for Products Proves Costly and Complicated," *Wall Street Journal,* 11 August 1977, p. 1.

6. Of the 175 cases, 25 percent were competitors' complaints, 11 percent were consumer challenges, 10 percent were referrals from local Better Business Bureaus, 52 percent resulted from NAD monitoring, and 2 percent were from miscellaneous sources.

7. Standardization of terminology is not to be confused with standardizing the product. It is one thing for government regulators to say that the manufacturer will produce only to certain specifications; it is far less constraining to tell the manufacturer that he can produce to whatever specifications he wants, but that he must adhere to certain definitions when using particular terms to describe the product or its performance.

8. See "Product Label Plan Forging Ahead Despite Protests from Appliance Area," *Advertising Age,* 6 June 1977, p. 18.

7. Almarin Phillips: "Regulation and Its Alternatives"

1. For similar and more recent lives like these, see Stigler and Friedland (1962); Posner (1974); Jordan (1972).

2. Fifteen years later, in Adams and Gray (1955: chapter 3, esp. pp. 58-72), the "new and socially superior institution" proposed for regulating reform was the force of competitive markets.

3. See, for example, Phillips (1975); MacAvoy and Pindyck (1973); Stigler and Friedland (1962); Posner (1974); Jordan (1972). A new journal, *Regulation,* published by the American Enterprise Institute, and publications by that institute, frequently argue the case for deregulation.

4. As this is written, the CAB is experimenting with new and more competitive approaches to airline regulation, the ICC has relaxed a small set of rail freight rates to promote intermodal competition, and the deregulation of natural gas is receiving its annual congressional consideration.

5. The dissent of Justice Brandeis in *New State Ice Co. v. Liebmann,* 285 U.S. 262 (1932), became the law with Justice Roberts's majority decision in *Nebbia v. New York,* 291 U.S. 502 (1934). Legislatures can almost always find some constitutional justification for regulation, whether or not there are scale economies.

6. See *U.S. v. Terminal Railroad Association of St. Louis,* 224 U.S. 810 (1912), and *Gamco, Inc., v. Providence Fruit and Produce Building,* 194 F. 2d 484 (1952). The difficulties of shared facilities are currently appearing in the context of electronic funds-transfer system. See National Commission on Electronic Fund Transfers (1977).

7. The term "fly-by-night operators" comes from this industry. In its early history, Delta Airlines moved back and forth from cropdusting to passenger and mail service. Interestingly, it was forced back to cropdusting when its commercial opera-

tions were effectively banned by exclusion from Post Office contracts.

8. The story of MCI and its rates, relative to those of AT&T, is pertinent.

9. The FCC has historically regulated to see that signals are available to low density population areas. This interest is manifested in recent rules concerning local origination of programs to the exclusion of network-originated programs. Regulators of telephone and electricity have also used cross-subsidization for low density service.

10. In the regulation of banks and bank holding companies, firms engaged principally in computer services and travel agents have sought and received restrictions on the performance of the services by banks.

11. This is a special case where owners of adjacent properties can recover from oil pools at long-run costs much lower than those of the original successful driller who bears the exploration costs.

12. The short-run marginal cost of an unemployed miner to use a pick and shovel to dig in an unused shaft or open strip is very low relative to long-run average costs. This is the story behind *United Mine Workers v. Pennington*, 381 U.S. 657 (1965), and, less directly, *Tampa Electric v. Nashville Coal Co.*, 365 U.S. 320 (1961). On this, see Williamson (1968).

13. In theory, this is the problem of separability.

14. The idea of using price discrimination to yield gross revenues at least equal to total costs dates back at least to Hadley (1885).

15. Unless one makes bold assumptions about compensated and uncompensated demand curves being identical, the result is not the competitive output in any case. Since so much has been written about regulatory bias and the A-J effect, this additional problem of optimal resources reallocation with rate of return regulation is omitted here.

16. It has been shown that a two-part tariff can also be used to extract revenues equal to the perfect price discrimination case; see Oi (1971). Thus the requirement of a fair return can sometimes be met by two-part tariffs, even when demand and cost functions run in terms of only one output variable.

17. It is ironic that, just at the time many regulators have been persuaded to the $P = MC$ rule, theory has shown it to apply in only a very special and restrictive case.

18. Just these reflections make a proposal to auction spectrum space more complicated than it appears.

9. Paul H. Weaver: "Regulation, Social Policy, and Class Conflict"

1. Each of these three theories proposes a different way to explain why regulatory behavior benefits special interests rather than the public. Invoking a military metaphor, Huntington (1952) posits an out-and-out political "capture" of the agency by the regulated industry. Bernstein (1955), preferring a Darwinian image, suggests that agencies begin by advancing the public interest but, through a natural evolutionary process, slowly lose their sense of mission and eventually lapse into serving special interests. Writing on the basis of historical research—and from very different political viewpoints—Kolko (1963) and others argue that the regulatory agencies have not in general lapsed from their proper mission, but were always intended to serve special interests. The FDA, Kolko maintains, was established at the behest of

big meat packers who wanted to eliminate price competition from small meat packers. According to other accounts, the ICC was created at the urging of some railroads anxious for government help to maintain the faltering railroad cartel in the late nineteenth century.

2. To some readers, perhaps, this use of the word "liberal" will seem unfamiliar, even far-fetched; Americans today are accustomed to attaching that honorable term to other sorts of values and institutions, e.g., redistributing wealth. Yet at least from the time of Locke himself, the idea of economic growth and individual prosperity has been as central to liberal political thought as the more widely recognized notions of individual rights, rule of law, and limited government. And the presence of this "materialist" aspect of the liberal tradition was no mere "historical accident." Economic growth, widespread enjoyment of material satisfactions, technological development, and other such phenomena are, in fact, necessary elements of the entire liberal vision of man and society and are inextricably interwoven with its other, more directly political and juridical features. Whosoever says "human rights" or "constitutional government" or "science" must also say "economic growth"—or, in effect, speak a kind of theoretical and practical nonsense, at least from the liberal viewpoint.

REFERENCES

Adams, Walter, and Gray, Horace. 1955. *Monopoly in America: The Government as Promoter*. New York: Macmillan.

Altman, Stuart H., and Eichenholz, Joseph 1976 "Inflation in the Health Industry—Causes and Cures." In *Health: A Victim or Cause of Inflation?*, ed. Michael Zubkoff. New York: Prodist.

Argyris, Chris. 1974. *Behind the Front Page*. San Francisco: Jossey-Bass.

———. 1976. *Increasing Leadership Effectiveness*. New York: Wiley-Interscience.

———, and Schön, Donald. 1977. *Organizational Learning*. Reading, Mass.: Addison-Wesley.

———, and Schön, Donald. 1974. *Theory in Practice*. San Francisco: Jossey-Bass.

Bardach, Eugene. 1977. *The Implementation Game: What Happens after a Bill Becomes a Law*. Boston: MIT Press.

Baumol, W. J. 1977. "Quasi-Optimality: The Welfare Price of a Nondiscriminatory Price System." In *Pricing in Regulated Industries: Theory and Application*, ed. John T. Wenders. Denver, Col.: Mountain States Telephone and Telegraph Company.

———. 1977. "Theory of Equity in Pricing for Resource Conservation." Presented to Conference on Natural Resource Pricing, Trail Lake, Wyoming (August).

———, and Bradford, D. 1970. "Optimal Departures from Marginal Cost Pricing." *American Economic Review* 60 (June).

Bernstein, Marver H. 1955. *Regulating Business by Independent Commission*. Princeton, N.J.: Princeton University Press.

Berry, Ralph E., Jr. 1976. "Prospective Rate Reimbursement and Cost Containment: Formula Reimbursement in New York." *Inquiry* 13 (September).

Bonner, Paul. 1976. "On-Site Utilization Review: An Evaluation of the Impact of Utilization Patterns and Expenditures." Doctoral dissertation, Harvard School of Public Health (February).

Braunwald, Eugene. 1977. "Coronary-Artery Surgery at the Crossroads." *New England Journal of Medicine* (22 September).

Breger, S. G., and MacAvoy, P. W. 1974. *Energy Regulation by the Federal Power Commission*. Washington, D.C.: The Brookings Institution.

Britton, Charles R. 1975. "Certificate of Need Legislation in Health Care Delivery." M.Sc. thesis, Sloan School of Management, Massachusetts Institute of Technology (May).

Brook, Robert, and Williams, Kathleen. 1976. *An Evaluation of New Mexico Peer Review*. Santa Monica, Ca.: The Rand Corporation.

Coase, R. H. 1966. "Externalities." *Journal of Law and Economics* 9 (October).

Cohodes, Donald R. 1976 (unpublished). "Certificate of Need Controls and Hospitals: An Outcome Assessment." Harvard School of Public Health (May).

Congressional Budget Office. 1977. *President Carter's Energy Proposals: A Perspective*. Staff Working Paper, 2d ed. Washington, D.C.: U.S. Government Printing Office (June).

Correia, Eddie. 1975. "Public Certification of Need for Health Facilities." *American Journal of Public Health* 65, 3 (March).

Davidson, P. 1963. "Public Policy Problems of the Domestic Crude Oil Industry." *American Economic Review* 53 (March).

————; Falk, L. H.; and Lee, H. 1974. "Oil: Its Time Allocation and Project Indendence." *Brookings Papers on Economic Activity,* no. 2. Washington, D.C.: The Brookings Institution.

Demsetz, H. 1968. "Why Regulate Utilities?" *Journal of Law and Economics* 11 (April).

Elmore, Richard F. 1977 (mimeographed). "Organizational Models of Social Program Implementation." Seattle, Wn.: Institute of Governmental Research, University of Washington.

Erickson, E. W., and Spann, R. M. 1974. "The U.S. Petroleum Industry." In *The Energy Question: An International Failure of Policy,* ed. E. W. Erickson and L. Waverman. Toronto, Canada: University of Toronto.

Erickson, E. W., and Waverman, L., eds. 1974. *The Energy Question: An International Failure of Policy*. Toronto, Canada: University of Toronto.

Executive Office of the President. 1977. *The National Energy Plan*. Washington, D.C.: U.S. Government Printing Office (29 April).

Feldman, Penny, and Roberts, Marc. 1978 (unpublished). "Implementing Health Care Regulation." Harvard School of Public Health (January).

Freeman, A. M., III. 1977. "Environmental Management as a Regulatory Process." Discussion Paper D-4. Washington, D.C.: Resources for the Future (January).

Friendly, H. J. 1962. *The Federal Administrative Agencies: The Need for Better Definitions of Standards*. Cambridge, Mass.: Harvard University Press.

Fuchs, Victor. 1974. *Who Shall Live*. New York: Basic Books.

Gibson, Robert M., and Mueller, Marjorie Smith. 1977. "National Health Expenditures, Fiscal Year 1976." *Social Security Bulletin* (April).

Gray, Horace M. 1940. "The Passing of the Public Utility Concept." *Journal of Land and Public Utility Economics* 16 (February).

Greyser, Stephen A., and Diamond, Steven. 1976. "Consumerism and Advertising: A U.S. Management Perspective." *Advertising Quarterly* (Spring).

Hadley, A. T. 1885. *Railroad Transportation: Its History and Its Laws.* New York: Putnam.

Heal, G. 1975. "Economic Aspects of Natural Resource Depletion." In *The Economics of Natural Resource Depletion,* ed. D. W. Pearce. New York: John Wiley.

Hellinger, Fred J. 1976. "Prospective Reimbursement through Budget Review: New Jersey, Rhode Island and Western Pennsylvania." *Inquiry* 13 (September).

HEW. 1976. *Papers on the National Health Guidelines for Setting Health Goals and Standards.* Washington, D.C.: U.S. Department of Health, Education and Welfare (September).

Hitch, Charles J. 1977. "Footnotes to the Future." *Journal of Marketing* 41, 2 (April).

Hoover, Edgar M., Jr., and Dean, Joel. 1949. *Readings in the Social Control of Industry.* Selection Committee for the American Economic Association. Philadelphia: Blakiston Company.

Huntington, Samuel P. 1952. "The Marasmus of the ICC: The Commission, the Railroads, and the Public Interest." *Yale Law Journal* (April).

Institute of Medicine. 1976. *Assessing Quality in Health Care: An Evaluation.* Washington, D.C.: National Academy of Sciences (November).

Jordan, W. A. 1972. "Producer Protection, Prior Market Structure and the Effects of Government Regulation." *Journal of Law and Economics* 15 (April).

Kamien, M. I., and Schwartz, N. L. 1977. "A Note on Resource Usage and Market Structure." *Journal of Economic Theory* 15 (August).

Kolins, Maura, and Baugh, David K. 1976(unpublished). "An Evaluation of Medicare Concurrent Utilization Review Project: The Sacramento Certified Hospital Admission Program." Washington, D.C.: The Social Security Administration.

Kolko, Gabriel. 1963. *The Triumph of Conservatism.* Glencoe, Ill.: Free Press of Glencoe.

Lave, Judith R., and Leinhardt, Samuel. 1976. "An Evaluation of a Hospital Stay Regulatory Mechanism." *American Journal of Public Health* (October).

Lewin and Associates, Inc. 1975. *An Analysis of State and Regional Health Regulations.* Washington, D.C. (February).

Lipsky, Michael, and Hawley, Willis, eds. 1976. "Toward a Theory of Street-Level Bureaucracy." In *Theoretical Perspectives in Urban Politics.* New York: Prentice-Hall.

MacAvoy, P. W. 1970. *Crisis of the Commissions.* New York: Norton.

———. 1965. *The Economic Effects of Regulation.* Cambridge, Mass.: Massachusetts Institute of Technology.

———, and Pindyck, R. S. 1973. "Alternative Regulating Policies for

Dealing with the Natural Gas Shortage." *Bell Journal of Economics* 4 (Autumn).

Malinvaud, E. 1976. *The Theory of Unemployment Reconsidered.* Yrjo Jahnsson Lectures. University of Helsinki (January).

Mead, W. J. 1977. "An Economic Appraisal of President Carter's Energy Program." *Science* 197 (22 July).

Meade, J. E. 1972. *The Controlled Economy.* Albany, N.Y.: State University of New York Press.

Mitchell, Wesley Claire. 1912. "The Backward Art of Spending Money." *American Economic Review* 2 (March).

Montgomery, W. D. 1977. "A Case Study of Regulatory Programs of the Federal Energy Administration." Social Science Working Paper, no. 147. Pasadena, Ca.: California Institute of Technology (January).

Motta, Roberto Paulo. 1976. "The Incompatibility of Good Planning and Bad Management: Implementation Problems in Development Administration." Conference, Latin American Public Sector, University of Texas (April).

National Commission on Electronic Fund Transfers. 1977. *EFT in the United States: Report by the National Commission on Electronic Fund Transfers.* Washington, D.C.: U.S. Government Printing Office.

Noll, R. 1971. *Reforming Regulation.* Washington, D.C.: The Brookings Institution.

Nordhaus, W. D. 1973. "The Allocation of Energy Resources." *Brookings Papers on Economic Activity,* no. 3. Washington, D.C.: The Brookings Institution.

————. 1977. "Economic Growth and Climate: The Carbon Dioxide Problem." *American Economic Review, Proceedings* 67 (February).

Oi, W. 1971. "A Disneyland Dilemma: Two-Part Tariffs for a Mickey Mouse Monopoly." *Quarterly Journal of Economics* 87 (February).

Page, T. 1977. *Conservation and Economic Efficiency: An Approach to Materials Policy.* Baltimore, Md.: Johns Hopkins University.

Pearce, D. W., ed. 1975. *The Economics of Natural Resource Depletion.* New York: John Wiley.

Pechman, J. A., ed. 1977. *Setting National Priorities: The 1978 Budget.* Washington, D.C.: The Brookings Institution.

Peltzman, S. 1976. "Toward a More General Theory of Regulation." *Journal of Law and Economics* (August).

Phillips, A. 1977. "Additional Notes on a Behavioral Theory of Regulation." In *Pricing in Regulated Industries: Theory and Application,* ed. J. T. Wenders. Denver, Col.: Mountain States Telephone and Telegraph Company.

————. 1975a. "Introduction." In *Promoting Competition in Regulated Markets,* ed. A. Phillips. Washington, D.C.: The Brookings Institution.

————, ed. 1975b. *Promoting Competition in Regulated Markets.* Washington, D.C.: The Brookings Institution.

Pitofsky, R. 1977. "Beyond Nader: Consumer Protection and the Regulation of Advertising." *Harvard Law Review* (February).

Porter, Michael E. 1976. *Interbrand Choice, Strategy, and Bilateral Market Power.* Cambridge, Mass.: Harvard University Press.

Posner, R. A. 1974. "Theories of Economic Regulation." *Bell Journal of Economics* 5 (Autumn).

"Product Label Plan Forging Ahead Despite Protests from Appliance Area." 1977. *Advertising Age,* 6 June.

Rice, P. 1976. "An Econometric Model of the Petroleum Industry." Doctoral dissertation, University of New York at Binghampton.

———, and Smith, V. K. 1978. "An Econometric Model of the Petroleum Industry." *Journal of Econometrics* (forthcoming).

Russell, C. S. 1977. "The Character of Effluent Charge Systems." Paper (June). Washington, D.C.: Resources for the Future.

Russell, M. 1977a. "Energy." In *Setting National Priorities: The 1978 Budget,* ed. J. A. Pechman. Washington, D.C.: The Brookings Institution.

———. 1977c. "The High Cost of Low Prices." Paper (16 May).

———. 1977b. "Testimony before the Committee on the Budget" (29 June).

Salkever, David S., and Bice, Tom W. 1976a. "The Impact of Certificate of Need Controls on Hospital Investment." *Health and Society* 54.

———. 1976b. *Impact of State Certificate of Need Laws on Health Care Costs and Utilization.* Final Report on Contract HRA 106–74–57, National Center for Health Services Research. Washington, D.C.: U.S. Department of Health, Education and Welfare.

Schultze, C. L. 1977. *The Public Use of Private Interest.* Washington, D.C.: The Brookings Institution.

Sentry Insurance. 1977. "Consumerism at the Crossroads." Louis Harris and Associates-Marketing Science Institute. In-house report.

"Setting Safety Rules for Products Proves Costly and Complicated." 1977. *Wall Street Journal,* 11 August.

Smith, V. K., ed. 1978. *Scarcity and Growth Reconsidered.* Forthcoming.

———, and Krutilla, J. V. 1978. "The Economics of Natural Resource Scarcity: An Interpretive Introduction." In *Scarcity and Growth Reconsidered,* ed. V. K. Smith. Forthcoming.

"Special Correspondence: A Debate on Coronary By-pass." *New England Journal of Medicine* (29 December).

Stigler, George J. 1975. *The Citizen and the State: Essays on Regulation.* Chicago: The University of Chicago.

———. 1961. "The Economics of Information." *Journal of Political Economy* 69 (June).

———. 1971. "The Theory of Economic Regulation." *Bell Journal of Economics* 2 (Spring).

———, and Friedland, C. 1962. "What Can Regulators Regulate? The Case of Electricity." *Journal of Law and Economics* 5 (October).

Stiglitz, J. E. 1976. "Monopoly and the Rate of Extraction of Exhaustible Resources." *American Economic Review* 66 (September).

—————. 1978. "A Neoclassical Analysis of the Economics of Natural Resources." In *Scarcity and Growth Reconsidered,* ed. V. K. Smith. Forthcoming.

Stiles, Samuel V., and Johnson, Katherine A. 1976. "Regulatory and Review Functions of Agencies Created by the Act: National Health Planning and Resources Development Act of 1974." *Public Health Reports* 91, 1 (January-February).

Stuart, Bruce, and Stockton, Ronald. 1973. "Control over the Utilization of Medical Service." *Millbank Memorial Fund Quarterly/Health and Society* 51, 3 (Summer).

Tobin, J. 1952. "A Survey of the Theory of Rationing." *Econometrics* 20 (October).

Walker, Weldon G. 1977. "Changing United States Life-Style and Declining Vascular Mortality: Cause or Coincidence?" *New England Journal of Medicine* (21 July).

Wenders, John T., ed. 1977. *Pricing in Regulated Industries: Theory and Application.* Denver, Col.: Mountain States Telephone and Telegraph Company.

Wennberg, John, and Gittelsohn, Alan. 1973. "Small Area Variations in Health Care Delivery." *Science* 182 (December).

Williamson, O. E. 1975. *Markets and Hierarchies.* New York: The Free Press.

—————. 1968. "Wage Rates as a Barrier to Entry: The Pennington Case in Perspective." *Quarterly Journal of Economics* 82 (February).

Worthington, Nancy. 1976. "National Health Expenditures, 1929–74." *Social Security Bulletin* (February).

Zarb, F. G., and MacAvoy, P. W., eds. 1976. *Report of the Presidential Task Force on Reform of Federal Energy Administration.* Washington, D.C. (December).

Zubkoff, Michael, ed. 1976. *Health: A Victim or Cause of Inflation?* New York: Prodist.

ABOUT THE AUTHORS

CHRIS ARGYRIS is James Bryant Conant Professor of Education and Organizational Behavior, Graduate Schools of Education and Business Administration, at Harvard University. As an authority on problems of executive development and productivity, he has been a consultant to numerous foreign governments, and to business firms in this country and overseas. He served as special consultant to the U.S. State Department, and to the Department of Health, Education and Welfare, the National Institute of Mental Health, the National Science Foundation, the Ford Foundation, and the U.S. Commissioner of Education. His many writings include *Increasing Leadership Effectiveness* (1976), *The Applicability of Organizational Sociology* (1972), *Intervention Theory and Method* (1970), and more than one hundred published articles.

A. LAWRENCE CHICKERING, Executive Director and Editor of the Institute for Contemporary Studies, served as Director of Research at the California Office of Economic Opportunity, and was Executive Assistant to the editor of the *National Review*. One of his articles appears in the Institute's publication *No Land Is an Island* (1975), and he was editor and contributor to two others—*Public Employee Unions* (1976), and *The Politics of Planning* (1976).

PENNY HOLLANDER FELDMAN is Assistant Professor of Political Science in the Department of Health Services, and Director of the Executive Program in Health Policy, Planning and Regulation, Harvard School of Public Health. Her interest in public policy, bureaucracy, and organizational behavior is reflected in a number of articles and papers, and in a forthcoming publication, "Regulating Professionals: A Political-Economic Approach."

RICHARD H. HOLTON, Professor of Business Administration at the University of California, Berkeley, served as Dean of the Schools of Business Administration at UC-Berkeley from 1967 to 1975. He has directed research on food distribution costs in Puerto Rico, and spent a year studying the marketing problems faced by firms involved in the economic development of southern Italy and Greece. In the U.S. government, he served as Special Assistant for Economic Affairs in the Office of the Secretary of Commerce, and was Assistant Secretary of Commerce for Economic Affairs from 1963 to 1965, when he became Chairman of the President's Consumer Advisory Council. He now serves as Chairman of the Public Advisory Committee on Truth-in-Lending, Federal Reserve System. His fields of interest include marketing, economic development, international business, and antitrust problems. Among his publications are *The Supply and Demand Structure of Food Retailing Services* (1954), *Management Education in Italy,* written with Neil C. Churchill and William C. Frederick (1973), and *Management of the Multinationals–Policies, Operations and Research,* edited with S. Prakash Sethi (1974).

DONALD P. JACOBS, Dean of the Graduate School of Management at Northwestern University, until 1975 was Director of the Banking Research Center and Chairman of the university's Finance Department. A consultant to corporations and government agencies, he has served as co-Staff Director of the Presidential Commission on Financial Structure and Regulation. He is co-author with R. D. Irwin of *Financial Institutions,* now in its 5th edition (1972), and of many articles on banking, financial structure, and business regulation. He also co-authored *The Financial Structure of Bank Holding Companies* (1975).

ALFRED E. KAHN was appointed Chairman of the Civil Aeronautics Board in June 1977. Since 1974 he had been Chairman of the New York State Public Service Commission, on leave from Cornell University, where he was Robert Julius Thorne Professor of Economics and Dean of the College of Arts and Sciences. Dr. Kahn served on the research staff of The Brookings Institution, was a member of the U.S. Attorney General's national committee to study antitrust laws, and a member of the senior staff of the President's Council of Economic Advisors in the mid-1950s. He is the author of numerous professional articles, and his books include *Fair Competition: The Law and Economics of Antitrust Policy,* with J. B. Dirlam (reprinted 1970), *Integration and Competition in the Petroleum Industry,* with M. G. de Chazeau (reprinted 1971), and *The Economics of Regulation* (1971).

PAUL W MacAVOY, Professor of Economics, Department of Economics and School of Organization and Management at Yale University, was Senior Staff Economist on the U.S. Council of

Economic Advisors until 1966, and spent the following two years as a member of the Presidential Task Force on Revision of the Antitrust Laws. Until 1975 he was editor-in-chief of *The Bell Journal of Economics and Management Science.* He was part of the Energy Policy Studies Group at the MIT Energy Laboratory from 1974 to 1975, and since 1976 has been Adjunct Scholar of the American Enterprise Institute. He is consultant to many government bodies and private organizations.The most recent of his publications include *Economic Perspective on the Politics of International Commodity Agreements* (1977), and, as editor, *Federal Energy Administration Regulation* and *OSHA Safety Regulation,* both also published in 1977.

ALMARIN PHILLIPS, Professor of Economics, Law and Public Policy, University of Pennsylvania, since 1963, is Visiting Professor at McGill University. He has been consultant to The RAND Corporation since 1964, and was Director of The Brookings Workshop on Regulated Industries from 1968 to 1973. He is a member of the National Academy of Science's Evaluation Panel for the Experimental Technology Incentives Program of the National Bureau of Standards, and a member of the Executive Committee of the National Bureau of Economic Research. A prolific writer, he is co-author of two forthcoming books: *Economics: Equity, Efficiency and Progress,* with L. R. Klein, and *Money and the Payments Mechanism,* with D. P. Jacobs.

V. KERRY SMITH is a Fellow in the Quality of the Environment Program, Resources for the Future, Inc. He spent two years as co-Director of the Economic Growth Institute, State University of New York, Binghamton, where he is Professor of Economics. In addition to many published articles on economics, his books include *Monte Carlo Methods: Their Roles for Econometrics* (1973), and *The Economic Consequences of Air Pollution* (1976).

PAUL H. WEAVER, Associate Editor of *Fortune* magazine, is a member of the Publication Committee of *The Public Interest,* spent five years as Assistant Professor of Government at Harvard University, and in 1970 was editor-in-chief of the President's Commission on Campus Unrest. He is a member of the Advisory Council to the Center for the Study of Government Regulation, American Enterprise Institute. He is co-editor with Irving Kristol of *The Americans: 1976* (1976, wrote "Liberals and the Presidency," *Commentary* (1975), and "On Adversary Government and the Liberal Audience" in *The Politics of Planning,* published by the Institute for Contemporary Studies in 1976.

RICHARD J. ZECKHAUSER, Professor of Political Economy in
the Kennedy School of Government at Harvard University, is consultant to the U.S. Occupational Safety and Health Administration,
the Senate Committee on Government Operations, and the Federal
Trade Commission. He is co-author of a major study on regulation
being sponsored by the American Bar Association. His articles on
economics, safety, and health have been widely published, and he
is co-author of two forthcoming books—*Primer for Public Choice,*
with Edith Stokey, and *Welfare of the Elderly,* with W. Kip Viscusi. He and Viscusi also co-authored the chapter on ''The Role of
Social Security in the Income Security of the Elderly'' in *The Crisis
in Social Security* published by the Institute for Contemporary
Studies in 1977.

Index

PUBLICATIONS LIST

THE INSTITUTE FOR CONTEMPORARY STUDIES

260 California Street, San Francisco, California 94111

Catalog available upon request

BUREAUCRATS AND BRAINPOWER: GOVERNMENT REGULA-
TION OF UNIVERSITIES
$6.95. 171 pages. Publication date: June 1979.
ISBN 0–917616–35–9
Library of Congress No. 79–51328
Contributors: Nathan Glazer, Robert S. Hatfield, Richard W. Lyman, Robert
L. Sproull, Paul Seabury, Miro M. Todorovich, Caspar W. Weinberger

THE CALIFORNIA COASTAL PLAN: A CRITIQUE
$5.95. 199 pages. Publication date: March 1976.
ISBN 0–917616–04–9
Library of Congress No. 76–7715
Contributors: Eugene Bardach, Daniel K. Benjamin, Thomas E. Borcherd-
ing, Ross D. Eckert, H. Edward Frech III, M. Bruce Johnson, Ronald N.
Lafferty, Walter J. Mead, Daniel Orr, Donald M. Pach, Michael R.
Peevey.

THE CRISIS IN SOCIAL SECURITY: PROBLEMS AND PROSPECTS
$6.95. 220 pages. Publication date: April 1977; 2d ed., rev., 1978.
ISBN 0–917616–16–2/1977; 0–917616–25–1/1978
Library of Congress No. 77–72542
Contributors: Michael J. Boskin, George F. Break, Rita Ricardo Campbell,
Edward Cowan, Martin S. Feldstein, Milton Friedman, Douglas R.
Munro, Donald O. Parsons, Carl V. Patton, Joseph A. Pechman, Sher-
win Rosen, W. Kip Viscusi, Richard J. Zeckhauser.

DEFENDING AMERICA: TOWARD A NEW ROLE IN THE POST-
DETENTE WORLD
$13.95 (hardbound only). 255 pages. Publication date: April 1977 by
Basic Books (New York).
ISBN 0–465–01585–9
Library of Congress No. 76–43479

258

Contributors: Robert Conquest, Theodore Draper, Gregory Grossman, Walter
Z. Laqueur, Edward N. Luttwak, Charles Burton Marshall, Paul H.
Nitze, Norman Polmar, Eugene V. Rostow, Leonard Schapiro, James
R. Schlesinger, Paul Seabury, W. Scott Thompson, Albert Wohlstet-
ter.

EMERGING COALITIONS IN AMERICAN POLITICS
$6.95. 530 pages. Publication date: June 1978.
ISBN 0–917616–22–7
Library of Congress No. 78–53414
Contributors: Jack Bass, David S. Broder, Jerome M. Clubb, Edward H.
Crane III, Walter De Vries, Andrew M. Greeley, S. I. Hayakawa,
Tom Hayden, Milton Himmelfarb, Richard Jensen, Paul Kleppner,
Everett Carll Ladd, Jr., Seymour Martin Lipset, Robert A. Nisbet,
Michael Novak, Gary R. Orren, Nelson W. Polsby, Joseph L. Rauh,
Jr., Stanley Rothman, William A. Rusher, William Schneider, Jesse
M. Unruh, Ben J. Wattenberg.

FEDERAL TAX REFORM: MYTHS AND REALITIES
$5.95. 270 pages. Publication date: September 1978.
ISBN 0–917616–32–4
Library of Congress No. 78–61661
Contributors: Robert J. Barro, Michael J. Boskin, George F. Break, Jerry
R. Green, Laurence J. Kotlikoff, Mordecai Kurz, Peter
Mieszkowski, John B. Shoven, Paul J. Taubman, John Whalley.

GOVERNMENT CREDIT ALLOCATION: WHERE DO WE GO
FROM HERE?
$4.95. 208 pages. Publication date: November 1975.
ISBN O–917616–02–2
Library of Congress No. 75–32951
Contributors: George J. Benston, Karl Brunner, Dwight M. Jaffe, Omotunde
E. G. Johnson, Edward J. Kane, Thomas Mayer, Allen H. Meltzer.

NEW DIRECTIONS IN PUBLIC HEALTH CARE: AN EVALUATION
OF PROPOSALS FOR NATIONAL HEALTH INSURANCE
$6.95. 277 pages. Publication date: May 1976.
ISBN 0–917616–00–6
Library of Congress No. 76 - 40680
Contributors: Martin S. Feldstein, Thomas D. Hall, Leon R. Kass, Keith B.
Leffler, Cotton M. Lindsay, Mark V. Pauly, Charles E. Phelps,
Thomas C. Schelling, Arthur Seldon.

NO LAND IS AN ISLAND: INDIVIDUAL RIGHTS AND GOVERN-
MENT CONTROL OF LAND USE
$5.95. 221 pages. Publication date: November 1975.
ISBN 0–917616–03–0
Library of Congress No. 75–38415

Contributors: Benjamin F. Bobo, B. Bruce-Briggs, Connie Cheney, A. Lawrence Chickering, Robert B. Ekelund, Jr., W. Philip Gramm, Donald G. Hagman, Robert B. Hawkins, Jr., M. Bruce Johnson, Jan Krasnowiecki, John McClaughry, Donald M. Pach, Bernard H. Siegan, Ann Louise Strong, Morris K. Udall.

NO TIME TO CONFUSE: A CRITIQUE OF THE FORD FOUNDATION'S ENERGY POLICY PROJECT *A TIME TO CHOOSE AMERICA'S ENERGY FUTURE*

$4.95. 156 pages. Publication date: February 1975.
ISBN 0-917616-01-4
Library of Congress No. 75-10230
Contributors: Morris A. Adelman, Armen A. Alchian, James C. DeHaven, George W. Hilton, M. Bruce Johnson, Herman Kahn, Walter J. Mead, Arnold B. Moore, Thomas Gale Moore, William H. Riker.

ONCE IS ENOUGH: THE TAXATION OF CORPORATE EQUITY INCOME
$2.00. 32 pages. Publication date: May 1977.
ISBN 0-917616-23-5
Library of Congress No. 77-670132
Author: Charles E. McLure, Jr.

OPTIONS FOR U.S. ENERGY POLICY
$5.95. 317 pages. Publication date: September 1977.
ISBN 0-917616-20-0
Library of Congress No. 77-89094
Contributors: Albert Carnesale, Stanley M. Greenfield, Fred S. Hoffman, Edward J. Mitchell, William R. Moffat, Richard Nehring, Robert S. Pindyck, Norman C. Rasmussen, David J. Rose, Henry S. Rowen, James L. Sweeney, Arthur W. Wright.

PARENTS, TEACHERS, AND CHILDREN: PROSPECTS FOR CHOICE IN AMERICAN EDUCATION
$5.95. 336 pages. Publication date: June 1977.
ISBN 0-917616-18-9
Library of Congress No. 77-79164
Contributors: James S. Coleman, John E. Coons, William H. Cornog, Denis P. Doyle, E. Babette Edwards, Nathan Glazer, Andrew M. Greeley, R. Kent Greenawalt, Marvin Lazerson, William C. McCready, Michael Novak, John P. O'Dwyer, Robert Singleton, Thomas Sowell, Stephen D. Sugarman, Richard E. Wagner.

THE POLITICS OF PLANNING: A REVIEW AND CRITIQUE OF CENTRALIZED ECONOMIC PLANNING
$5.95. 367 pages. Publication date: March 1976.
ISBN 0-917616-05-7
Library of Congress No. 76-7714

Contributors: B. Bruce-Briggs, James Buchanan, A. Lawrence Chickering, Ralph Harris, Robert B. Hawkins, Jr., George W. Hilton, Richard Mancke, Richard Muth, Vincent Ostrom, Svetozar Pejovich, Myron Sharpe, John Sheahan, Herbert Stein, Gordon Tullock, Ernest van den Haag, Paul H. Weaver, Murray L. Weidenbaum, Hans Willgerodt, Peter P. Witonski.

PUBLIC EMPLOYEE UNIONS: A STUDY OF THE CRISIS IN PUBLIC SECTOR LABOR RELATIONS

$6.95. 251 pages. Publication date: June 1976; 2d ed., rev., 1977.
ISBN 0–917616–08–1/1976; ISBN 0–917616–24–3/1977
Library of Congress No. 76–17444

Contributors: A. Lawrence Chickering, Jack D. Douglas, Raymond D. Horton, Theodore W. Kheel, David Lewin, Seymour Martin Lipset, Harvey C. Mansfield, Jr., George Meany, Robert A. Nisbet, Daniel Orr, A. H. Raskin, Wes Uhlman, Harry H. Wellington, Charles B. Wheeler, Jr., Ralph K. Winter, Jr., Jerry Wurf.

REGULATING BUSINESS: THE SEARCH FOR AN OPTIMUM

$6.95. 260 pages. Publication date: April 1978.
ISBN 0–917616–27–8
Library of Congress No. 78–50678

Contributors: Chris Argyris, A. Lawrence Chickering, Penny Hollander Feldman, Richard H. Holton, Donald P. Jacobs, Alfred E. Kahn, Paul W. MacAvoy, Almarin Phillips, V. Kerry Smith, Paul H. Weaver, Richard J. Zeckhauser.

TARIFFS, QUOTAS, AND TRADE: THE POLITICS OF PROTECTIONISM

$6.95. 330 pages. Publication date: February 1979.
ISBN 0–917616–34–0
Library of Congress No. 78–66267

Contributors: Walter Adams, Ryan C. Amacher, Sven W. Arndt, Malcolm D. Bale, John T. Cuddington, Alan V. Deardorff, Joel B. Dirlam, Roger D. Hansen, H. Robert Heller, D. Gale Johnson, Robert O. Keohane, Michael W. Keran, Rachel McCulloch, Ronald I. McKinnon, Gordon W. Smith, Robert M. Stern, Richard James Sweeney, Robert D. Tollison, Thomas D. Willett.

THE THIRD WORLD: PREMISES OF U.S. POLICY

$5.95. 332 pages. Publication date: November 1978.
ISBN 0–917616–30–8
Library of Congress No. 78–67593

Contributors: Dennis Austin, Peter T. Bauer, Max Beloff, Richard E. Bissell, Daniel J. Elazar, S. E. Finer, Allan E. Goodman, Nathaniel H. Leff, Seymour Martin Lipset, Edward N. Luttwak, Daniel Pipes, Wilson E Schmidt, Anthony Smith, W. Scott Thompson, Basil S. Yamey.

UNION CONTROL OF PENSION FUNDS: WILL THE NORTH RISE
AGAIN?
$2.00. 52 pages. Publication date: July 1979 .
ISBN 0–917616–36–7
Library of Congress No. 78–66581
Author: George J. Borjas

WATER BANKING: HOW TO STOP WASTING
AGRICULTURAL WATER
$2.00. 56 pages. Publication date: January 1978.
ISBN 0–917616–26–X
Library of Congress No. 78–50766
Authors: Sotirios Angelides, Eugene Bardach.